CRIMINAL LAW
FOR
POLICEMEN

NEIL C. CHAMELIN

University of Georgia

KENNETH R. EVANS

University of Mississippi

2nd edition

CRIMINAL LAW FOR POLICEMEN

PRENTICE-HALL, INC., *Englewood Cliffs, New Jersey*

Library of Congress Cataloging in Publication Data

CHAMELIN, Neil C   (date)
    Criminal law for policemen.

    (Prentice-Hall series in law enforcement)
    Includes index.
        1.–Criminal law—United States.   2.–Police—
United States—Handbooks, manuals, etc.   I.–Evans,
Kenneth R., (date)   joint author.   II.–Title.
KF9219.3.C45–1975   345' .73'00243632
ISBN   0–13–193862–2   75–17941

Prentice-Hall Series in Law Enforcement
James D. Stinchcomb, *Editor*

© 1976, 1971 by Prentice-Hall, Inc.,
Englewood Cliffs, New Jersey

10   9   8   7   6   5   4   3   2   1

Printed in the United States of America

PRENTICE-HALL INTERNATIONAL, INC., *London*
PRENTICE-HALL OF AUSTRALIA, PTY. LTD., *Sydney*
PRENTICE-HALL OF CANADA, LTD., *Toronto*
PRENTICE-HALL OF INDIA PRIVATE LIMITED, *New Delhi*
PRENTICE-HALL OF JAPAN, INC., *Tokyo*
PRENTICE-HALL OF SOUTHEAST ASIA (PTE.) LTD., *Singapore*

To Vicki and JoAnne

CONTENTS

3

4

5

6

MATTERS AFFECTING CRIMINAL RESPONSIBILITY 60

7

HOMICIDE 86

8

ASSAULT AND OTHER RELATED CRIMES 101

PREFACE
TO FIRST EDITION

Throughout the United States, undergraduate programs for the development of college-trained professional law enforcement officers have been established. Such programs cover a wide range of subjects including evidence, investigation, administration, and substantive criminal law, among others. Substantive criminal law, as a course, endeavors to help the law enforcement officer understand the essential elements of crimes and the rationale underlying the criminal law. Armed with these elements, his investigative prowess is improved. If he knows what the prosecution must prove and why it must be proved, he can be more thorough and searching. Hopefully, such a course would enable him to have a keener appreciation of the judicial arena and the adversary system.

An instructor in a substantive law course must either prepare his own materials or must select prepared materials from law texts. These texts are written for lawyers, judges, and law students by lawyers. Too often they are written in "lawyerese." More important, these books are written in the adversary context, the after-the-fact process.

To expand the choices available to the substantive criminal law instructor we have written a book on the subject. Written by lawyers for non-lawyers, the book attempts, in non-lawyerese to educate. This book contains no original materials. It is not our purpose to create law but only to simplify the explanation of the already existing law that law enforcement officers must understand to effectively perform their sworn responsibilities. Wherever the law is not settled, however, we have indicated what our opinion is so that it may be distinguished from settled law.

The book places emphasis on materials not generally covered in training academy situations. The nature of jurisdiction, the criminal act, the criminal state of mind, and matters affecting responsibility for criminal conduct are all touched upon. We did not intend this book to be a text used for a course in the processes of the administration of criminal justice, but rather one designed for the law course itself.

The law covered by this book isn't localized to a particular area of the country. It is composed of general legal principles applicable throughout the majority of the states. We have tried to use many examples to illustrate the complex rules discussed herein. We did not include footnotes for our public domain references for the simple reason that their usefulness in an undergraduate course of this type is limited and they would only be in the way.

It is impossible to prepare any book on a legal subject that does not contain some erroneous material, especially when written for a national audience. Any errors that might appear in this work due to local statutory or case modifications we apologize for, and we hope we can correct them in future editions. Our purpose is to present generally recognized legal principles.

We mentioned that, through this book, we are attempting to present an educational tool rather than a training tool. Admittedly, the last portion of the book, dealing with specific offenses, is an area where training and education overlap. It is our belief, however, that the approach taken is more educationally oriented. We, by no means, mean to imply that education has no practical value. If we believed this, we would not subscribe to police education programs, but we do believe there is, and should be, a distinction maintained between education and training. Training is a process whereby one learns how to perform a task; education is the process whereby one learns what tasks to perform and why to perform them. It is our hope that this book helps in an understanding of "what" and "why."

The format of the book is dictated by the principles of law discussed. Some chapters are longer than others. Those who are used to assigning materials by chapters will encounter some difficulty using that method with this book. We have provided a detailed table of contents and suggest that the material be assigned by sections rather than by chapters. This way the instructor will be able to plan his daily and weekly tasks much as he did under assignment by the chapter method.

We would like to acknowledge the help and the patience of Ann Scotta, Anne Connelly, and Reba Souders who played an important part in the preparation of this book.

Neil C. Chamelin
Kenneth R. Evans

PREFACE
TO SECOND EDITION

Neither the philosophy nor approach taken in the preparation of the second edition of *Criminal Law for Policemen* has changed from the first edition. Our sole purpose in preparing the second edition was to update, expand, clarify, and further illustrate the principles presented in this text.

Although substantive criminal law is not as rapidly changing a field as is procedural law, several sections of the text have been affected by court decisions in recent years. Therefore, we have updated the sections on Insanity, Abortion, and Obscenity and Pornography. In addition, we have both expanded and updated the chapters on Alcohol and Narcotics, Crimes By and Against Juveniles, and the section on Gambling. Several changes have also been made in the chapters on Jurisdiction and Robbery to clarify principles which led to some confusion earlier. Further examples have been added throughout many sections of the text to further illustrate and clarify the principles discussed.

A number of chapters on the substantive topics of Robbery, Theft Offenses, Burglary, Arson, and Forgery and Related Offenses have been rearranged to improve the organizational flow of the materials in the book.

As a result of many fine suggestions from users of the first edition, sections on Treason, Criminal Contempt, and Slander have been added to appropriate chapters. These are topics not treated in the first edition. The second edition also contains expanded coverage of federal jurisdiction. A new chapter on organized crime has been added. Finally, this edition contains a glossary of legal terms used throughout the book which we hope will be of considerable assistance to both students and faculty in comprehending the materials.

We are grateful for the assistance in preparation of this manuscript to Linda Marlow, Cathy Spencer, and Terry Zinn without whose assistance and typing capabilities, the preparation of this manuscript would not have been possible. Thanks also to Walter Barry for his research efforts.

Neil C. Chamelin
Kenneth R. Evans

CRIMINAL LAW
FOR
POLICEMEN

Chapter 1

HISTORICAL BACKGROUND OF CRIMINAL LAW

1.0 The Nature of Law

A. Why Law?

The question, "What is law?" invites a multiplicity of answers, for "law" is a broad concept with many definitions. For purposes of this book, law can be defined as a group of rules governing interaction. Law is a set of regulations governing the relationship between man and his fellow men, and between man and the state.

The need for law lies in the history of the human race. In early times, when man first appeared on this earth and was living alone in caves, laws were not needed for conflicts did not arise, but when men began to live in groups, communities, and societies, laws became necessary. Men still remained individuals whose desires, needs, and wants differed from those of other men. These differences caused conflict. Law was necessary as a means of social control attempting either to alleviate these conflicts or settle them in a manner most advantageous to the group.

B. Law as Language

Law is nothing more than language. Just as a carpenter uses a hammer and saw, a lawyer's tool is his ability to communicate. Communication is defined not merely as the conveyance of words but, more properly as the conveyance of words with the ability to make one's self understood to the listener or reader. The more one studies and delves into the complexities of the law, the more one realizes the truth of the statement that language is the essence of law. The importance of being able to communicate in terms that mean the same thing to the parties on both the sending and receiving ends of a communication cannot be overemphasized. What the law strives for is uniformity of interpretation. The question then arises, "Well, why are not the laws so pointedly written that everyone knows exactly what they mean?" This question is relatively easily answered when the problem is seen in proper perspective. Laws must be stable yet flexible enough to be interpreted so that they may be molded to fit the problems of a complex and changing society. If every law were written to cover only one specific fact situation, two major problems would arise. First, the number of laws would increase at least one hundred times over, each law covering a specific subject. The civil law systems in France and Germany are subject to this weakness. Second, many of these laws would become obsolete so quickly legislatures would spend most of their time repealing laws. However, when laws can be interpreted flexibly, they can be read to include new and unexpected situations that arise. The United States Constitution operates on the same principle and we use that document to illustrate this point. The framers of the Constitution could not foresee the problems of the twentieth century. If the Constitution had been prepared only for the problems of 1789, it would have collapsed many years ago. It would not function today because the problems of society in the twentieth century are not the same as the problems encountered by the framers of the Constitution in the eighteenth century. Thus, the Constitution was purposely drafted to be stable and yet flexible in the sense that it was capable of being interpreted in light of contemporary problems.

Any number of contemporary problems could be used to illustrate this point. Let us consider a few. At one time, the federal government's right to regulate commerce between the states was limited to prohibiting the erection of such barriers as tariffs. Georgia couldn't prevent Florida from shipping chickens to Georgia merely to protect Georgia chicken farmers. But certain related commerce problems arose. States were unwilling to prevent certain abuses to members of the labor force. As a result, our federal labor laws came into being. Congress cited the commerce clause of the Constitution as authority for these acts. The Supreme Court upheld the labor laws so that today wages, working conditions, and hours are regulated. This problem was not foreseen by the framers of the Constitution. Years ago, segregation was said to be supported by the Constitution. However, due to the changing times and attitudes of the people, in 1954 segregation was said to be in opposition to the Constitution. Finally, the right to counsel, which is found in the Bill of Rights, was said to apply only to federal courts and federal cases. However, in the now famous *Gideon* case, the right to counsel was said to apply to state courts and state criminal cases. The same document was used; the times had changed.

1.1 Crime Defined

Not all violations of the law are crimes. One need only refer to the local statutes to see that the criminal law is only a small part of the entire legal field. For example, if the state statutes require two witnesses for a valid will, having only one witness will render the will invalid but will not result in criminal charges. Perhaps the best way to clarify this point is by defining crime. A crime may be defined as a public wrong. It is an act or omission forbidden by law for which the state prescribes a punishment in its own name. What does this mean? A crime must be a wrong against the public not merely a wrong against a particular individual. There are many laws, in many jurisdictions, governing the rights and duties of man in his relationship to other men. However, only those violations which wrong the public are considered criminal and make up the body of the substantive criminal law.

The determination as to whether a particular act is criminal or merely civil in nature is a function of the law-making body of each jurisdiction. In tribal times, this decision was made by the people. They considered criminal those acts which they felt injured the welfare of the entire community. Today, this function rests with the legislatures of the states.

Crimes differ from civil wrongs in many respects, but the sole reason they differ is that the legislature says they differ. In other words, only a fine line distinguishes crimes from civil wrongs, and that line is drawn by the legislature where and when that body so desires within the limits of what the public will tolerate.

Crimes are prosecuted by the state in its own name. In a civil case, the action is instituted by the wronged individual. Persons convicted of crimes are punished by fines, imprisonment or death, while defendants who lose civil cases are usually ordered to pay the injured party. A crime is a public wrong, while a civil wrong is private in nature, not involving the state as a party. Punishment is prescribed and must be prescribed for convictions of criminal acts but there is no set amount of damages to which a wronged person is entitled in a civil suit. These are only a few of the major differences between crimes and civil wrongs, differences which exist solely as a consequence of the legislature having attached the label "crime" to one act and not the other. This is not to say that the legislature has only an "either or" choice. The lawgivers may choose to declare a particular act both a crime and a civil wrong, as in the case of assault and battery. An act of this nature may be both criminally and civilly wrong, in which case the victim may proceed civilly and the state may prosecute. Both avenues are open and the outcome in one does not affect the proceedings in the other.

The purpose of the criminal law is twofold. First, it attempts to control the behavior of human beings. Failing in this, the criminal law seeks to sanction uncontrolled behavior by punishing the law violator.

Within the framework of criminal law, punishment may take one of three forms: fine, imprisonment, or death. The advantages, disadvantages, and effectiveness of imprisonment and death involve some of the most controversial social problems in society today. However, an in depth study of these problems is beyond the scope of this book.

1.2   Early Development of Criminal Law

Criminal law is an offspring of personal vendetta. At some time in the development of each society, when one individual injured another, it became the responsibility of the victim or his family to seek redress. The community in no way became involved. This led to the theory of retributive justice. The Code of Hammurabi, circa 2100 B.C., codified the rules which called for punishment to fit the crime: "An eye for an eye." Eventually, despite the setback of the Dark Ages, societies began treating certain offenses as crimes against the sovereign, and the state began punishing individuals who committed offenses against the public. This practice became the keystone of modern criminal law.

During this developmental period, the law did not take the responsibility of the accused into consideration. That is, the law did not ask why an individual had committed a crime or whether he was accountable for his actions. Defenses such as insanity, justification, excuse, intoxication, infancy, and the like were not considered. The mere doing of the act was all that was required to show the commission of a crime. Today, of course, this is no longer true in most instances. The fact that a person commits a wrongful act does not make that act criminal until the perpetrator is convicted, due to the defenses which may bar his conviction. These defenses are discussed in Chapter 6.

The key to the doctrine of responsibility is the legal approach to human psychology. The law is based on the assumption that man acts of his own free will. His fate is not predetermined or predestined. Therefore, the law may hold man accountable for his actions. If the law accepted the concept of determinism, it would hold that man is not responsible for his conduct; everything man does would be predestined, determined by his early environment and his genetic history. The individual should not be on trial for his criminal acts but rather, fate should be on trial. This theory, for obvious reasons, would be totally unacceptable in any society as a legal theory. Many deterministic theories have been propounded throughout the history of criminal law. Some of them have either been wholly or partially rejected. The great Italian sociologist, Lombroso, felt that he could predict criminality and guilt by measuring the accused's head, ears, nose, or some other area. Fortunately, this theory was rejected. Of more current interest is the very controversial "XYY" chromosome theory. In 1968 an Australian court acquitted a man charged with murder on the theory that he was born with imbalanced chromosomes and, that as a consequence of this physiological deficiency, he was destined to commit crimes for which he could not legally be held accountable. The defendant in this case had the support of several professional medical men. Shortly after the decision of this court, a commission was appointed in the United States to research the feasibility of applying this theory. Their conclusion, released in the summer of 1969, was that there was no correlation between the existence of "XYY" chromosomes and criminality.

1.3 Legal Systems and the Beginning of the Common Law

There are two major legal systems prevailing throughout nine-tenths of the civilized world. They are the civil law and common law systems. The civil law system is the predominant legal system of the civilized world, while the common law system is prevalent in England, its dominions, and North America. These systems had their beginnings in completely different ways.

The common law began as a result of the habits of individuals and the customs of groups. These habits and customs were so entrenched in society that they became the acceptable norms of behavior. When courts developed, violations of these customs produced the cases heard. The courts began recording their decisions, and judges looking for assistance started following previous court decisions when confronted with new cases. This procedure became known as *stare decisis*—the following of precedents. Thus, the customs of the common people became the source of the common law, the law of the common people.

The remainder of the world grew under a different system of law, the civil law. We can trace this system back at least as far as the Roman Empire, where laws were written and codified by the rulers of the "state" and imposed on the people. As will be seen, the law of the United States is a combination of common law and civil law. The two systems of law began at opposite ends of the legal spectrum. The common law was developed by the common people and was imposed on the rulers of the country. The civil law was developed by the rulers and imposed on the people. Of course, this is a highly simplified explanation of the development of the legal systems but it will serve as a useful frame of reference.

1.4 Common Law in the United States

The English colonists who settled America brought with them a large part of the body of law to which they were accustomed—the English Common Law. As a consequence of this, and of their political dominancy, this system predominated in the colonies with certain modifications— modifications caused by the feeling that certain English laws were oppressive, and that it was these laws the colonists came to America to escape.

Under the federal-state relationship established by our Constitution, each of the United States is sovereign under a federal government. Consequently, each state is free to decide whether it will select the common law system or the civil law system as the basis for its criminal law. The basic difference between the way these systems operate is that under the common law, any act that *was* criminal under the old common law remains criminal today, even though it is not found in statutory form. Under the civil law, all crimes are statutory. In the absence of a statute, there can be no crime.

Presently, nineteen states have expressly abolished common law offenses and all offenses in those jurisdictions are statutory. In seven states, the common law offenses have been impliedly abolished or their status is uncertain. In the remainder of the states, the common law survives either expressly or by implication.

Even in jurisdictions which have abolished the common law, reference is still made to the common law for definitional purposes. For example, the State of Georgia has abolished all common law offenses. The Georgia statutes make murder a crime, however, and explain the situations under which that crime may be charged. But nowhere in the

Georgia statutes is the word murder defined. Thus, it is necessary to look to the common law for a definition of the term.

Today, when most crimes are statutory, how significant is the distinction between the common law system and the civil or statutory law system? The common law states have a distinct advantage in being able to reach back into the common law to find additional offenses which might not be covered by statute in their jurisdictions. Although this a rare occurrence, these states have the power to look to the common law if an offensive act occurs that is not covered by statute. If the offense was punishable at common law, then it is punishable in those states today. An example of this reaching back to the common law occurred in Pennsylvania in 1955.

In *Commonwealth* v. *Mochan*, 177 Pa. Super 454, 110 A 2d 788 (1955), the defendant made numerous obscene telephone calls to the complainant. Apparently, Pennsylvania had no statute governing this type of behavior, so the trial court looked to the common law and found a misdemeanor which in substance was defined as "contriving and intending to debauch and corrupt the morals of the citizens." The court invoked this offense and convicted the defendant. The conviction was affirmed on appeal. This conviction could not have been obtained in a jurisdiction that had abolished the common law offenses if there were no statute making this type of conduct criminal. Any number of offenses which are the constant subject matter of police investigation today were unknown to the common law. The inventive genius of the criminal mind, accompanying the various stages of historical, industrial, and sociological development, has created new antisocial conduct against which society needs protection. Legislatures, in response to these new pressures, have established new offenses by statute. The list of legislatively established crimes could go on here for a number of pages. We shall examine most of them in this book. But as an example of legislative response, the authors note that embezzlement, as discussed in Chapter 10, was created by statute and was not a common law crime.

The federal judiciary has no power to exercise common law jurisdiction. This comes about not by choice but by mandate. The federal government has only certain enumerated powers. This means that it can only exercise those powers which have been granted to it by the people. The people have given the Congress the power to enact laws, but not to adopt the common law. Therefore, the judiciary can only exercise authority over crimes enacted by Congress. The federal judiciary, however, like the states, must look to the common law for definitions to aid in interpreting federal laws.

Questions for Discussion

1. John has committed an act which under the common law of England would be criminal. The same act is not made criminal by any statute of any state nor by federal statute. Can such an offense be successfully prosecuted in the federal courts or in your state? Why?

2. In the study of criminal law, why is it essential to understand the significance of the common law and its effect on the law of the United States?

3. What is meant by the statement that the Constitution must be stable yet flexible?

4. Of what significance is the concept of "responsibility" with regard to the criminal law today?

Chapter 2

FUNDAMENTALS OF CRIMINAL LAW

2.0 Morality and the Law

The first-time student of criminal law must be able to approach the subject with an open mind and as objectively as possible. There is often a difference between what is morally wrong and what is legally prohibited. Legal problems should not be settled by resorting to emotion, because people who fall prey to emotion discover many wrong answers. This is not to say that there is necessarily a right or wrong answer to a legal question. If this were true, our system would not require the services of attorneys and judges. The facts of a particular case could be fed into a computer and the "right answer" retrieved mechanically.

An act may be committed which is obviously morally wrong in the eyes of most people but for which there is no legal penalty. In such a case, it would be unlawful for the police officer to make an arrest. He would be subject not only to embarrassment but to civil liability as well. If this happened, it would be because the officer acted emotionally, based on what he felt to be right, instead of approaching the problem with the analytical mind required of any good law enforcement official.

Suppose a young girl has swum too far from shore and is struggling to keep from drowning. A man on the beach observes this activity but takes no action to save the girl even though a rescue attempt would involve no danger to his own safety. Instead, he remains on shore and takes photographs of the drowning girl with the thought of having them published in a national magazine. The girl drowns. Most people would agree that this man's conduct was morally wrong and that there probably is some clear-cut crime here with which he should be charged. Although morally this conduct cannot be tolerated, legally no offense has occurred.

Of course, criminal law, like other areas of law, is not completely devoid of moral considerations. The next section of this chapter concerns itself with the classification of crimes. Historically, offenses have been classified according to their severity and the threat they pose to the public welfare. It must be recognized that this categorization was based on the precepts of society at the time of classification. The seriousness of the offenses is really a moral consideration.

2.1 Classification of Crimes

Crimes are classified in many ways. Among them is the distinction made between offenses *mala in se* and *mala prohibita*. Crimes *mala in se* are defined as those bad in themselves; those morally as well as legally wrong. Murder and rape would be among the crimes classified this way. Historically, all common law crimes were *mala in se*. Statutory crimes were not classified this way by legal philosophers even at common law. *Mala prohibita* crimes are those which are wrong simply because they are prohibited and they involve no moral turpitude.

Basically moral turpitude is depravity or baseness of conduct. Most authorities, including the courts, agree with this. However, whether a particular prohibited act constitutes depravity or baseness depends on the attitude of the people. A criminal act which may be *mala in se* (involving moral turpitude) in one jurisdiction may not be in another.

The most popular common law classification of crimes—into the three categories of treason, felonies, and misdemeanors—is perhaps the most workable. This basic distinction remains today in most, if not all, jurisdictions.

Although treason is considered to be the most serious of all crimes because it threatens the very existence of the nation, its rarity of occurrence and the unlikelihood that a police officer will ever be confronted with such a case necessitate only a brief mention of its history and substance. Treason is the only offense specified or defined in the federal Constitution. Article III, Section 3, says, "Treason against the United States, shall consist *only* in levying war against them, or in adhering to their enemies, giving them aid and comfort" [emphasis added]. The word *only* is emphasized for the simple reason that Congress does not have the power either to extend or restrict the crime; its power over the subject is limited to prescribing the punishment. The reason for this restriction may be found in the historical development of the crime of treason.

At early common law the crime was divided into high treason and petit treason. High treason included acts directed particularly against the sovereign, such as killing the king, queen, or prince, levying war against the king, or adhering to his enemies. Petit treason involved a malicious homicide of particular persons of importance but of less stature than the king, such as a husband by his wife, a master or mistress by his or her servant, or a prelate by a clergyman. Such persons were held in high esteem in early English society and a homicide of this type required exceptionally special and brutal punishment. For example, the most common punishment for petit treason committed by a man was to be drawn and hanged, and by a woman to be drawn and burned. "Drawing" consisted of tying the malefactor behind a horse which dragged him or her along a rough road. Eventually, the special brutality provided by the common law for the punishment of petit treason disappeared. As a result, the need for a separate crime disappeared, and petit treason became merged with murder. This left only one crime of treason.

A most significant development in the early common law was the tendency to enlarge greatly the scope of the offense of treason so that it included many acts not originally intended. Because of this continuing expansion, Parliament was required to limit and define the crime of treason. In 1350 Parliament enacted the Statute of Treasons, which specified exactly what acts constituted high treason.

Due to the fact that Parliament found this restriction necessary, and to the fact that special brutality punishments were never tolerated in the United States, the separate crime of petit treason was never recognized in this country, and the framers of the Constitution specifically prohibited Congress from expanding the definition.

Although the wording of the Constitution might imply that treason may be committed by three separate methods, in actuality only two are recognized. One is levying war against the United States. The second consists of two elements: adhering to its enemies and giving them aid and comfort.

Levying war means that there must be a war directed at the government of the United States. No formal declaration is needed. A treasonable act must be one directed toward the overthrow of the entire government rather than for a private purpose.

Adhering to its enemies, giving them aid and comfort, includes such acts as buying a ship and fitting it for service in aid of the enemy, delivering prisoners and deserters to the enemy, or selling critical materials with knowledge of the fact that the purchaser buys them to use in the manufacture of gunpowder for the enemy. Adhering to the enemy provides the mental element of the crime, while giving aid and comfort is the physical element. Under this definition, the enemy must be a hostile foreign power, not merely citizens of the United States who might be rebelling against the government.

Proof of the crime of treason requires (1) an overt physical act tending toward the accomplishment of the treasonable objective and (2) that the act must be proved by two witnesses or confessed by the defendant in open court. The gist of the offense of treason is breach of allegiance. Therefore, treason must be committed by a citizen (by birth or naturalized) or by a resident alien who does owe some allegiance to this country.

Treason does not require proof of any specific intent. It is sufficient that the defendant intended to do the prohibited act. He is then held responsible for the natural and probable consequences of that act (see Chapter 5).

Treason may be committed against a state by armed opposition to its laws or by forcibly attempting to overthrow its government. Treason against the United States is not necessarily an offense against the laws of a particular state. Conversely, treason against a state is not necessarily treason against the United States.

Every person owing allegiance to the United States (or to a state), having knowledge of the commission of treason against the (particular) government, is obligated to disclose that knowledge as soon as possible. Failure to do so makes one guilty of misprision of treason, against either the United States or the particular state. (See misprision of felony in Chapter 4 for more detail.)

A felony was defined as any crime for which the perpetrator could be compelled to forfeit his property—both real and personal—in addition to being subjected to punishment through the normal procedures of death, imprisonment, or fine. The common law felonies were: murder, manslaughter, rape, sodomy, larceny, robbery, arson, and burglary. Statutes today make other crimes felonies, but these were the only felonies at common law. The key to distinguishing felonies from misdemeanors was not the punishment that could be imposed but whether forfeiture was required.

The word felony, like misdemeanor, is just a label used to define a class of offenses, and these labels do not apply uniformly throughout all jurisdictions. Each jurisdiction is free to call criminal violations by any name it chooses and to impose such punishment for violations as it desires, providing it does not violate the Eighth Amendment of the United States Constitution protecting individuals from cruel and unusual punishments. There are some absurdities as a result. The following is an excerpt from an item published by the Associated Press Wire Service in 1965. "It is a misdemeanor in Maryland to use a machine gun to perpetrate a crime of violence but it is a felony to break open a hogshead of tobacco . . . conviction for burglary with explosives, a misdemeanor, carries a maximum penalty of 40 years in prison. On the other hand, conviction for the felony of injuring a race horse would mean a maximum sentence of three years. . . . Larceny after trust with a five-year maximum is a felony. But abduction of a child under 12 with a 20-year maximum, escape from the penitentiary with a 10-year maximum, and bribery with a 12-year maximum are all simply misdemeanors. Among other misdemeanor and maximum penalties are: abduction of a female under 18, eight years; injuring a railroad car, five years; stealing fish, two years; dueling, penalty up to court; marrying close relatives, banishment from the state forever."

Today, the law does not require forfeiture of property for committing a felony and therefore the common law rule is no longer applicable. However, most jurisdictions still maintain the distinction between felonies and misdemeanors. Some jurisdictions distinguish on the basis of where the imprisonment is to take place. Twenty-two states distinguish felonies from misdemeanors based on the place of imprisonment. The remaining jurisdictions seem to use a combination of place of imprisonment and character of the offense or both to make this distinction. In many of these latter states, the criteria are difficult to comprehend. In some, the length of imprisonment is the deciding factor while in other states it is difficult to determine what criteria are used to differentiate between felonies and misdemeanors.

The American Law Institute has proposed the Model Penal Code. Several states have adopted this code with some qualifications and changes. The Model Penal Code (MPC) creates different classes of crimes.

Under the MPC a crime is a felony if it is so designated no matter what the penalty. Any crime that creates a punishment exceeding one year is also a felony under the MPC.

Further, the MPC creates degrees of felonies. First and second degree felonies are those so labeled in the MPC. A crime that is a felony but for which there is no designated degree is a third degree felony. This creation of degrees is for the purpose of sentencing. Certain fines attach to the various degrees of felonies as a result. A first or second degree felony carries a $10,000 fine; a third degree felony a $5,000 fine, unless higher (or lower) amounts are specifically attached to a specific offense. Likewise, the felony degrees each fix a maximum and minimum imprisonment ranging from one year to life, to one year to five years.

A misdemeanor is one designated as such by the MPC no matter what the penalty is. The MPC also adds a new term, petty misdemeanor, and says that a petty misdemeanor is a crime so designated as such or one where the penalty is for less than a year. A misdemeanor carries a $1,000 fine, and a petty misdemeanor a $500 fine, unless higher (or lower) amounts are attached to a specific offense. Like previous law, an undesignated offense providing a sentence is a misdemeanor under the MPC.

The MPC also creates a new class of offense called the violation. A violation usually is either named as such or, and most important, provides no jail sentence. It involves only a fine or forfeiture. Since a violation is not a crime, there is to be no disability or legal disadvantage for someone convicted of a violation. Many of the *mala prohibita* offenses are violations under the MPC.

A number of states, although not having adopted the MPC *in toto*, have adopted its method of classifying offenses.

On the federal level, persons convicted of crimes for which imprisonment is imposed are all sentenced to federal prisons. Thus, the distinction between felonies and misdemeanors on the federal level cannot be the place of imprisonment but rather, must be based on the length of imprisonment. A felony under federal law is any crime for which the penalty is death or imprisonment for a term exceeding one year.

Why is it important to know the distinction between a felony and a misdemeanor? Much of the treatment of the accused hinges upon this distinction. The procedural steps that may be taken by police officers in the performance of their duties depend on whether they are dealing with a felony or a misdemeanor. As will be illustrated in detail later (Chapter 6.14), the amount of force an officer may use to apprehend a person for commission of a crime will be based on the type of crime for which the individual is to be arrested. In addition, one convicted of a felony will lose his civil rights, while a convicted misdemeanant will not. Even more important, the arrest powers that an officer or private citizen has are governed by the classification of the crime for which the arrest is being made.

Police officers are often confused as to how the punishment actually administered by a court affects the classification of a crime. Whether a crime is a felony or a misdemeanor is governed by the maximum punishment that can be imposed by the courts for a conviction of the offense and not by the punishment that is actually imposed. For example, if Andy commits grand larceny in a state where a felony is defined as any crime punishable by imprisonment in the state prison, assuming grand larceny carries a maximum penalty of five years in the state prison in that state, Andy is guilty of a felony regardless of the fact that the court may only sentence him to spend six months in the county jail.

All crimes carrying penalties less than those imposed for the commission of felonies are misdemeanors. Thus, by the process of elimination, it may be determined which crimes are misdemeanors in any particular jurisdiction.

2.2   Enacting and Interpreting Statutes

Most police officers automatically think of recent Supreme Court decisions the instant the word "constitutionality" is mentioned. Constitutional law is a broad subject in its procedural applications and is beyond the scope of this book. The following is a highly simplified explanation of who enacts laws and on what authority laws are enacted, in addition to a short summary of a few basic rules observed when a statute is interpreted.

Two phrases, "grant of power" and "limitation on power," are essential to an understanding of this subject. The federal government exists because the people of the various states, in whom rests total sovereignty, created it. It has only the authority specifically given to it by the people of the states. The instrument by which the people granted this authority is the United States Constitution. In essence, the people stripped their state governments of certain powers, such as governing commerce, coining money, and conducting wars.

For this reason we call the United States Constitution a "grant of power." The federal government exercises this authority through acts passed by Congress. To determine the constitutionality of these acts, the courts look to the Constitution to see if the people gave the federal government the power to pass laws on the particular subject with which a Congressional act deals. If the power and authority can be found in the Constitution, and if Congress acted within the limits set by the people in dealing with the particular subject of the act, it is constitutional. If Congress was without the authority or acting outside the scope of that authority, the act is unconstitutional.

Turning to the state constitutions, which are called "limitations on power," it can be seen that any powers not specifically granted to the federal government through the United States Constitution are reserved to the states or its people. Thus, the states are free to exercise any legislative power not given to the federal government unless there are certain rights that the people of the states wish to reserve to themselves, not allowing even their own state legislatures to have a say in this regard. Thus, the people, through their respective state constitutions, limit the powers of the state legislature. They may prohibit their state from having an income tax or prohibit gambling which would otherwise be permissible. It is for this reason that state constitutions are referred to as limitations on power. State constitutions are therefore usually negative in their application, if not in their language. State legislatures may enact laws on any subject for which authority has neither been granted to the federal government nor prohibited to them by the people of the state.

To test the constitutionality of a state statute, the state courts first determine if the authority to legislate in the particular area has been granted exclusively to the federal government. For example, if a state enacted a criminal statute prohibiting counterfeiting of money, the court would find that this power has been exclusively granted to the federal government. In this case, the state would not have the authority to pass such a law and the statute would be unconstitutional.

If this authority has not been granted to the federal government through the United States Constitution, the court must then look to the state constitution to determine if the people forbade the legislature from enacting such a law. Finding no such prohibition, the court can declare the statute constitutional.

In addition to this brief explanation, two other important principles deserve mention. It is a principle of law that courts will make every effort to hold statutes constitutional. Only when there is no way of so holding, will they declare them to be unconstitutional.

This section has implied that the authority to enact laws on any particular subject rests either with the federal government or the state legislatures. However, there are times when the two levels of government will have concurrent jurisdiction. Federal legislation must apply uniformly to all states on any subject, while each state legislature can enact laws on the same subject pertaining only to its geographical boundaries. As a result there are differences among the states on the same subject matter.

One further principle governs the determination of the constitutionality of statutes. Since people are entitled to know what conduct is prohibited by the law, statutes cannot be written in such broad terms as to make unclear the type of conduct prohibited. Such statutes will be held unconstitutional for vagueness.

Our legal system is based on the theory that every benefit of the doubt will be accorded to the defendant in criminal cases. This is like the famous rule in baseball games that "a tie goes to the runner." Based on this principle, we take the view that criminal statutes are to be strictly construed when they work against the accused in a criminal case and liberally construed when they benefit the accused. This means that if the statute works against the defendant, it would be interpreted in its narrowest sense so that only the specified conduct would be included.

If, however, the statute works a benefit to the defendant, it is broadly construed so that his conduct would be interpreted in the most favorable way.

2.3 Ex Post Facto Laws

The United States Constitution, in Article I, Sections 9 and 10, prohibits the passage of *ex post facto* laws either by the federal or the state governments. In brief, an *ex post facto* law is one which alters the laws regarding a particular act in such a way as to be detrimental to the substantial rights of an accused person. This can occur in any of three ways. First, if at the time an individual commits an act, that act is not criminal but is subsequently made a crime by legislative action, the individual cannot then be prosecuted for its violation. Any attempt to prosecute in such a case constitutes an *ex post facto* application of the law. A person is entitled to know what, if any, violation occurs at the time he commits an act. Thus, if the act is not criminal at the time committed, no punishment can be imposed.

The second situation to which the rule applies involves the increasing of punishment for a specific crime after it has occurred. Suppose, for example, Fred commits grand larceny for which the maximum penalty is five years imprisonment. Before his trial, the legislature increases the maximum penalty to ten years imprisonment. Any application of the more severe penalty to Fred would be *ex post facto* since it does affect his substantial rights. He can only be punished to the extent provided at the time he committed the criminal act.

Third, the *ex post facto* rule applies to decreasing the state's burden of proof. It is *ex post facto* if the legislature decreases the amount of proof the state will be required to produce in order to convict for a crime. The reason for this is that it would be detrimental to the rights of the accused if the state could convict him more easily than it could have at the time the act was committed. But, other changes in the rules of evidence, which do not materially affect the defendant's rights, can be made.

If the reverse of any of these situations exists, for instance, when the punishment is decreased or the burden of proof on the state is increased between the time of the commission of the crime and trial, these changes will benefit the defendant and will not be considered *ex post facto*.

Similarly, if the statute making a certain act criminal has been repealed after the accused committed the act, proceedings against him must be dropped. The act must be criminal both at the time of the act and during the course of proceedings to punish him. This is true even if the crime is repealed any time before final appeals have been exhausted.

Generally, changes in the law which relate to procedure and jurisdiction and which are to be applied retroactively do not come within the prohibition against *ex post facto* laws.

2.4   Status of Municipal Ordinances

Municipal police officers spend most of their working time enforcing municipal ordinances. This is not criminal law enforcement because violations of ordinances are not crimes. The distinction between crimes and violations of ordinances lies in the definition of crime and in the nature of municipal corporations.

A crime has been defined as a public wrong created by the state and prosecuted by the state in its name. Public wrong is interpreted as a wrong affecting the people of the entire state, not just of a particular portion of the state. Municipal ordinances are not enacted by the state legislature nor are they punished by that lawmaking body. Ordinances are enacted by city councils or commissions, affecting only the municipality, and are punished by the city in its name when violated.

A municipality is a corporation like any other corporation except that it is a public corporation. Municipalities are created by the state legislature and exist at the whim of that body. Municipalities can be dissolved when and if the legislature so chooses unless they have been established under constitutional home rule.

Like other corporations, municipal corporations are required to have a charter granted by the state. Private corporations have rules for governing internal operations, called bylaws. Municipal ordinances are the bylaws of municipal corporations. Violations of some ordinances do not carry penalties and therefore are of little concern to municipal police officers. Violation of other ordinances do carry penalties, and subject the violator to arrest and trial, but these are not crimes. They are more closely associated with civil wrongs. For this reason, violations of ordinances are often called quasi-criminal in nature. It is difficult to define this term except to say that it lies somewhere between a criminal wrong and a civil wrong.

Since the state enacts crimes, and because such offenses must be applicable throughout the state on a uniform basis, the state legislature cannot delegate this power.

It would appear that an individual may be fined or imprisoned for violation of a municipal ordinance in the same manner as he might for the commission of a crime. In theory a fine is treated as civil damages for wronging the municipality. Failure to pay a fine subjects the violator to imprisonment. This is not imprisonment for nonpayment of a debt but imprisonment for failure to obey a lawful court order. The student may then wonder how a municipality can impose both a fine and an imprisonment for violations of municipal ordinances. Some states follow this practice. The authors question the constitutionality of the practice and await a challenge to arise in the courts of those states. A municipal court is empowered to assess a fine. If the fine is not paid, only then can the defendant be imprisoned under the theory that he has failed to comply with an order of the court. This theory is followed in the states of Georgia, Louisiana, Minnesota, Missouri, Montana, New York, and Wisconsin.

The student should check his own municipal ordinances to see if violations are punishable by fine or imprisonment *or both*. The "or both" language represents an attempt by the municipality to raise the status of ordinances to criminal statutes, which, of course, only the legislature can enact.

2.5 Corpus Delicti

For a police officer to fully understand what is necessary to prove a case in court, he must be aware of the factors that constitute a particular crime. This involves the concept of *corpus delicti*.

Contrary to some popular belief and most comic strip detectives, the *corpus delicti* is not the body of the victim of a homicide, but rather the body of the crime. Every offense consists of distinctive elements, all of which must exist for a particular crime to be proven. If one or more of these elements is missing, the crime thought to have occurred, in fact, could not have been committed. What might have been committed was another crime requiring proof of those elements which do exist. The combination of these elements in a particular offense is called the *corpus delicti*.

At common law, the *corpus delicti* of burglary consisted of the following elements: breaking, entering, dwelling house, of another, in the night time, and intent to commit a felony therein.

All these elements had to exist before the crime of burglary could properly be charged at common law. If, instead of a dwelling house, a store had been broken into, then burglary had not been committed because one element was not present. Instead, another crime had been committed. If the defendant were charged with burglary, the state would have been unable to prove that burglary had been committed and the case would have been thrown out of court.

The reader will observe that nothing mentioned in the above paragraphs involves guilt or innocence of the accused as a necessary part of the *corpus delicti*. Guilt or innocence is not material at this point. Before someone can be charged with a crime or arrested for committing a crime, it must first be established that a crime has, in fact, been committed.

The prosecuting attorney must prove the *corpus delicti* at trial before he can attempt to prove the defendant guilty. An investigating police officer should follow the same pattern in his investigation. Before arresting a suspect, the officer must be aware of the charges he will bring. To accomplish this effectively, he must be able to organize his investigation in terms of the elements required for the offense he thinks occurred. Then he can determine whether that crime has, in fact, been committed. Only then can he confidently determine that when he does have a suspect, the arrest will be based upon the proper charge corresponding to the crime actually committed and provable in a court of law.

Questions for Discussion

1. Why is it important for the police officer to know and understand the difference between a felony and a misdemeanor?

2. Distinguish between the violation of a state criminal statute and the violation of a municipal ordinance.

3. By what process is a state statute declared constitutional or unconstitutional?

4. Joe is charged with petty larceny in violation of a section of the municipal ordinances of Senior City. He had taken city property. After prosecution in the city court the state seeks to prosecute Joe under its statutes. Among other contentions, Joe argues that he has twice been put in jeopardy for the same offense. Is his double jeopardy plea valid?

Chapter 3

JURISDICTION

3.0 Introduction and Definition

In designing a system that will efficiently handle disputes which arise in a complex society, two decisions must be made. First, man seems to find it essential to write down guidelines for all members of society. These we call laws. But the process is only half complete. A place for interpretation and enforcement of these laws must be established. Without such a place, law enforcement would depend on the individual likes and dislikes of each person. Tyranny would become probable.

Through a slow process, most civilized countries have developed courts, in one form or another, to interpret and enforce their laws. Even these courts are bound by guidelines for the conduct of matters before them. The guidelines, called rules of procedure, govern the conduct of all the parties concerned in a case. The rules are carefully thought out to assure procedural fairness for everyone involved. One would think that these rules would be all that is needed to insure a person's rights. But before these rules can effectively come into play, the right of a particular court to handle the case before it must be determined.

The fact that a court has a judge or judges, a place to meet, and officers to enforce its commands does not automatically give that court the power to try a case. The court must have jurisdiction. Without jurisdiction no court can validly try and sentence a person. Jurisdiction is defined by the legislature under common law principles and subject to state or federal constitutional provisions.

Jurisdiction, then, is the power of a court to handle a case. That some courts have power to handle some matters and are denied this power in other areas is simply a matter of convenience and order. We will attempt to demonstrate the basic jurisdictional problems in this chapter. Jurisdiction has three apects: territorial, personal, and subject matter.

3.1   Territorial Aspects of Jurisdiction

The first principle of territorial jurisdiction is that no state can enforce the criminal laws of another state or sovereign. The second principle is that a state can enforce its laws only when those laws have been broken. Normally, the arm of the law of a state cannot reach outside the state boundaries. With these rules in mind, let us consider this problem. John, a citizen of New York, goes into Delaware and murders Sam. John returns to New York and is immediately arrested by New York authorities under a warrant charging John with murder. Since New York's law against murder has not been broken, John cannot be tried on the New York charge nor can New York enforce the laws of Delaware. Therefore, New York has no jurisdiction.

Suppose John poisons Sam in Maryland. Sam appears to be dead and John intended to commit murder. John puts Sam in the trunk of a car and drives to Virginia. While in Virginia, John lops off Sam's head. John hoped to leave the head in one place and the torso elsewhere so that identification would be difficult. For the first time it is realized that Sam was not dead. Can Maryland try John for the murder or can they try him only for attempted murder? The common law rule was that the crime was committed where the injury occurred. In a homicide case, the place where death happened was immaterial. However, death must be the proximate result of the act which inflicted harm before this rule applies. In the above example, the poisoning of Sam was not the cause of his death. What actually caused death was John's act of chopping Sam into pieces. Thus, the common law view of this situation would hold that the crime was committed in Virginia, and only that state could prosecute John for murder. John did, however, attempt to murder Sam in Maryland and therefore an attempted murder charge would be proper in that state.

Some modern statutes have changed the common law rule by enacting statutes providing, in effect, that any crime begun in that state but completed in another is chargeable in the first state. Conversely, many of these same states provide that any crime begun in another state but completed in the second state is a chargeable crime in the completing state. Thus, if two adjoining states have identical statutes of this type, it is conceivable that a crime begun in State A and completed in State B would be chargeable in both states without any double jeopardy implications.

A somewhat analogous problem exists in the multielement crime. Suppose we have a four element crime recognized in each of four states, A, B, C, and D. John boards a plane in State A which has as its destination State D. While flying over each of the states, John commits the first element of the crime over State A, the second over State B, the third over State C, and the fourth over State D. Who has jurisdiction to try John? Assuming each state has an identical statute, each would have a territorial infringement of its laws which would allow each to try John. The same rule applies to any crime committed in transit when it cannot be determined in which jurisdiction the harm was actually inflicted.

3.2   Jurisdiction Over the Person

No court can validly try a man for a crime unless that defendant is in the courtroom and is known to the court. This is so because the Bill of Rights insulates us against the obvious tyranny that could be imposed if this were not so.

How does a court get jurisdiction of the person? First of all, a person can consent to jurisdiction without an arrest. He can also consent to jurisdiction by waiving his right to complain of an illegal arrest. This type of consent is no good unless the court also has jurisdiction of the subject matter. (See 3.3)

Second, jurisdiction over the person attaches when the arrest made is proper. But don't be misled. The court has jurisdiction whether the arrest was illegal or legal. The court does not inquire into the manner in which the defendant got before the court as long as he is there. It is up to the defendant to raise the issue of the correctness of his arrest. Practically speaking, even if the defendant wins his protest on the validity of the arrest, sound prosecutors will have prepared the proper papers to make a valid arrest before thè defendant leaves the courthouse. The main reason for objecting to an improper arrest is to prevent the state from using evidence illegally obtained during the arrest.

One problem in this area involves the extradition of an accused from one state to another. When it is discovered that an accused, who is sought by one state, is residing in another state, the state seeking to prosecute the accused has two choices. It can either kidnap him or it can use the channels provided by the United States Constitution and statutes for extradition. This procedure is handled at the executive level of government and not in the courts. It can be used only in criminal matters. A person can be extradited on a misdemeanor charge as well as a felony.

3.3   Jurisdiction Over the Subject Matter

As essential as the territorial and personal aspects of jurisdiction is the requirement that any court which seeks to try an accused must have jurisdiction over the subject matter. Here again, the legislature, limited by constitutional principles, determines which courts can hear which matters. For instance, no federal court within the continental United States, except in Washington, D.C., can grant a divorce. Even if the parties to a divorce action were to consent to the federal court's handling of such a matter, the judgment given by the federal court would be void. A judgment rendered by their friendly butcher would be as good.

It is possible for the legislature to confer subject matter jurisdiction on their courts in such a way as to create overlapping or concurrent jurisdiction. If two courts claim jurisdiction in such a situation, which court has jurisdiction? The court which first assumes jurisdiction of the person and begins prosecution will have the exclusive power over the case until it waives its priority by legally and voluntarily abandoning it.

Suppose Al robs a bank in State X insured by the Federal Deposit Insurance Corporation. As he is leaving the bank, he is arrested by federal authorities who were advised of Al's conduct. Al is arrested and taken to the county jail where he is housed awaiting trial. Federal authorities often use state facilities to house federal prisoners awaiting trial. When the federal authorities seek to secure the prisoner from custody, the state officials refuse to surrender him saying that they are going to prosecute him under the state law. Who has jurisdiction? It has been held in such cases that the sovereign first having jurisdiction over the person has the initial right to try him. Thus, the state would be compelled to turn the prisoner over to federal authorities since they made the initial arrest.

How do legislatures confer subject matter jurisdiction? Some states with a simple court system confer jurisdiction based on the felony-misdemeanor distinction. This system is satisfactory as long as the terms are consistent. (See Chapter 2 for a detailed discussion of these terms and the problems they involve.) Other states, because of definition problems, spell out the specific crimes which each court may properly handle. Further, some states grant power to their courts not on the basis of labels or names but on the penalty which may be imposed. Of course, these factors may be used in combination with each other.

The final matter to be considered under subject matter jurisdiction involves distinguishing which courts have original jurisdiction, which have appellate jurisdiction, and which have both.

Original jurisdiction is power to try a case which has never been tried before. Trial courts are courts of original jurisdiction. One cannot be tried in a court unless that court has original jurisdiction. The power to review a case that has been heard in trial court is called appellate jurisdiction. Purely speaking, a trial court does not have appellate jurisdiction. Circumstances have caused legislatures to set up a hierarchy of courts which allows some to have both types of jurisdiction. Appellate jurisdiction, when granted to general trial courts, is limited to review of cases heard in courts of a lesser nature. One court cannot review its own decision under this power nor can it review the decisions of equal or higher courts.

Although the right to have one's case reviewed is not a right guaranteed by the United States Constitution, it is a privilege granted by all levels of government in the United States. This review privilege takes one of two forms. The first form is the appeal. Appeal is the direct review of a case which the statute says an appellate court must hear if all of the procedural steps are followed. The second form of review is *certiorari,* discretionary review of a case by a higher court. One attempts to get *certiorari* by a petition. The court looks at the petition, considers it, and then determines whether or not to review the case. When a court denies *certiorari,* it does not mean that everything was done correctly in the lower courts; it simply means that the court does not want to review the case.

Probably one of the most common phrases we use is "there ought to be a law." Over the years, our system has developed a group of special relief writs to fill that need. These writs are called the extraordinary writs, of which *certiorari* is one. The others commonly recognized by most states are *mandamus,* prohibition, *quo warranto,* and *habeas corpus.*

The extraordinary writ most often used in criminal law is *habeas corpus.* Primarily a procedural tool best left to other courses, we mention it here to make you aware of what it is and why it is used. It is a writ which asks the question "Why and by what right do you detain this person?" Its determination cannot be delayed. It can be used instead of, in conjunction with, or after all other judicially employed remedies.

3.4 Concurrent and Overlapping Jurisdiction

Many students ask, if an individual commits an act which happens to violate both a federal and a state law, can he properly be convicted in both jurisdictions without being able successfully to argue double jeopardy as a defense? The answer to this logical question is yes. Even though the crimes arose out of a single act, that act violated the laws of two separate sovereigns and each has the authority to try and convict the offender. Bank robbery, as an example, would constitute both a federal and a state offense, and both jurisdictions could prosecute. As a practical matter, this is rarely done, unless the crimes are dissimilar in nature or the sovereignty first assuming jurisdiction prosecutes unsuccessfully. In any case, however, both sovereigns may legally prosecute. These instances do not constitute double jeopardy. Double jeopardy occurs when the *same* sovereign prosecutes the *same* individual for the *same* act and the *same* crime.

The United States Supreme Court, in *Bartkus* v. *Illinois*, 359 U.S. 121 (1959), said that it would be a "derogation of our federal system to displace the reserved power of States over state offenses by reason of prosecution of minor federal offenses by federal authorities." Several states prohibit a prosecution if the defendant has already been tried by another government for a similar offense. These statutes usually bar the prosecution when the federal and state statutes are very much alike and not when great differences as to elements or penalties exist. Following the *Bartkus* decision the attorney general of the United States issued a directive that no federal case be prosecuted after there has been a state prosecution for substantially the same act or acts without the approval of his office. This policy is still in effect.

Until recently, a similar relationship existed between violations of state criminal statutes and municipal ordinances. If an act violated both a state statute and a municipal ordinance, both jurisdictions had the power to prosecute, and the outcome in one would not affect the decision to prosecute in the other. Thus, an individual who violated a state statute and a municipal ordinance by committing a single act was subject to punishment in both jurisdictions. Again, as a practical matter, this was rarely done but it was legally permissible. The United States Supreme Court ruled that a municipality is an extension of the same sovereignty as the state. Therefore, a single act which violates both state law and municipal ordinance can be prosecuted in one or the other, but not both. The court held that to rule differently would constitute double jeopardy.

3.5 Venue and Its Relation to Jurisdiction

Territorial jurisdiction discussed above is determined by showing venue, the place where the crime was committed. Beyond that, venue is a procedural matter which directly affects the place where the trial may take place and from where the jury is selected. Generally, a person has a right to be tried where the offense took place unless he waives that right by failing to object to the change of trial location or by asking to have the trial changed to a place where he feels he can get a fairer trial.

Questions for Discussion

1. Sam Spud, a detective with the Middleburg, New Hampshire, police department, has been sent to New York City to work with the detectives' bureau. Sam is to learn the latest detection techniques. While in New York, Sam sees a man whom he knows is wanted for murder in New Hampshire. Sam asks this man to lunch. Sam mentions that he is from New Hampshire but not that he is a policeman. The suspected murderer says he would like to see his family but has no way to get to New Hampshire. Sam tells the man he is going there and that he will be glad to take him. They leave New York City and as they cross into New Hampshire Sam stops the car, tells the man he is under arrest, handcuffs the man, and takes him back to the town where he is wanted. The man's attorney urges that the court has no jurisdiction. Can this be validly raised? Why or why not?

2. Bill wants to kill Charlie. Bill, who is standing in State A, looks and sees Charlie standing a few feet from him, but in State B. Bill shoots and kills Charlie. Who has jurisdiction to try Bill? Why?

Chapter 4

THE CRIMINAL ACT

4.0 The Criminal Act in General

Every crime requires an act. The criminal act may take a variety of forms and consequently may lead to a variety of complex legal problems which form the subject of this chapter. As will be seen at the beginning of the next chapter, the law, in its own peculiar way, will not allow a man to be formally punished by society merely for what he thinks. Nor does the law generally punish one who commits an act without some form of evil state of mind. The problem of concurrence of act and intent will be discussed in detail later. These rules are noted here to help the student understand this chapter so that it may be studied in light of the significance of Chapter 5.

4.1 Possession as an Act

At common law, possession of an article was considered a very weak act, and therefore possession was usually not chargeable. Because it is an act, state legislatures have the authority to make possession a crime. To be a crime, however, the possession must be coupled with an evil state of mind as required by the legislature. Possession of contraband is an exception to this rule. Contraband is defined in criminal law as the possession or trafficking of articles so detrimental to the welfare of society that public policy demands that it be unlawful to possess such articles regardless of the reasons for possession. This will vary with the changing attitudes of society. Since no legal justification for possession exists, the mere possession of articles like untaxed whiskey (moonshine), numbers slips (bolita), or unprescribed narcotics is illegal regardless of reason or intent. Refer to your local statutes on possession of various articles such as guns or burglary tools, and it should become clear that the state of mind or mental element, often called intent, is stressed throughout these statutes. The reason is a logical one. Consider the plight of an officer who stops a motorist at three o'clock in the morning, finding the motorist in possession of a set of lock picks. After arresting the motorist for possession of burglary tools, the officer finds that the man is a locksmith by trade and was called out of bed at that early hour by worried parents whose two-year-old child had locked himself in the bathroom. And what about the man arrested for possession of a concealed weapon who later turns out to be a store owner on his way to make a nightly bank deposit and who has a written permit from the police chief to carry a weapon while performing this task? Thus, with the exception of contraband articles, possession can be innocent. It is for this reason that the state of mind is so important in possession cases. Therefore a person who is unaware that he possesses something which is or could be used for criminal purposes is not criminally liable. Generally, possession must be conscious and knowing before it can be punishable.

4.2 Procuring as an Act

Unlike possession, procuring, even at common law, was a sufficient act to give rise to criminal liability if coupled with an evil state of mind. The theory was that one had to do some act in order to procure, while possession was more closely connected to a status or condition, without requiring any physical effort on the part of the possessor. Nevertheless, it must be repeated that the act of procuring can also be innocent and must be coupled with an evil state of mind in order to be criminal. For example, one may procure narcotics, but if one has a prescription, this is not criminal procurement.

The criminal law references to procurement fall into three categories. Procurement can involve obtaining articles with the intent of using them for criminal purposes. The case law in this category is sparse due to the difficulty of proving the criminal purpose intended. The few cases that can be found arose a number of years ago in the British Empire.

The category commonly associated with procurement involves prostitution statutes and the prohibition against those who procure, or "pimp," for the prostitute.

The third category involves the act of procuring another to commit a crime. Statutes like these are usually classified under the topic of accessory before the fact which will be treated in 4.11.

4.3   Status as an Act

Status can be defined as a condition or state of being. Attempts have been made to treat a status as an act and punish one for simply being in a particular condition. The United States Supreme Court has ruled that a statute making it a crime to be a narcotics addict is invalid because the state of being addicted was insufficient to constitute the act necessary for a crime. This law, therefore, violated the Eighth Amendment's prohibition against imposing cruel and unusual punishment. Being an alcoholic falls into the same class as addiction, but public drunkenness is recognized as an act rather than a status. Why the distinction? A person can suffer from the physiological or psychological illnesses of alcoholism or addiction, whether voluntary or not, without the illness affecting that person's mobility. On the other hand public drunkenness is a voluntary observable fact which, through its effect on mobility and mental stability, presents a threat to society or to the intoxicated person himself. This potential for danger is one from which the society can justifiably protect itself.

The question arises as to whether vagrancy is considered an act or a status. State and federal courts have upheld the validity of vagrancy statutes.

One court recommended that a vagrancy arrest should not be made unless it is clear that a person is a vagrant of his own volition and choice. This statement indicates that one who becomes a vagrant by voluntary or intentional conduct has performed a necessary act sufficient to support a criminal charge.

4.4   Methods Used to Commit the Act

Ordinarily, when thinking of the commission of a crime, we think of the offender acting with his own hand, by shooting a gun, breaking open a window, or driving an automobile, for instance. The law does not limit criminal liability to cases where the perpetrator acts by his own hand. There are three more ways an offense may be committed. An offense may be committed through an inanimate agency. Using the mails to send poisoned candy from California to a potential victim in Florida, knowing the victim will eat the candy and die, is an example. In this case, the mail becomes the tool by which the offender produces the desired effect.

An innocent *human* agent may also be used to commit a crime. For instance, Able, intending to burglarize Sam's house, obtains the assistance of Chuck, a passerby, to climb a ladder and break open a window on the second floor. Able pretends the house is his own and he has locked himself out. Chuck agrees because Able explains that he has a bad leg and cannot climb the ladder. Able is just as guilty as if he had climbed the ladder himself and broken into the house.

Finally, a nonhuman agency such as an animal may be used to commit a criminal act. The case of the organ grinder who trained his monkey to enter homes through partially opened windows and remove wallets and purses from dressing tables serves as an example.

4.5 Crime by Omission or Negative Act

A crime may be committed by doing some affirmative act or by doing nothing. A person may be guilty of a crime for failing to act when and where the law imposes a legal duty upon him to act. This rule points up the fact that legal duties do not always correspond to moral or ethical duties. A situation that appears to involve criminal liability for failure to act in a given case, may, in fact, involve no legal guilt. The classic example used to illustrate this point is the case involving the magazine photographer who, while at the beach, observes a young girl in the water crying for help. He makes no attempt to rescue her but instead stands on the shore and takes photographs for his magazine. The photographer is an expert swimmer. In such a case, if he has no legal relationship to the drowning girl, the photographer is in no way liable for the girl's death.

The legal duty to act generally falls upon one who has some influence over the victim or offender through some legal relationship such as marriage, parenthood, or contract, which could have been exerted to prevent the injury.

Law enforcement officers should also remember that the crime charged in cases of failure to act is the same crime that would be charged had the accused produced the same result by acting affirmatively. An evil state of mind must be proved in either case.

4.6 Causation

One of the most complicated legal problems regarding the criminal act involves the law of causation. The rules of causation establish nothing more than a cause and effect relationship between the act of the accused and the resulting harm. Establishing this relationship is a prime function of the prosecutor in any criminal case. Generally this presents little, if any, problem to the police officer. However, because of its connection with the criminal act, it deserves mention in this area.

The majority of criminal cases involve a direct cause and effect relationship. For example, Sam fires a gun at Fred; the bullet strikes Fred and he is injured. In this case, it is not difficult to convince a jury that Sam's act produced the result in order to convict Sam of the crime. The situation becomes more complex when, after Sam shot him, Fred was taken to a hospital where he died, not from the bullet wound, but from an infection caused by a doctor's failure to sterilize his instruments before removing the bullet from Fred. Another example involves the case where Fred is mortally wounded by Sam but, an hour before he would have died, Young stabs Fred in the back causing instant death. Is Sam solely liable for the homicide, or is Young solely liable, or are both liable, or is either one liable? In cases such as those, investigating police officers would generally be correct in arresting any or all of the participants who could possibly be liable and letting the attorneys and courts determine which, if any, of these people will be held responsible for the criminal result. Of course, the facts in each case must be such as to give the officer probable cause for making an arrest or obtaining an arrest warrant.

Several legal principles apply in situations like these. First, a man is presumed to intend the natural and probable consequences of his acts. This is often referred to as foreseeability. Suppose Bill threatens to shoot Adam, who has a weak heart. Adam is frightened so badly by this threat that he suffers a heart attack and dies. Bill will be held to have foreseen that this might occur as a consequence of his act and might therefore be held liable for Adam's death.

A second rule that applies to these situations is that the accused takes his victim as he finds him. For example, if Joe strikes Art without the intent to kill but, unknown to Joe, Art is a hemophiliac and bleeds to death because of the injury inflicted by Joe, Joe can be liable for the death.

In these instances the prosecutor must establish more than a simple physical cause and effect relationship. He must prove the defendant's act was the *proximate* cause of the injury or harm resulting. The difference between these two concepts can best be explained by example: If Dick shoots a gun at Pete and the bullet strikes and injures Pete, any fact or circumstance surrounding or contributing to this incident can be considered a physical cause of Pete's injury. Thus, the fact that Company X manufactured the weapon used by Dick would be a physical cause. The production of the ammunition by Company Y would also be a physical cause. Obviously, it would be ridiculous to attempt to hold Company X or Y liable for Pete's injury simply on the theory that Pete would not have been injured if these companies had not produced the gun or the ammunition.

Proximate cause exists when a particular act or omission is the direct cause of harm, and when this cause will be recognized by the law as the act responsible for the injury.

There are three rules used for determining the existence of proximate cause with modifications existing from jurisdiction to jurisdiction. First, proximate cause is established by showing a direct cause and effect relationship: Art shoots at Bob, the bullet strikes Bob, and Bob is injured. No other act interfered in producing this result.

The second method of establishing proximate cause is by showing that the act of the accused set a chain of events in motion which indirectly caused the harm. This is commonly referred to as the "but for" test and is illustrated by the examples where Bill threatens to shoot Adam and Adam dies of a heart attack from fear of Bill's threat or where Joe strikes a person he does not know is a hemophiliac and the victim subsequently bleeds to death. In each of these instances, but for the act of the accused, the victim would not have suffered the harm. Thus, the accused is criminally liable in each case.

Finally, proximate cause may be shown by establishing that the act of the accused placed the victim in a position that substantially increased the risk to the victim of being harmed by some other cause. Thus, where Al shoots Ben in the leg knocking Ben into the street where he is run over and killed by a passing automobile, Al's act is the proximate cause of death, and Al is criminally liable.

The above examples illustrate only some of the problems that can occur in any given criminal situation. Court decisions throughout the states have discussed and decided many of the questions raised. Police officers should understand the possibility that more than one person may be liable for a single harm even though they were acting independently of one another.

4.7 Attempts

When can a police officer properly make an arrest for an attempt to commit a crime? This is not an easy question to answer. Even lawyers have difficulty understanding and applying the complex rules for determining what constitutes an attempt.

As a basis for much of our discussion on this topic, consider the following example. Sam, a wealthy man, invited Red to be his house guest. Red discovered that Sam had a safe in his bedroom and found the combination on a piece of paper in a desk drawer. Red decided to rifle the safe one night. After waiting in his room until he believed Sam was asleep, Red emerged, taking with him the paper with the combination and a revolver. Red's bedroom was on the first floor and the safe was in Sam's bedroom in the rear of the second floor. Red had taken but two or three steps from his bedroom when he stopped, thinking he saw the outline of a man's head at the end of the hallway. Believing it was Sam and that he, Red, would be apprehended, Red shot at the outline. Sam was actually in the hall at that time but behind Red when he shot. What Red thought was a man's head was actually a post at the foot of the staircase. In this example, has the crime of attempt been committed?

Statutes categorically spell out at least three significant elements of the crime of attempt: (1) the doing of an act, (2) tending toward the commission of an offense, (3) but which falls short of completion so that the target crime is, in fact, not consummated. The difficulty arises not in stating these elements but in applying them to a specific fact situation. For example, what is an act? When does an act tend toward the commission of an offense? When is a crime completed?

An attempt is not a part of the target crime, but is a separate offense punishable by statute. Like most other crimes, it requires the combination of an act and an intent. Care must be taken to distinguish an attempt from the concept of intent.

A. Subelements of Attempt

It is necessary to subdivide the three elements of attempt into component parts, which may be called subelements for lack of a better term.

1. Legal Impossibility

Simply stated, if the result the accused sought to achieve would not have been a crime, even if the act he attempted were completed, he cannot be charged with an attempt. This is only logical, for unless the accused was trying to commit a crime, he cannot be charged with an attempt. It is immaterial whether the accused thought he was committing a crime. If it would have been a crime had he completed it, this element is satisfied. On the other hand, if the accused thought he was committing a crime, but was mistaken in his belief and no crime would have resulted from his completed act, he cannot properly be charged with attempt.

To illustrate, before the 1969 legislative session, it was a crime to sell liquor in Big City. However, the legislature repealed that law and made it legal for anyone to sell liquor in Big City. Neither the Sheriff nor John, a bootlegger, knows of the repeal. John does all other steps necessary to constitute an attempt but before he can sell the liquor the Sheriff arrests him. John cannot be charged with an attempt. Even though his motive was evil, he could not have committed the crime for there was none to commit.

Let us vary the problem. Suppose it was legal to sell liquor in Big City before 1969. The legislature met and made such sales illegal. John, still thinking he could sell liquor in Big City, takes all steps short of actual sale when he is arrested. His belief that his conduct was legal will not relieve him of criminal liability.

2. Intent

The intent required of an accused charged with an attempt is a specific intent as distinguished from a general intent or guilty state of mind. In order to charge for an attempt properly, the prosecution, through the police officer's investigation, must be able to prove the specific intent an accused had at the time he attempted to commit a crime. That specific intent must be the intent to commit the target crime.

Intent is a complex subject and is treated more exhaustively in Chapter 5. For the present, it is enough to realize that it is impossible to look into a man's mind and tell his actual intent at the time he committed a crime. The only practical way to determine someone's intent is to infer it by what he did and said. For this reason, the law may imply intent from the facts and circumstances surrounding the attempted commission of a crime. If the specific intent can be shown, the intent element has been satisfied. Thus, in the illustration in the preceding subsection, John's purposeful, attempted sale of liquor, even though he thought it to be legal, would be sufficient to supply the intent required because he specifically intended to commit the prohibited act of selling liquor. Even though the completed crime may or may not require an intent, the attempt to commit any crime always requires a specific intent.

3. Nonconsummation

By definition, the attempt must fall short of successfully completing the target crime. If the crime is completed, there is no attempt. Statutes specify that an attempt is an act tending toward, but failing in, the commission of a crime because the accused is somehow prevented or interrupted before completion. If the crime is completed, the attempt merges into the completed crime and can no longer be charged as a separate substantive offense, since completion removes a necessary element.

Statutes in some jurisdictions may change the logical result regarding merger and allow the prosecution to elect to charge either the completed crime or the attempt even though the crime was completed.

4. The Act

An overt act tending toward, but failing in, the completion of the crime is necessary to an attempt charge. What constitutes an act and when it is sufficient to warrant the charge are difficult problems. It is a universal rule that the conduct must have gone beyond mere preparation. A close analysis of this statement may leave the reader in doubt.

To complicate the situation slightly, it can be said that the exact point where preparation leaves off and an act commences is a matter of degree. Each case must be decided on its own facts.

The act done must be capable of being directly connected with the crime for which an attempt is being charged. For example, if Dan buys a gun with the intent to kill Al and does nothing more, this is not a sufficient act. The mere buying of a gun cannot be directly linked only to the purpose of killing Al, so this constitutes mere preparation. Similarly, if Dan buys a mask and hires a taxi to drive him to a bank he intends to rob, this is mere preparation in most states. In and of itself, it is not illegal to buy a mask and hire a taxi. Since the law will not punish intent alone without some wrongful act, no attempt charge will be upheld. Some states would disagree with this interpretation and would find an attempt to have occurred somewhere in that taxi. We feel this ignores the "point of no return" concept essential to the logical distinction between preparation and the act necessary for an attempt. On the other hand, if Dan walks into the bank with gun in hand and announces his purpose, but is somehow prevented from taking the money, he is guilty of an attempt.

Consider the problems raised by the illustration at the beginning of this section. Did Red, by stepping from his room on the first floor of Sam's home armed with the revolver and safe combination, satisfy the requirement of an overt act necessary for an attempt, or was his conduct merely preparatory?

5. Physical Impossibility

What happens if, for some reason, it is physically impossible for the accused to complete the target crime? In an attempt to commit murder, what result if the gun is not loaded? This is the problem of physical impossibility. By the great weight of authority, if the physical impossibility is unknown to the accused when he acts and, despite this factor, all surrounding circumstances indicate an apparent possibility of committing the crime, an attempt can properly be charged. On the other hand, if the accused knew at the time that the gun was not loaded, he cannot be charged with an attempt, for then he would not have the intent to commit the crime.

Another example of physical impossibility involves the situation where a pickpocket can be charged with an attempt where he puts his hand into the victim's pocket and finds the pocket is empty. Here, the accused performed an act with the requisite intent which would have been a crime had it been completed, but due to a factor he did not know about, it was physically impossible to complete the crime.

Refer again to the problem set forth earlier in this section where Red fired a gun at a post thinking it was Sam, who was actually standing behind Red. In this instance, due to a fact unknown to Red, it was physically impossible for Red to complete the target crime of murder. Yet, because Red did not know that fact, the physical impossibility will not prevent him from being successfully prosecuted for an attempt.

6. Factual Impossibility

Closely allied to physical impossibility is the subelement of factual impossibility, which refers specifically to the adequacy of the means used to commit the crime. Physical and factual impossibility are often difficult to distinguish.

Different jurisdictions follow different tests to determine the adequacy of the means used. Some courts hold that the means must have, in fact, been adequate before an attempt can be charged. Others hold that the means must have appeared to the defendant to be adequate. Most courts hold that the means need only be apparently adequate under the circumstances. Thus, an attempt-to-murder charge is proper when a gun is used, since the means are apparently adequate notwithstanding the existence of a physical impossibility in that the gun was unloaded. On the other hand, if a man tries to kill another using a child's popgun, the means are obviously inadequate and an attempt cannot be charged.

B. Abandonment of Attempt

Ordinarily, one can withdraw before the commission of a crime and be relieved of criminal liability either because the crime is never committed or because it is committed by coconspirators after the accused has manifested his intent to withdraw and has actually withdrawn before the others committed the crime.

The law of attempts is a little different. If the act has gone far enough toward consummation, it is an attempt even though the accused may abandon his intent to complete the crime. If he fails to abandon his intent in time, he can still be charged with attempt, even though he had decided not to complete the crime.

Al, Ben, and Sid walk into Big City Bank to rob it. Once inside with guns drawn, Al decides he does not want any more to do with this crime. He makes his intentions known to Ben and Sid, turns and walks from the bank. Al has probably successfully withdrawn from the commission of the robbery, which Ben and Sid complete, but at the time of Al's withdrawal the conduct of the group had gone far enough to constitute an attempt and Al could not withdraw from that. Consequently Al would be prosecuted for attempted bank robbery, while Ben and Sid would be prosecuted for the completed bank robbery.

4.8   Assaults Distinguished from Attempts

Any discussion of the law of attempts requires a brief mention of the law of assaults. The substantive aspects of assault will be covered more fully in Chapter 8. It is referred to here solely to distinguish assaults from attempts.

Actually, there are few dissimilarities between assaults and attempts. Assaults are defined as acts tending toward the commission of a crime against the person of another. An attempt is directed toward the commission of any offense prohibited by law. The act leading toward the commission of the completed crime must go beyond mere preparation in both assault and attempt cases.

Most assaults require the accused to have acted with a specific intent as is required in attempts. Modern aggravated assault statutes in many states are an exception to this rule. The specific intent in an assault case is intent to cause bodily harm or intent to place the victim in fear of bodily harm. It is here that assaults differ from attempts in one important aspect. Assaults may be committed not only by attempting a battery, but also by placing the victim in a position where the victim fears imminent bodily harm even though no battery was actually intended by the accused. This difference leads to situations where an assault charge may be proper but a charge of attempt would be improper.

For example, Art points an unloaded gun at Bill. Bill does not know it is unloaded but Art does. Under the better point of view, described in 4.7, an attempt could not be charged because the specific intent to complete the crime of battery is absent. Under assault law, however, it would be immaterial whether the accused knew the gun was unloaded. If the victim did not know the gun was unloaded, but thought it to be loaded and feared imminent bodily harm, the crime of assault would be complete.

Many states have enacted statutes covering assaults with intent to commit felony. It is often difficult to distinguish these statutes as they are applied to specific fact situations from the law of attempts which exists in all states. Confusion in this area would only arise in crimes against persons. In many of these states, even the courts are at a loss to explain the difference. For example, Florida is compelled to recognize the existence of such a distinction by statute. The Florida statutes create the separate offenses of attempt and assault with intent to commit a felony. The courts faced with this problem have been unable to supply factual distinctions but have relied instead on rules of statutory construction as the basis for justifying the difference on the theory that the legislature would not have enacted separate offenses without some valid reason. It appears that the validity of that reason remains secreted in the minds of the state legislators.

See also, *Devoe* v. *Tucker*, 152 So. 624, 626 (Fla. 1934). "There is a distinction between an 'attempt' to commit an offense . . . and an 'assault with the intent to commit' such offense. While there is considerable similarity between the two offenses, they are not in all respects the same. Our legislature has recognized this by enacting two separate statutes. . . . It may be that in some cases the conduct of the accused would constitute a violation of both these statutes, while in other cases, this would not be true . . . to hold that the two deal with the identical offense would be to impute to the Legislature the enactment of a useless and unnecessary statute." However, Professor Rollin M. Perkins, in his treatise entitled *Criminal Law*, 2d ed., page 578, takes a bold step when he distinguishes the two. In essence he says that in the majority of cases there is no distinction, but that an assault with intent to commit a felony must come much closer to success to be chargeable than a chargeable attempt.

To illustrate this point, let us consider these examples. First, Art, intending to kill Bill, enters Bill's room thinking Bill is asleep in his bed. Art is armed with a loaded revolver. Although it appears to Art that Bill is in bed, in fact no one is in the bed or in the room for that matter. Art takes careful aim and fires six shots into the empty bed. Art cannot be charged with assault to commit murder because of the absence of the victim from the scene, thus making the proximity of success too remote for an assault. However, he can be charged with an attempt to murder because all elements have been satisfied. The defense of physical impossibility is not available to Art since Bill's absence was unknown to Art.

Changing the facts somewhat, assume that Bill was, in fact, in the bed when Art fired. Assume also that Art missed Bill with all six shots. On these assumptions of fact, Art can now be charged with assault to commit murder because he came so close to succeeding. In fact, his conduct came so dangerously close to completion that no other reasonable outcome was probable. Of course, we do not want to lose sight of the fact that Art could be charged with attempted murder instead of assault with intent to commit murder. The choice is up to the prosecutor.

Professor Perkins notes one more distinction. In some states, for an assault with intent to commit a felony, it is necessary that the accused have the actual, present ability to commit the battery, whereas for an attempt this is not necessary. This will be discussed more fully in Chapter 8.

4.9 Conspiracy

Conspiracy means concert in criminal purpose. The crime of conspiracy is defined as the combining of two or more persons to accomplish either an unlawful purpose or a lawful purpose by unlawful means. This crime was a misdemeanor at common law regardless of whether the purpose was to commit a felony or a misdemeanor. Many modern statutes make conspiracy either a felony or a misdemeanor depending on the nature of the target crime.

Conspiracy is a separate crime and does not depend on commission of the conspired crime. The gist of conspiracy is an agreement to commit a crime or to commit a lawful act by criminal means. In a few jurisdictions, conspiracy cannot be charged unless some overt act tending toward commission of the target crime has occurred. In these states, however, the act required is not the same as for an attempt. Most states do not require any act beyond agreement. Because of the social threat created by persons agreeing to commit crimes, conspiracy by itself was criminal under common law whether or not the ultimate objective was ever accomplished or even attempted.

Although an intended participant in the commission of a crime may withdraw before the target crime is committed, this is not true of conspiracy. Once the agreement has been made, parties are coconspirators, and withdrawal to escape a conspiracy charge is impossible.

A formal written or verbal agreement is not necessary for a chargeable conspiracy. It is sufficient if the parties act in concert, working together understandingly with a single design for the accomplishment of a common purpose. It is not necessary that each conspirator know or see the others. Each conspirator need not know all the plans. Al masterminds a bank robbery and employs Ben, Sid, Dan, and Ed, all specialists in one facet of bank robbery. Ben, Sid, Dan, and Ed are assigned to perform their particular art knowing others are involved but not their identities. Only Al knows all the participants. Ben, Sid, Dan, and Ed never meet together before carrying out their assignments, yet they are all liable for conspiracy.

One person alone cannot commit conspiracy since, by definition, it requires at least two people. If one coconspirator is acquitted of the conspiracy charge, the other must also be acquitted. In such a case, the law says that if one did not conspire, the other could not have conspired alone. This is true when only two people are involved in the conspiracy. If there are three or more involved, however, some may be acquitted as long as there are at least two left who could be convicted.

This rule does not apply if one coconspirator dies or pleads guilty before the trial of the second. Neither death nor a guilty plea renders the person innocent. This can be done only by acquittal. Similarly, if one is convicted of conspiracy and the case against the second is *nolle prossed,* the conviction against the first will stand since a *nolle prosequi* is not equivalent to an acquittal. It is simply a decision by the prosecutor not to prosecute at the present time. The rules are deceptively simple. Local case law must be consulted because of the complex variations from one state to another and often within the same state. A detailed analysis of these variations would consume too many pages for the intended scope of this book since these are matters of procedure.

Conspiracy does not merge into the target crime even when that crime is consummated. This general rule has a few exceptions; for instance, when a statute specifies that if the crime is completed, conspiracy cannot be charged or when, by its very nature, the target crime is one that can only be accomplished by two people, such as adultery where only the participants are involved. A third person, however, may conspire for the commission of adultery.

The elements that must be shown to support a charge of conspiracy are: (1) that the individuals charged knew the unlawful purpose of their agreement; (2) that each individual intended to associate himself with the promotion of that unlawful purpose; (3) that each made clear his intent to promote the unlawful purpose; and (4) that each was accepted by the other coconspirators as a participant in the conspiracy.

Joe, Fred, and Art reach an agreement. On the way to the intended crime scene, Dick joins in. At that point, can Dick be charged with conspiracy? The answer is yes. By adopting the purpose of the agreement, he became a party to the agreement.

All participants in the conspiracy are responsible for acts of the others that are natural and probable consequences of the original plan. Thus, when Art, Bill, and Cal conspire to commit robbery and arm themselves for that purpose, all are liable for the homicide committed by Art during the robbery even though killing was not specifically a part of their original plan. This would be true even though one of the coconspirators was absent from the scene of the crime at the time of the killing.

However, if one coconspirator acts in a manner completely foreign to the intended plan and its natural and probable consequences, the other coconspirators will not be liable. This is always a question for the jury. To illustrate, suppose Ed, Bill, and Sid conspire to commit and do commit the crime of auto theft. This is not a crime of violence, but unknown to Bill and Sid, Ed is armed. As the trio drives the stolen car away from the curb, Ed sees his arch enemy, Walt, walking down the street. Before Bill and Sid can react, Ed pulls the revolver from under his coat and shoots Walt, killing him. Bill and Sid could not be held liable for Walt's death since Ed's conduct was beyond the scope of the conspiracy to commit auto theft.

If someone knows a crime is going to be committed, is he liable for conspiracy when he assists the conspirators in what would otherwise be an innocent manner? John, the owner and operator of a retail food store, had for some months been selling large quantities of sugar and empty gallon jugs to George and Red. John learned that George and Red were using these raw materials to make moonshine whiskey, but did not stop selling the raw materials to them. John received no profit from the sale of the moonshine nor did he have any connection with the operation of the still. Some months later, George and Red were arrested for making the illicit liquor. Empty sugar bags were found at the site of the still and traced to John's store. Having learned the facts outlined above, officers arrested John for conspiracy to violate the federal liquor laws. Was the conspiracy charge proper?

The courts have come to an unusual conclusion in cases like this by holding that if the target crime is not a violent one involving the threat of death or serious bodily harm, mere knowledge is insufficient to make someone a coconspirator. On the other hand, if a violent crime is intended, for instance, when Al sells a machine gun to Ben knowing Ben intends to use it to commit murder, the attitude of the courts is likely to be different.

4.10   Solicitation

Counseling, procuring, or hiring another person to commit a crime was a common law misdemeanor called solicitation. Solicitation is a substantive offense. Its existence does not depend on the commission of the crime solicited. It is immaterial whether the person solicited even accepts the offer.

Like conspiracy, solicitation does not proceed far enough to be an attempt; yet, the courts have no difficulty saying that soliciting another to commit a crime is enough of an act to be punishable.

The justification for making solicitation a crime, as for conspiracy, is public policy. In a 1923 Connecticut case, *State* v. *Schliefer,* 9 Conn. 432, 121A, 805 (1923), the court stated the philosophy: "The solicitation to another to a crime is as a rule far more dangerous to society than the attempt to commit the same crime. For the solicitation has behind it an evil purpose, coupled with the pressure of a stronger intellect upon the weak and criminally inclined. . . ."

There is little doubt that solicitation is chargeable in cases where the crime solicited is a felony. Courts are split, however, as to whether solicitation to commit a misdemeanor is a crime. Most authorities agree that the better view is that solicitation to commit a misdemeanor should be a crime.

4.11   Parties to Crimes—Participation

Since an act is required for the commission of every crime, a person's mere presence at the scene of a crime during its commission will not support a criminal charge. The fact that a person is present, even though he may mentally concur in the commission of the criminal act, does not make him liable for the crime. To be liable, he must participate in some manner. In the rest of this chapter, we will strive to make clear just when someone does participate in committing a crime, in what capacity he will be liable, and the punishment to which he will be subjected.

At common law, parties to crime were grouped into broad categories called principals and accessories. Each of these groups was further divided into principals in the first degree, principals in the second degree, and accessories before and after the fact.

At common law, all parties to the commission of treason or to the commission of misdemeanors were treated as principals no matter how they participated. An exception to this rule was made for anyone who helped a misdemeanant after the crime was committed. Because of the petty nature of misdemeanors, the law did not treat such persons as participants in the offense. Only in felonies were these distinctions important.

A. Principal in the First Degree

At common law, a principal in the first degree was the actual perpetrator of the crime, that is, the person who, with his own hand or through some inanimate agency or some innocent human agent, committed the crime. (See 4.4.)

B. Principal in the Second Degree

A principal in the second degree at common law was one who was either actually or constructively present at the commission of the crime and who aided and abetted in its commission even though he was not the actual perpetrator. Mere presence at the commission of the crime would not justify charging a person with the crime. He had to aid and abet. This meant he had to assist the perpetrator either by doing some affirmative act or by providing advice. Aiding and abetting also involved criminal intent which had to be proven before a conviction could be obtained.

A person might be a principal in the second degree without rendering physical assistance. It was not necessary, therefore, that the principal in the second degree be actually present when the crime was committed. Only constructive presence was required. Constructive presence meant being sufficiently near to render some type of assistance if necessary. For example, Al, Ben, and Frank conspired to break and enter a store owned and operated by George to steal goods. They agreed that in order to facilitate the crime and lessen the danger of detection, Al would entice George from the store to a house about two miles away and keep him there while Ben and Frank broke into the store and stole the goods. Under these facts, Al would be liable for the crime as a principal in the second degree under common law since despite his distance from the scene of the crime, Al was aiding and abetting during its commission and was, therefore, constructively present.

C. Accessory Before the Fact

An accessory before the fact at common law was someone who, although not actually or constructively present nor aiding or abetting in the commission of a crime, was a participant by his prior acts of procuring, counseling, or commanding. This is the basis of the distinction between being an accessory before the fact and soliciting. For a person to be an accessory before the fact, the crime must have been committed. If no crime was committed, no accessory charge could be made and the only alternative was to charge solicitation.

D. Participation Under Modern Law

The foregoing distinctions between principals in the first and second degrees and accessories before the fact, although still essential, have caused considerable procedural difficulties for our courts.

At common law the penalty for persons convicted as principals or accessories before the fact were the same. Statutes have complicated this otherwise simple procedure by providing different penalties for each type of participation. As a result, if the indictment failed specifically to spell out the level of participation, the indictment would be invalid.

Although at common law the principal in the second degree could be tried and convicted before a principal in the first degree was convicted, this was not true with respect to someone charged as an accessory before the fact. This was the second major problem created by distinguishing the participants. An accessory before the fact could not be convicted unless a principal was convicted first. The common law based this on the idea that there could be no accessoriship unless the identity of the principal was known. Illogically, this was true even though it could be shown that a crime was committed and that the accused was directly related to that offense as an accessory before the fact.

Conversely, even though a principal was identifiable and had been convicted before the accessory's trial, the accused accessory before the fact could still attempt to prove that the principal should not have been convicted. He was permitted to do this by introducing facts which were not produced at the trial of the principal.

Recognizing the complexity of the problems often caused by their statutes, the legislatures of many states have taken steps to correct them.

Some states have abolished all distinctions between principals in both degrees and accessories before the fact, labeling them all principals without reference to degrees. In these states, it is still important to define a participant by resorting to the common law distinctions to prove an accused's participation. But the penalty and trial problems do not exist in these states. Among the states that have selected this alternative are Alabama, California, Connecticut, and Florida.

Other states have retained the distinctions but eliminated the requirement that a principal be convicted before the accessory before the fact can be convicted. In these states, being an accessory before the fact is a separate offense. The prosecution need only prove that a crime has been committed and that the accused participated as accessory before the fact. Colorado, Massachusetts, North Carolina, South Carolina, and Tennessee follow this course.

A third group of states have returned to the common law approach of standardizing the penalties for all three categories but have eliminated the procedural problems mentioned above. Among the states in this category are Delaware, Mississippi and New Jersey.

What is the importance of the distinctions between principals and accessories? Besides differences in penalties and the use of these classifications to prove participation, there is one further loophole. This involves certain persons' capabilities to commit crimes.

A classic illustration of this point raises the question: Can a woman forcibly rape a man? The answer to this is an obvious no. However, criminal liability may attach to a woman involved in a rape. Can a woman be convicted of rape? The answer to this question is an obvious yes. The opposite answers to these two questions can only be reconciled by understanding the subject of parties to crimes. The fact that a female cannot be the actual perpetrator, that is, a principal in the first degree, does not affect her liability as a principal in the second degree or as an accessory before the fact under common law. If she procures a man to commit rape or if she aids and abets in the commission of a rape, she is just as guilty of the crime as the actual perpetrator.

As you can see from this example, the purpose of classifying parties to a crime is to prevent a person from escaping criminal liability when he is not the actual perpetrator of a crime, but has done more than merely observed its commission.

E. Accessory After the Fact

The previous discussion made no mention of the fourth common law participant. Accessories after the fact should not be referred to in connection with the problems raised by accessories before the fact and principals. The liability of an accessory after the fact does not arise until after the crime is completed. Because of this, all states retain the classification of accessories after the fact despite what they have done to the other participant classifications. Since an accessory after the fact does not commit the crime, the penalties, which are usually less severe than those involved in the precommission and commission stages of the crime, are easily justified.

An accessory after the fact is defined as one who personally receives, relieves, comforts, or assists another knowing that the other person has committed a felony. To convict someone as an accessory after the fact, it must be shown that a felony was, in fact, committed and that it was completed at the time the supposed accessory rendered assistance. It must also be shown that the accused knew a felony had been committed by the person he assisted. The last, and possibly most significant, factor to be shown is that assistance was rendered to the felon personally. Although the common law required a felony to have been committed, it is possible today under some statutes to be an accessory after the fact to a misdemeanor. This appears to be the rule in Arkansas, Colorado, Georgia, Indiana, and New Hampshire. This is contrary to the common law, which distinguished between principals and accessories only in felony cases.

Mere failure to disclose the commission of the felony is not personal assistance making one liable as an accessory after the fact unless there is a statute requiring disclosure. However, one could be convicted at common law for the separate offense of misprision of felony, a misdemeanor. This involved acts like concealing the commission of a felony or nonpersonally assisting the felon. Concealing stolen property or concealing the commission of a felony without agreeing to do so would make one liable for misprision of felony at common law. However, since modern statutes cover acts like this that do not constitute personal assistance, the misprision of felony offense has fallen into disuse, and exists by statute today only on the federal level—18 U.S.C. 4 (1964). It is interesting to note that no conviction for violation of this statute has ever been affirmed on final appeal.

If an accused concealed a felony by agreeing with the felon to do so, without going so far as to give personal assistance and become liable as an accessory after the fact, he would be chargeable with a common law crime called compounding a felony. In substance, compounding a felony consisted of agreeing to conceal a felony, or agreeing not to prosecute, or agreeing to withhold evidence. The agreement was an essential element of this offense. Compounding a felony remains a statutory offense in many states.

At common law, the only person exempt from prosecution as an accessory after the fact was the wife of an accused. The bases for this exception were maintenance of the confidential relationship between spouses, preservation of the unity between husband and wife recognized by common law, and recognition to the presumed bond of love and affection. Under modern statutes, most states have extended the exempted class to include certain relatives of the accused, recognizing human frailties caused by such relationships.

Questions for Discussion

1. D struck B with his fist. B was drunk at the time. The blow caused the death of B, who would not have died had he been sober at the time according to the testimony of the medical examiner. Is D liable for the death of B? Explain.

2. X, a wealthy man, invited A to be his house guest. A discovered that X had a safe in his bedroom and A located the combination on a piece of paper in a desk drawer. A decided to rifle the safe one night. Waiting in his room until he believed X was asleep, A emerged, taking with him the paper with the combination and a revolver. A's bedroom was on the first floor and the safe was in X's bedroom in the rear of the second floor. A had taken but two or three steps from his bedroom when he stopped, thinking he saw the outline of a man's head at the end of the hallway. Believing it was X and that he, A, would be apprehended, A shot at the outline. X was actually in the hall at that time but behind A when he shot. What A thought was a man's head was actually a post at the foot of the staircase. A is charged with, among other things, (1) attempted theft and (2) attempted homicide. Discuss the propriety of these two charges.

3. A, B, and C conspired to break and enter a store owned and operated by D for the purpose of stealing goods. They agreed between them that in order to facilitate the crime and lessen the danger of detection, A would entice D from the store to a house about two miles away and detain him there while B and C broke into the store and stole the goods. Under these facts, in what capacity will A be liable for the resulting crimes if any? Explain.

4. X, the owner and operator of a retail food store, had for some months been selling large quantities of sugar and empty gallon jugs to B and C. X learned that B and C were using these raw

materials to make moonshine whiskey, but did not stop selling the raw products to them. X received no profit from the sale of the moonshine nor did he have any connection with the operation of the still. Some months later, B and C were arrested for making the illict liquor. Empty sugar bags were found at the site of the still and traced to X's store. Upon learning the above facts, officers arrested X for conspiracy to violate the federal liquor laws. Was the charge of conspiracy proper? Explain.

Chapter 5

THE MENTAL ELEMENT

5.0 The Mental Element—General
5.1 Intent—Introductory Comments
5.2 Types of Intent
5.3 Recklessness
5.4 Negligence
5.5 Mala Prohibita Offenses

5.0 The Mental Element—General

We saw in Chapter 4 that in order for conduct to be criminal, some act, either affirmative or negative, must occur. In this chapter we will discuss the need for showing that the act was committed with a certain state of mind.

As a general rule most crimes require a combination of an act and an intent. When both are required, the act and intent must be simultaneous. If the act occurs without the intent required, later formation of the intent will not make the injuring party criminally liable. For example, if John by accident and with no criminal responsibility kills Fred, John cannot be tried for a crime even if John later decides he is glad he killed Fred. The result would be the same if John planned to kill Fred on Tuesday but abandoned that intent and on Wednesday, by accident and without a criminal state of mind, kills Fred. Therefore, the prosecution must not only prove that the criminal state of mind existed but that it existed at the time the injurious act occurred.

There is no specific length of time that the intent must exist before the act as long as both exist and do so concurrently. The intent may be formed at the time of the act or it may be formed over a longer period of time. John may see his hated enemy Fred and in that instant intend to and, in fact, kill Fred. Or John may plan for weeks the method of killing Fred and merely await the proper moment for execution. The most difficult time problem associated with intent is the continuing intent fiction employed in criminal law. In Chapter 3 we saw an example of this. Suppose John poisons Sam in Maryland. Sam appears to be dead and John intended to commit murder. John puts Sam in the trunk of a car and drives to Virginia. While in Virginia, John lops off Sam's head. John hoped to leave the head in one place and the torso elsewhere so that identification would be difficult. Until John cut his head off, Sam was not dead.

John intended to kill Sam by poisoning in Maryland. Unknown to John, Sam did not die of poisoning but rather died of the wounds inflicted by decapitation in Virginia. The act causing death occurred in Virginia. However, did the necessary mental element exist at that time? By using the continuing intent fiction, courts generally hold that John would be liable for Sam's death in Virginia. The reason for this is that John intended Sam's death. The method by which this was to be accomplished has no bearing on the intent. Thus, John's intent continued from Maryland to Virginia where Sam's death occurred.

The mental element in criminal law may take any one of several forms—all often mislabeled intent. Intent in its legal sense is only one of several forms. The following sections of this chapter will discuss the various mental elements.

Proof in court is the object of any discussion of the mental element or state of mind. It must be recognized that it is impossible to look into a man's mind in the literal sense. It would be much easier if we could see a picture of the state of mind that existed when the injuring act occurred. Since we cannot do this, we must resort to objective tests to determine the apparent subjective mental state. This is accomplished by permitting the fact finders, the jury or judge, to presume or infer the accused's state of mind at the time he committed the act. This inference is based on what the accused did, what he said, and all other circumstances surrounding his act. Admittedly, this "Monday morning quarterbacking" is imperfect but it is the best system available today. There are constitutional, moral, and philosophical questions as to whether we ever want to be able to read a man's mind perfectly.

Perhaps one of the best known principles of constitutional law is that a man is presumed innocent until proven guilty. Proof offered by the prosecution must rise to a very high standard. The proof offered must be "beyond and to the exclusion of any reasonable doubt"—a greater standard than required in a civil suit, which requires only a "preponderance of the evidence," or 51 percent to 49 percent split. Once the prosecution has presented evidence that the act was committed, that the accused committed it, and shown all the surrounding circumstances, the finder of fact, as mentioned in the last paragraph, may presume that the necessary mental element existed because each man is presumed to intend the natural and probable consequences of the acts he commits. Of course, this presumption is rebuttable. The accused can offer contradictory evidence which, if believed or reasonably thought to be true, can destroy the presumption and require that the accused be acquitted.

Although one can abandon his intent before committing the act in most instances, the accused cannot escape criminal sanction by repenting after completing the act. The crime is a breach of society's standard and the attempt to make the injured party whole or by saying "I'm sorry" will be of no avail as far as guilt is concerned. This is not to say that it may not in some way mitigate or lessen the sentence imposed. But this is solely the function of the court in most cases.

5.1   Intent—Introductory Comments

Intent is the primary form of the mental element the prosecution seeks to prove through evidence found by the investigator. Two points of confusion often arise in the police officer's mind. Too often he does not realize that there is a distinction between the word "intent" in its legal sense and "intention." When we speak of doing something intentionally we refer to voluntary conduct with a specific objective in mind. Although in a number of instances criminal intent can be proven by showing such voluntary conduct with a specific objective, criminality may also be proven by showing either voluntary or involuntary harm resulting merely from a determination to act in a certain way. For example, if John shoots at Fred voluntarily, John is said to have acted intentionally. If John commits this act in order to injure Fred, he is said to have the requisite criminal intent. If John intentionally shoots at Sam but the bullet strikes Fred, a person John had no intention of hitting, John will nonetheless be liable for his act because of his intent to do harm.

The second point of confusion arises over the meaning of "motive" and the part it plays in criminal law. Very often, motive is thought to be the same as intent. It is not. It is important for the investigating officer to realize that there is a vast distinction between these two concepts.

Watching Perry Mason or some other courtroom television program would lead one to believe that proof of motive is essential. Motive, good or bad, is never an essential element of a crime. Neither the presence nor the absence of a motive ever has to be proven at a trial regardless of the nature of the case. In no crime does motive constitute a part of the *corpus delicti* (2.5).

Motive can be defined as those desires which compel or drive a person to intend to do something. Motive involves judgment, but we do not judge a man's motive for doing something. He may have the best of motives, as where a man kills a known assassin or mass killer to get rid of him. He may have done society a service, but he is nonetheless guilty of a crime unless his act falls within the bounds of the standard defenses to homicide. (See Chapter 7.) Neither do we convict a man for doing an innocent act merely because he had an evil motive.

This is not to say, however, that motive has no use whatsoever in a criminal case. Motive can play an important role in determining the existence or absence of intent. It can be one of those surrounding circumstances which help to prove intent, since it is impossible to determine exactly what thoughts were in the mind of the accused when he committed the offense. It is important to remember, however, that motive is only one factor that can be utilized in finding intent. Motive alone is never sufficient to prove intent.

An example of the difference between motive and intent may help to illustrate: Mr. Smith is lying deathly ill in a hospital bed. He is in misery. Death within a short time is inevitable, but the doctors are doing everything possible to keep him alive. Mr. Smith begs his son to do something to put him out of his misery. Son, realizing his father's pain, procures some sleeping tablets and gives them to his father. The father takes the entire bottle and dies. In this example, Son had good motives. He could no longer bear to see his father suffer. Still, his intent was to kill and he is criminally liable for the death of Mr. Smith despite his good motives.

A man may be responsible for unintended consequences of his conduct. As long as the accused commits an unlawful act accompanied by a wrongful state of mind, he is held to intend the result of his conduct. This is true even when the specific result he achieves is not the specific result he intends as long as the actual harm he does would normally flow from such an act under rules set out by law. This is the basis of reasoning the rule that a man is responsible for the natural and probable consequences of his act. If he intends to commit the act, he is held to intend all probable consequences.

A corollary rule derived from the concept of responsibility for unintended consequences is the doctrine of transferred intent. Suppose John fires a gun at Sam intending to kill him. The bullet misses Sam and strikes Bill who is standing a short distance away. Bill dies as a result. Although John did not want to cause Bill's death, he is responsible for that death because the law will transfer his homicidal intent from Sam to Bill.

5.2 Types of Intent

Intent is divided into two categories known as the *mens rea,* or general intent and specific intent. Some crimes only require proof of general intent or general evil state of mind. Other crimes require proof of a specific state of mind or intent to commit a specific crime.

A. Mens Rea

The *mens rea,* or general criminal intent, is all that is required in most crimes. All that has to be shown is that the accused acted with a malevolent purpose—that he knew what he was doing was wrong. Unless more is required, evidence which will convince a jury that the defendant had this evil state of mind at the time he committed the act will be enough to raise the presumption which must be overcome by the defense. A specific intent, when required, must be proved and cannot be presumed.

B. Specific Intent

Some crimes require proof of a specific intent. It must be shown that the actor desired the prohibited result. A specific intent cannot be presumed but must be proved like any other element of a crime.

For example, John opens a door to someone's house and enters it to escape the rain. Has he broken and entered the dwelling house of another with intent to commit a crime? No. The prosecution would be unable to prove the required specific state of mind by presumption. The jury would not be permitted to presume that merely because John was in another's house that he was there to commit a crime. However, they could presume from the evidence of his being in the house that he trespassed, since criminal trespass requires only a showing of general intent. It would then be up to John to prove a proper defense to his action, if he has any, to escape liability for his act. There are some exceptions to the rules we have discussed under the specific crimes noted in following chapters. We will attempt, in our discussion of the crimes, to indicate whether it is a specific or general intent crime. The reader is cautioned to note that certain crimes which required only a general intent at common law require a specific intent under modern statutes. We will attempt to point out these changes, but local statutes should be consulted to determine the type of intent required in the reader's home state.

5.3 Recklessness

A less wrongful state of mind than intent is that called recklessness. Committing a prohibited act with a reckless state of mind is nonetheless criminal and will often justify holding an individual criminally liable even though intent cannot be proved.

A reckless state of mind implies that one acts, not intending harm, but with complete disregard for the rights and safety of others, causing harm to result. To put the rule another way, if John voluntarily commits an act without intending to hurt anyone but his conduct is so dangerously done that he is not concerned with the consequences, he is acting with a reckless state of mind. The accused must foresee that his voluntary act would possibly or probably cause the result, and that he acted unreasonably under circumstances he knew about. The defendant's actual state of mind must be shown. Suppose John decides to do some target practice with his new .22 caliber target pistol in front of his house on Christmas morning in a busy residential neighborhood. There are children playing in the street but John is determined to test his new weapon. He fires once at the tire of a passing car and misses. The bullet strikes and kills a child playing across the street. John intended to hurt no one. His reckless state of mind would nevertheless make him criminally liable, but probably for a lesser degree of homicide than if he had acted with the intent to kill.

5.4 Negligence

The final type of mental element we will discuss is negligence. We will attempt to show what type of negligence will render one criminally liable and what type will not. There are four elements of negligence: a standard of care; breach of that standard; proximate cause; and harm or injury produced. In any discussion of negligence, it would appear that only conduct is being examined. Although it is difficult to separate or compartmentalize the state of mind and the conduct involved in negligence, it is enough to say that negligence, which involves acts of omission as well as acts of commission, will, in any number of instances, render one guilty of a crime. Negligent acts are usually voluntary but do not rise to the level of intended conduct.

The first element, standard of care, concerns everyone's legal responsibility to act or refrain from acting in ways dangerous to others. Every individual owes some duty to every other person not to infringe upon someone else's welfare or safety. When one individual harms another, it must first be determined whether a duty was owed. If a duty was owed, this element is satisfied. The duty may be fixed either by statutory or common law. For example: the duty owed to a child by a parent. The duty may arise when someone who owes no duty to another performs an act directed to that other person. This is best illustrated by an example: A passerby owes no duty to save a stranger in distress.

Once the passerby begins to save the stranger, he has a duty to act with reasonable care.

Once the duty is found, it becomes essential to determine if there was a breach of that duty. Did the person owing the duty meet the standard of care? This factor involves what is known to the law as the "reasonable man" test. This test is applied by asking whether the accused exercised the same amount of care that a reasonable, prudent man exercising ordinary caution would have used under similar circumstances. If the accused did not act this way, the duty has not been fulfilled. Unfortunately, there is no model man we can turn to for this standard. The "reasonable man" is a legal fiction. The standard may vary from jurisdiction to jurisdiction and from case to case because the trier of fact examines the circumstances of each case and determines what the reasonable man would have done under similar circumstances.

The reasonable man criterion will vary according to the skill of each individual. In a case involving need for medical attention, a doctor would be required to exercise more care than an ordinary passerby.

If a duty has been discovered and if it is thought that the duty has been breached, it is necessary to determine if that breach was the proximate cause of the alleged injury. This determination is based on all the rules of causation discussed in Section 4.6.

Of course, there cannot be liability unless an injury or actual harm has occurred. The harm, however, need not be severe. The slightest injury to person or property will support this element of negligence.

All of these elements define both civil and criminal negligence. The elements of civil negligence, often called simple or ordinary negligence, are the same as the elements of criminal negligence. Criminal negligence is often called gross or culpable negligence, but all these terms are interchangeable. The difference between civil and criminal negligence is solely a matter of degree and is usually a question to be settled by the fact finder. The distinction will depend on the facts of the particular case and not on any hard and fast legal principles. The guidelines the jury uses to distinguish civil and criminal negligence are based, not on the severity of the harm or injury that results, but on the severity of the breach itself.

Negligence differs from recklessness in one important aspect. In recklessness, conduct is governed by the actual state of mind of the accused. In negligence it is possible that the accused is actually not aware of the consequences of his conduct even though a reasonable man would be.

The same conduct can render one both civilly and criminally liable if the conduct is grossly negligent. On the other hand, if the harm resulted from only simple negligence only a civil action can be supported.

It can be seen that law enforcement officers are often required to make a value judgment at the scene as to the degree of negligence involved in a particular case. If the officer, based on the above guidelines, determines that there has been a duty owed by one to another, and that the standard of care has been breached, that as a proximate result a harm requiring police investigation has occurred, he may justifiably make an arrest. If he finds that the accused acted with a criminally negligent state of mind, the officer will be protected. This is so even though the prosecutor or jury later find only simple negligence.

Negligence will not support a charge for a crime requiring a specific intent.

The following examples will serve to consolidate the principles of negligence. Suppose John is driving down the street and is obeying all traffic laws. John takes his eyes off the road for a second to light a cigarette and unintentionally runs through a stop sign striking another automobile crossing the intersection, killing the driver of that car. John, of course, owed a duty to others on the road constantly to be aware of traffic conditions. He breached that standard of care by taking his eyes off the road, which proximately resulted in the harm. There is no doubt that John was negligent, but to what degree? At most, John would be civilly liable for his negligence because the breach of the standard of care was not so severe as to constitute culpable negligence, notwithstanding the amount of injury inflicted.

On the other hand, suppose John had been driving while intoxicated instead of merely lighting a cigarette when he ran through the stop sign. Here, John's breach of reasonable conduct was so severe that a jury could justifiably find gross negligence and hold John criminally liable.

5.5 Mala Prohibita Offenses

All common law crimes were considered moral wrongs or wrongs in themselves and were labelled *mala in se*. These common law crimes all required proof of intent whether general or specific. Since that time, offenses have been created which involve no moral turpitude but which are designed to protect the health, safety, or welfare of society. These offenses are not wrongs in themselves but rather are wrongs because the lawmakers say so. These offenses are called *mala prohibita*. A large number of these offenses require no proof of intent or other state of mind but merely proof that the act was done. A number of academicians say that these offenses are not crimes. That may be so in a pure sense, but in each *malum prohibitum* offense, a man's property or life may be restricted. The Supreme Court guarantees the right of trial by jury, and all other constitutional rights are extended to one charged with such an offense.

Among the many types of offenses considered to be *malum prohibitum* are: (1) illegal sales of intoxicating liquor by such conduct as selling of a prohibited beverage or selling to minors; (2) sales of impure or adulterated food or drugs; (3) sales of misbranded articles such as selling oleomargarine as butter or shortweighting a customer by having produce or meat scales improperly balanced so that the customer is overcharged. Violations of most traffic regulations and motor vehicle laws also are considered *malum prohibitum*. Running a red light, speeding, improper passing, driving without a license, and others are violations enacted for the safety, health, and well-being of the community. Most such violations are not inherently opposed to the moral concept of what is wrong. These types of offenses are wrong only because they are prohibited. The fact that the existence of a guilty state of mind at the time of commission need not be proved is only of secondary importance in distinguishing such conduct from crimes *malum in se*. It is the history and nature of the offense that controls its classification as *malum prohibitum* or *malum in se*, rather than the requirements regarding proof of a guilty state of mind. It is thus improper to believe that any offense which does not require proof of intent or guilty mind, either general or specific, is, by that very fact, *malum prohibitum*. Statutory rape is a good example of this principle. Some view statutory rape as a *malum prohibitum* offense because proof of a criminal state of mind is not an element of the crime needed for conviction. The mere doing of the prohibited act is all that need be shown. Although this is true, when analyzed in terms of the nature of the offense, statutory rape takes on moral overtones that clearly reflect the opinion of society to treat that conduct as being morally unacceptable as well as legally prohibited; hence, *malum in se*.

It may then be concluded that although most *mala prohibita* offenses do not require proof of intent as an element leading to conviction, this strict liability factor is not the sole criterion for distinguishing acts which are *malum prohibitum* from those which are *malum in se*.

Questions for Discussion

1.   Albert, a city police detective assigned to the vice detail, managed to gain the confidence of a group operating a commercialized gambling operation. One night Albert sat in on a card game for the purpose of learning the identity of participants for eventual use in prosecutions for violating the state gambling laws. Several hours after the game started, the house was raided

by sheriff's deputies and state investigators. All the participants were arrested and charged with gambling, including Albert. At trial, Albert argued that his intent was only to gain the evidence he was seeking and not to gamble. The jury convicted Albert, after an instruction by the court stating, in effect, that Albert's motive was to get the evidence, but his intent was to gamble. Albert immediately appealed. What should be the decision of the appellate court?

2. A defendant ran through a stop sign while driving an automobile and convincingly showed he did so unintentionally. Should the court have acquitted him?

3. Sam was an olympic medalist in swimming. He secured a job as a lifeguard at Euclid Beach Park. Things were not too exciting so Sam decided to have a few drinks while he was on duty. Sam was feeling no pain when he heard a cry for help. He saw a person in great difficulty about 100 yards offshore. Sam stumbled and finally reached the water. He was unable to get to the victim before she drowned. Under what theory, if any, would Sam be liable for the death of the drowning victim?

Chapter 6

MATTERS AFFECTING CRIMINAL RESPONSIBILITY

6.0 Introductory Remarks

A police officer often becomes frustrated when an accused walks out of the courtroom a free man if it appears to the officer that the defendant did, in fact, commit a prohibited act. Many of these acquittals result from improper procedures followed by officers in the areas of arrest, search, seizure, and so forth. Other "nonconvictions" occur because some court has decided that a procedure, formerly permissible, is no longer correct under modern constitutional interpretation. A third group of cases is decided to the dissatisfaction of police and prosecuting officials because of some substantive rule of criminal law which constitutes a defense to the commission of a criminal act, operating to the benefit of the accused.

The defenses available in a criminal case are the subject of this chapter. If the rationale underlying them can be understood, perhaps their existence can be better appreciated and accepted by working law enforcement officers.

As was observed earlier (1.2), the early history of criminal law did not take a man's responsibility for his actions into account. All that was necessary to convict for a criminal offense was to show that the accused did, in fact, commit the forbidden act. The law during that time was not concerned with the reasons or justifications for committing the act. If this rationale held true today, persons killing other persons in self-defense, police officers killing fleeing felons or killing to prevent a felony, and persons forced to commit crimes against their will under threat of death or serious bodily harm, among other examples, would all be guilty of serious crimes without any opportunity to justify their acts. As a result, there is little doubt that society would soon crumble.

Our system of justice is predicated on the theory that man acts of his own free will. To maintain this system, the law must allow some tolerance to those accused of crimes when they act against their own free will, either because they were insane or because their free will was exercised in such a way that they were compelled to commit an act in order to avoid more serious consequences, as in the case of self-defense or duress, or because they were compelled to act in the performance of a legal duty, as in the case of a police officer killing a fleeing felon.

With this purpose in mind, let us now examine a number of these defenses.

6.1 Insanity

Insanity is a legal defense in criminal cases. The word legal should be emphasized because insanity is a legal, not a medical, concept. The term itself implies a sharp line distinguishing normality from abnormality. Those of the medical profession who specialize in personality disorders (psychiatrists) believe there is no such line of demarcation; that normality and abnormality are extremes of a continuum with variations in between. However, it is a fundamental principle of law that a person cannot be convicted of a crime if, at the time he committed the offense, he was not responsible for his actions. A dividing line must, therefore, be drawn somewhere to separate those who are responsible from those who are not. This line is the difference between sanity and insanity.

Everyone is presumed to be sane at the time he commits an offense. This rule benefits the state since it eliminates the necessity of proving that every defendant in every criminal case is sane, before the trial can proceed. However, if the defense does present some question about the defendant's sanity, the state must take the time to prove the defendant's sanity. The method by which this is done is governed by state statutes and rules of court procedures.

The issue of insanity may arise at any stage of the process of administering justice. The substantive criminal law is concerned with insanity at the time the act was committed, not insanity before, during, or after trial begins. These are procedural questions and they generally have no bearing on the question of whether the accused will ultimately be liable for his prohibited conduct. For example, if an accused claims insanity at the time of trial and he is adjudged incompetent at a special hearing held for that purpose, he cannot stand trial until he is declared competent at a later date. The test to determine competence to stand trial is whether the accused is capable of understanding the nature of the proceedings against him and whether he is able to help his counsel in preparing a defense. If not, he is incompetent to stand trial. This does not mean he cannot be tried for the crime with which he is accused. It simply means his trial will be postponed until he is adjudged competent again in another hearing held for that purpose. Likewise, a man may not be executed for a capital offense if he is insane.

This section is concerned with insanity at the time the act is committed, for this determines liability for the commission of criminal acts. The procedural aspects are left, with the exception of the brief mention above, to the research of the individual student.

The origin of the insanity defense is not to be found in the statute books, but has developed through the case law process. In the beginning of legal systems, madmen were not acquitted of criminal charges. After they were convicted by a special verdict declaring their "madness," the king granted pardons. Later, the test of insanity became known as the "wild beast test," under which an accused was excused from liability if he were totally deprived of reason, understanding, and memory and did not know what he was doing any more than a wild beast would be aware of its actions. Subsequently, a type of right-wrong test was established under which the defendant was declared insane if he were unable to distinguish between what was morally right and morally wrong or between good and evil.

In 1843 Daniel M'Naghten killed the secretary to Sir Robert Peel. M'Naghten claimed that at the time he committed the act, he was not of a sound state of mind. The decision of this case became the cornerstone of the test of insanity in modern times. The decision established the rule that, if at the time of committing the act, the defendant was laboring under such a defect of reason from disease of the mind as not to know the nature and quality of the act he was doing; or, if he did know the nature and quality of the act, but did not know that what he was doing was wrong, he was legally insane and not responsible for his acts. This test became popularly known as the "Right-Wrong" test of insanity. The nature and quality of the act, as referred to in this test, deals with the ability of the accused to act in a rational manner and his ability to evaluate the circumstances at the time he commits the act.

The M'Naghten Rule was not totally acceptable in all jurisdictions and, consequently, additional tests were developed. For example, the State of Alabama in 1886, in *Parsons* v. *State*, 81 Ala. 577, 60 Am. Rep. 193, extended the M'Naghten Rule to include a test called irresistible impulse. In essence, that test declared that if by reason of a mental disease, the accused had so far lost his power to choose between right and wrong that he was unable to avoid doing the act in question, he was insane.

The M'Naghten test was severely criticized on the grounds that it was arbitrary, that it only applied to a small percentage of the people who were actually mentally ill, that it underemphasized emotional strain on an individual, that it required psychiatrists to give a yes or no answer about a person's sanity in an age when psychiatry had become much more of a science than in the past, and that it took into account only one aspect instead of the whole personality of an individual. In 1954 the United States Court of Appeals for the District of Columbia broadened the M'Naghten test in favor of what has become known as the Durham Rule, 94 App. D. C. 228, 214 F. 2d 862 (1954). The Durham case held that an accused is not criminally responsible if his unlawful act was the product of mental disease or mental defect. Mental disease is defined as a condition capable of either improving or deteriorating, while a defect is a condition considered not capable of either improving or deteriorating. This broad test of insanity has only been adopted by a few states.

The Durham Rule has also been criticized on opposite grounds from M'Naghten in that the Durham Rule is too broad and places too much power in the hands of psychiatry in determining the legal issue of insanity. Critics fear that too many people will be able to escape punishment for crimes if this test is applied.

In a long line of cases following the Durham decision, the district court attempted to clarify the rule so that its application would be more understandable to juries who were required to apply it. One of the greatest problems faced by the court was in its attempt to restrict the impact of the rule on juries so that they would base their decisions as to the defendant's sanity on factual details relating to the evidence presented rather than simply on medical conclusions testified to by experts. The evidentiary distinction between the right of an expert witness to give opinions or draw conclusions on matters of a technical nature and the function of the jury to draw conclusions on factual matters became fuzzy. By early 1971, the dissatisfaction with the Durham Rule in the District of Columbia courts became patently irreconcilable. As a result, the District rejected the Durham Rule in 1972 in the case of *United States v. Brawner*, 471 F.2d 969 (D. C. Cir., 1972), in favor of the Model Penal Code test proposed by the American Law Institute and described below. All federal courts except the First Circuit (which includes the states of Maine, New Hampshire, Massachusetts, and Rhode Island, and Puerto Rico) are following the Model Penal Code test.

The Model Penal Code, which, as we said earlier, was adopted in 1962 by the American Law Institute, proposed the following test: the accused is legally insane if he "lacks substantial capacity either to appreciate the criminality of his conduct or to conform his conduct to the requirements of law."

Some jurisdictions recognize an insane delusion test under which the accused may have been partially insane in respect to the circumstances surrounding the commission of the crime, but sane as to other matters.

Another suggested test goes by the name "policeman-at-the elbow" test. The essence of this proposal is that the accused is not guilty if he would still have committed the crime even if there had been a policeman standing at his elbow. In such a case, the accused must have been insane.

All of these tests rest on the premise that the accused is *non compos mentis,* that is, that the accused is unable, due to his mental illness, to form the intent necessary to commit a crime. As may be observed from the conflicting tests described, there is no one test that is universally acceptable, and all are subject to valid criticisms.

The law does not recognize any degrees of insanity. There are no gray areas. One is either sane or insane. Likewise, the law is not concerned with the causes of insanity. It is felt that this is the concern of the medical profession. Even delirium tremens, resulting from excess consumption of alcohol, is treated as a type of insanity and will be a defense, notwithstanding the fact that it was probably induced voluntarily by the accused over a period of time.

With only a few exceptions, most courts agree that low intelligence or mental weakness is not the same thing as, nor will it support, a claim of insanity. A person may be an idiot, moron, or imbecile but if he possesses sufficient capacity to know the rightness and wrongness of his acts, he is legally sane. The only situation in which mental weakness may operate as a defense is where the limited intelligence may prevent the individual from having the capacity to form a specific intent where one is required. In such a case, the intent cannot be proved and, hence, no conviction. This is not based on a plea of insanity nor will it be decided on the tests of insanity.

Related to insanity cases, but not quite constituting insanity, are the problems of persons referred to as criminal sexual psychopaths. The problems of this type of individual are usually treated separately by each jurisdiction and are generally covered by statute. See Chapter 9 for a more complete discussion of this point.

6.2 Intoxication

Intoxication is usually thought of in the context of alcoholic beverages. Many jurisdictions, however, also apply the same rules to intoxication resulting from use of narcotics and dangerous drugs. Intoxication as a defense may fall into either of two categories.

Voluntary intoxication is ordinarily not a defense. If a person voluntarily becomes intoxicated, he is held to be responsible for the consequences of his acts committed while in that condition. There are, however, two exceptions to this rule. In those cases where the crime committed requires proof of a specific intent, the accused's state of voluntary intoxication may be such that he was incapable of forming the specific intent, and, therefore, he cannot be convicted (5.2). Also, if the crime requires knowledge of certain facts, extreme voluntary intoxication may make the defendant incapable of having this knowledge; thus, an essential element could not be proved. This might apply in a case such as "knowingly receiving stolen property."

If, however, the defendant forms his intent before becoming voluntarily intoxicated, the intent remains until the act is committed, and the intervening intoxication will not be a defense. If a legally insane person is also voluntarily intoxicated at the time he commits a prohibited act, the intoxication will not affect his defense of insanity.

In those few cases where a person claims he was so intoxicated that he was incapable of forming a specific intent, the jury must decide the truth of the claim. There is no set point where voluntary intoxication will serve as a defense in these cases. It is a matter of degree, for it is well known that intoxicants affect different people in different ways and to different extents. Suffice it to say that in the authors' experience, it is difficult to convince a jury to accept voluntary intoxication as a defense and rarely is it successfully argued.

Involuntary intoxication, on the other hand (liquor forcibly poured into someone who then commits a crime, for example) is ordinarily a defense. There is a question, however, as to whether the degree of involuntary intoxication is important. If involuntary intoxication were an absolute defense, any individual could claim that the one small drink he was forced to take was sufficient to excuse his commission of a subsequent crime. Most authorities would agree that the degree of intoxication is an important factor in determining criminal liability under these circumstances.

6.3 Infancy

To repeat, the key to successfully prosecuting someone charged with criminal conduct is the ability to prove intent. Children are sometimes not old enough or mature enough to be capable of forming a criminal intent so they may not be held liable for acts which would otherwise be criminal. With this in mind, the common law set some arbitrary rules regarding the capability of children to form a criminal state of mind. The rules have no foundation in the actual abilities of children, nor do they take into consideration the actual abilities of the individual child except within the framework of the rules.

A child under the age of seven years was conclusively presumed incapable of entertaining a criminal intent and therefore could not be held accountable for otherwise criminal conduct. It could not be shown in these instances that a particular child was sufficiently intelligent to know his act was wrong.

A child between the ages of seven and fourteen years was rebuttably presumed incapable of entertaining a criminal intent. This meant that although he was presumed incapable, the state could offer evidence to show that the particular child did possess sufficient intelligence to know the difference between right and wrong and did have the capacity to act with an evil state of mind. Unless the state could show he had this capability, the presumption remained and the child could not be convicted.

Children over fourteen years of age were presumed capable of forming a criminal intent. This presumption was also rebuttable, as in the case of adults, by showing that the accused suffered from some deficiency which prevented him from acting with an evil state of mind.

This breakdown by age bracket has been modified by statute in many states and the student should become familiar with the local law.

6.4 Immunity

The fact that granting immunity is now common in some criminal trials does not mean the law is new. Actually, immunity was a recognized common law doctrine.

There are basically two types of immunity that may be granted to an individual—common law immunity and statutory immunity. In order to convict persons accused of committing crimes, it is sometimes necessary that one or more participants be given immunity so that their testimony may be used to help convict other participants. This is the purpose of granting immunity. It is rarely done if there is sufficient evidence to convict without statements from the participants themselves.

Common law immunity, sometimes called an agreement not to prosecute or contract of immunity, exists as a matter of public policy and may prevent an individual from relying on the self-incrimination clause of the Fifth Amendment to the United States Constitution.

Police officers should be aware that the prosecutor, and not the police, is the only party authorized to grant immunity. In all cases, the court in which the case is being heard should be made a party to the agreement. A few jurisdictions require the court to consent, but in all jurisdictions it is a recommended policy.

The agreement may take any of three forms. It may take the form of an agreement not to prosecute the individual to whom immunity is granted, or it may be an agreement to the effect that the individual will be prosecuted but that no sentence will be imposed. Third, it may be agreed that the compelled testimony will not be used against the witness in any subsequent proceeding. Common law immunity is a three-party agreement involving the prosecutor, defendant, and court, and can be granted only with the consent of the defendant.

Statutory immunity is not an agreement of the type existing at common law. Under statutes of the various jurisdictions, immunity from self-incrimination is involuntarily taken away from the defendant by the state and by the statutes. In cases where statutory immunity is granted, the state is subsequently prevented from prosecuting an individual against whom the statute was imposed as to all evidence obtained as a result of compelled testimony. If, however, there is other sufficient evidence aside from the compelled testimony on which to prosecute, a charge may be brought against the individual.

Generally, immunity will apply to any testimony given which has any relevance to the issue in question, even though the response indicates the defendant committed an act not thought to be relevant or connected in any way.

6.5   Statutes of Limitations

At common law there was no time limit on prosecuting for the commission of a crime. If the offender was not apprehended for twenty or thirty years, he could still be prosecuted after that time, the only problem being the possibility of loss or destruction of evidence or the unavailability of witnesses.

Most jurisdictions today still place no limitation on prosecutions for capital offenses or murder in noncapital punishment states. However, in most states statutes have been enacted providing that the state has only a certain period of time after a crime is committed in which to initiate the criminal process. This time period differs from state to state and is established arbitrarily. The reason for statutes like this is that evidence and witnesses will usually be unavailable after that period of time so that prosecutions would be fruitless.

What constitutes the initiation of the criminal process is one of the prime questions under such statutes. The criminal process begins with either the issuance of an indictment, the filing of an information, or the issuance of a valid arrest warrant. When any of these events occurs, the statute of limitations will stop running and there will no longer be a time limit imposed by the statute of limitations for that crime.

The statute of limitations for any offense begins to run from the moment the crime is committed, not when it is discovered or when the defendant is actually identified, unless otherwise specified.

Besides issuance of an indictment, filing of an information, or issuance of a valid arrest warrant, the statute may stop running when the accused is a fugitive from justice. A fugitive from justice is one who hides himself. If he openly lives in any state or nation without intending to conceal himself, he is not a fugitive and the statute is not interrupted, but continues to run.

6.6   Mistake of Fact

One who commits a prohibited act in good faith and with a reasonable belief that certain facts exist which, if they actually did exist, would make the act innocent may base his defense on mistake of fact. Thus, where John takes property belonging to Bill, believing it to be his own, his defense will be that he was operating under a mistake of fact. In this example, the mistake prevents John from having a criminal intent, so he cannot be charged with larceny. This is true provided John's mistake was made in good faith and was a reasonable mistake that anyone could have made under the circumstances. If the facts actually were as he believed them to be, his act would have been innocent.

The mistake must be an honest one not caused by the defendant's own negligence or deliberation. The decision in any case as to whether the mistake was honest rests with the jury.

There are three cases when mistake of fact will not operate as a defense. First, in those few offenses where intent is not a necessary element of the offense and the mere doing of the act is sufficient to convict, mistake of fact is irrelevant since there is no intent element to be negated by the mistake. A statute designed to protect consumers of goods from being shortweighted by retailers, therefore, makes the seller of goods criminally liable for overcharging a customer by shortweighing the goods sold. This is a *malum prohibitum* misdemeanor (wrong only because it is prohibited) not requiring intent. Once the act is committed, mistake of fact will be no defense and the seller's contention that he did not know his scales were unbalanced will not be a valid defense.

The second type of case to which this defense will not apply is one in which the accused intended to commit some wrong but did not intend the actual consequences of his act. If the initial wrong was intended, the defense will not apply because of the rule that a wrongdoer is responsible for the natural and probable consequences of his acts. If Joe strikes Bob with his fist intending to injure Bob and Bob accidentally trips over a log, striking his head on the pavement, and dies, Joe cannot claim mistake of fact as a defense because he intentionally struck Bob and is liable for all natural and probable consequences of his act.

The third exception to the rule involves crimes committed through the culpable negligence of the accused. Since culpable negligence is a different type of mental element than intention, and results from a gross failure to exercise due care, there is no intent to be negated by the mistake and it will not be a defense. Suppose the groundskeeper of a children's playground leaves parathion, a deadly poison, within the reach of the children. As a result, one of the children, thinking it to be face powder, applies it to her face and arms and dies within a few minutes. The groundskeeper cannot claim mistake of fact as a defense to his culpable negligence by showing that he was unaware of the presence of any children in the area.

6.7 Mistake of Law

There is an old cliche that "ignorance of the law is no excuse." This is true in ninety-nine percent of the cases, because everyone is presumed to know the law. It is true for aliens and citizens alike. Suppose it is permissible in a middle eastern country for a man to kill another when the other has stolen his purse. Can the alien do the same thing in the United States and escape punishment? No, because he is held to the same standards as our citizens under our law. Less exaggerated is the example often given concerning the American tourist who travels through the United States. Suppose our tourist comes from a state permitting right-hand turns when the light is red. If he goes to a state which prohibits such turns, he cannot use his home state law as a defense nor can he use ignorance of the law as a defense, if the prosecution wishes to pursue the matter.

When a person acts in a prohibited manner, and knows the facts surrounding his actions, the law will presume he had an evil state of mind at the time and intent will be implied. But, as was observed in the previous chapter, there are two kinds of intent. Mistake of law will not apply to any case involving *mens rea* or general criminal intent, but mistake of law may be a defense in cases involving a specific intent.

Where the crime charged requires proof of a specific intent (5.2), and the accused can show a mistake of law to an extent that would nullify his forming the specific intent, the defense will be available. Admittedly this is a rare occurrence. We have been unable to discover a pure mistake-of-law case which negated a specific intent. Research reveals any number of cases which state this rule, but which, in fact, involved primarily a mistake of fact and its effect on the specific intent required. For example: Sam takes a book believing it belongs to Joe, intending to steal it, when, in fact, it is Sam's own book. Here, the specific intent cannot be fulfilled because Sam did not take the property of another. Lack of knowledge of the existing law will not, of itself, establish the defense. It must be shown that because he lacked this knowledge, the accused did not actually form the specific intent required for commission of the specific offense.

There is one further way mistake of law may be a defense. When a legislature enacts a law, constitutional principles require that it be presumed valid until and unless a proper court holds to the contrary. Anyone who obeys the law as it is written cannot be prosecuted for following it even if a court subsequently declares the law to be invalid. The most difficult problem concerns the status of one who bases his conduct on a lower court's determination that a specific statute is unconstitutional when the decision is later reversed by a higher court and the law is held to be constitutional. The accepted view in situations like this is that the statute was constitutional from the beginning and that the lower court's determination of unconstitutionality must be ignored. This rule creates a dilemma for people who conduct themselves in accordance with the lower court's determination of unconstitutionality. They are placed in a position where they must act at their own peril in deciding whether to obey the law. To illustrate, suppose state A enacts a law prohibiting the importation of alcoholic beverages. John imports alcoholic beverages and is brought to trial for violating the law. The court, at John's trial, declares the statute to be unconstitutional and releases him. Bill, hearing of this decision, begins to import alcoholic beverages relying on the decision of the lower courts. Unknown to Bill, the lower court's decision was appealed to the supreme court of the state, which reversed the lower court and declared the statute constitutional. Even though Bill relied on the lower court's decision, he is subject to prosecution for violating the statute. It is possible, however, for the law to take a practical look at the dilemma caused, and in each case determine whether or not mistake of law will be a defense.

6.8 Entrapment

The key word in the area of entrapment is inducement. When an officer of the law induces an otherwise innocent person to commit a crime in order to have him punished, the accused can raise the defense of entrapment. Notice the two key elements of entrapment—inducement of a person, by a law enforcement officer.

Inducement means the accused person did not intend to commit a crime before being induced to do so by the law enforcement officer. If the officer placed the idea of committing the crime in the mind of the accused, the defense is available to the accused, and the case will be dismissed. Williams, an undercover officer with the Big City Police Department, manages to gain the confidence of Burke. Williams proceeds to convince Burke that Burke should rob Johnson. Burke had no intention of robbing Johnson until Williams talked him into it. Burke commits the robbery and is immediately arrested by Williams. If Burke raises the defense of entrapment, his case will be dismissed. Let us distinguish this from merely presenting the accused with the opportunity to commit the crime: Paul, another undercover agent for the Big City Police Department, is walking along the street and observes Roger, a known "mugger" approaching from the other direction. Paul pretends to be a staggering drunk and falls down in Roger's path. Seizing this inviting opportunity, Roger takes Paul's wallet and turns to leave, at which point Paul places Roger under arrest. This is not entrapment. In such a case, there is no entrapment because merely presenting the accused with an opportunity to commit a crime in no way has any bearing on his intent. If the accused, without outside assistance or pressure, forms the intent to commit a crime, he cannot raise the defense of entrapment. Likewise, there is no entrapment where officers, knowing a crime is about to be committed, allow the accused to commit the act before arresting him. Entrapment is not the same thing as trapping the accused during the commission of, or immediately following the commission of, a crime.

The courts will not allow law enforcement officers to force, pressure, persuade, or influence a man into committing a crime which he would not otherwise have committed, merely for the purpose of punishing him for doing the act.

Note that entrapment is referred to here as a defense. In order to raise the defense, the defendant must, in fact, admit he committed the crime. Thus, he is guilty of doing the act charged but the courts refuse to punish him under such circumstances because the government which punishes is also the government that compelled this man to commit the crime in the first place, and such a situation is unacceptable in our society.

The second major element of entrapment is that it must be accomplished by an officer of the law or some other government official. That is, it does not extend to acts induced by a private citizen who is not an officer of the law. If the private citizen is acting for, or on behalf of, or by direction of an officer of the law, he is treated as being an officer of the law for that purpose and any arrest resulting from the commission of crimes induced this way will be subject to the defense of entrapment.

If an officer cooperates with a suspect in order to influence the suspect to participate in committing a crime, and the officer commits the act himself without intending to commit a crime, but solely for the purpose of charging the suspect as a principal in the second degree, the suspect is not guilty of the crime because the officer, the one who actually committed the act, is not guilty of a crime.

If one merely requests another to commit a prohibited act which the other would not normally commit unless he were ready and willing at the time of the request, no entrapment results. Thus, when Arthur approaches Bob and asks Bob to sell him some narcotics, there is no entrapment if Bob complies, because there is no inducement, only an opportunity presented to someone ready and willing to violate the law. Similarly, if Alice, an undercover policewoman, approaches a suspected abortionist and requests an abortion, the abortionist cannot raise the defense of entrapment at his trial because he was merely given an opportunity to apply his skills and he was ready and willing to perform.

6.9 Consent

The victim of a crime, in most cases, can consent to the crime being committed, and the defendant will often be able to use this consent as a defense. This is true specifically where the crime is directed against an individual, such as larceny. On the other hand, if the act is the type of offense that affects the public at large, as in the case of fighting in public or disturbing the peace, consent of the individuals involved will not be a defense for they are all wrongdoers to a certain extent.

When lack of consent is a necessary element of the crime, as in cases of forcible rape, robbery, larceny, burglary, and so forth, lack of consent can usually be presumed. If, however, the accused raises consent as a defense, the state must then prove the defendant acted without the victim's consent.

There are four elements to the defense of consent. First, the person giving consent must be capable of giving consent. Consent would not be available as a defense to statutory rape because the class of persons protected by these type statutes are incapable, by law, of giving consent. Consent by insane people or infants will not be legally recognized.

Second, the offense must be of the type for which consent may be given. Breaches of the peace, including affrays and disorderly conduct, are the offenses for which consent cannot be given, and therefore the defense is unavailable. Similarly, murder and mayhem are nonconsentable crimes. This would also be true in many *mala prohibita* offenses, such as the sale of mislabeled goods.

The third element is that the consent not be obtained by fraud as to the nature of the act to be committed. Fraud can take one of two forms which must be distinguished because one applies to the defense of consent while the other does not. Fraud in the execution refers to the fact that the victim agreed to an act, the nature of which he was unaware. For example, Ann goes to Doctor Borman for an illness. Borman advises Ann that she needs an operation to which Ann agrees. Under anesthetic, Borman proceeds to have intercourse with Ann. This "consent" was obtained by fraud as to the nature of the act and, therefore, consent will not be a defense in Doctor Borman's trial for rape. On the other hand, suppose Doctor Borman has intercourse with Ann after telling Ann that this will cure her ailment. Ann later learns that this was just a ruse on the part of Doctor Borman to have intercourse with her. In his subsequent trial for rape, Borman's defense of consent would be applicable. In this case, Ann did consent to the act, knowing full well its nature. However, she was induced to give her consent by fraud. Here, fraud will not negate her consent because the law is not concerned with her reasons for consenting as long as she was aware of the nature of the act to be performed. This is called fraud in the inducement.

The fourth element is that the person giving consent have the authority to consent to the commission of the crime. Arthur may consent to have his property stolen, but his consent is no good when he agrees to allow Bill to take property belonging to Charlie.

All four of the above elements must be satisfied before the accused can raise the defense of consent.

If consent to perform a certain act is given, the accused may still be liable if he goes beyond the bounds of the consent. If Alan gives Bob permission to take a one-dollar bill from the dresser in Alan's bedroom and Bob takes ten dollars instead, Bob has exceeded the bounds of the consent and will be liable for the theft of the extra nine dollars.

Consent given under threat or fear of reprisal will not be a good defense if the threat or reasonable fear was so strong that agreeing was a better alternative than allowing the threat to be carried out. The reasonableness of the fear will vary according to the type and seriousness of the act. If Al says to Ben, "If you don't give me all of your money, I will never speak to you again," this is not sufficient threat or fear to negate Ben's consent when he agrees to hand over the money. If, on the other hand, Al forces Betty to consent to intercourse under threat of death, Betty's agreement will not constitute consent for the purpose of his defense.

6.10 Duress

Duress implies that one is not acting of his own free will. Our system of criminal law emphasizes responsibility. We look to the facts of any given case to determine whether an individual may be held accountable for his actions. If not, we will not punish his conduct. Most crimes require both the intent and the act. Duress acknowledges that a person may act wrongfully without having any criminal intent. For duress to be available as a defense, one person's will must have been substituted for that of another. The person commanding the crime forms the intent and, by imposing his will, forces another to commit the crime.

When one is compelled or commanded to commit a crime under fear or threats against his person, this will be a defense to his committing the act provided certain elements are present. As soon as the threat or fear under which the accused was operating ceases, he must stop his wrongful conduct. If he continues his conduct, he alone will be held liable for his criminal acts. Suppose Art commands Bert at gunpoint and under threat of death to commit a robbery. If this threat continues up to the point where Bert commits the robbery, Bert will not be liable, for duress will be a defense. However, if Bert discovers that Art's threat is withdrawn before committing the act, but continues because it seems like a good idea, Bert will be liable. Bert failed to stop his wrongful conduct when the threat ceased.

To be a defense, duress must involve a threat against the person, not just a threat to destroy or deprive one of his property. Finally, the threat must be present and impending, not future. Someone who says, "If you do not help me commit this robbery, I will come back next week and kill you," is not imposing an immediate threat. A crime committed under these conditions cannot be defended on grounds of duress.

Most authorities feel duress is not a defense when it requires the taking of another's life in order to preserve the accused's own life. This is based on the theory that if the choice comes down to losing one's own life or taking that of another, a man is supposed to sacrifice his own life rather than kill. Admittedly, the practicalities of this rule of law are questionable.

6.11 Custom

If a statute or common law rule is in force, the fact that the law has never before been enforced is no defense. If the act is prohibited, the custom of not enforcing the rule against it can never justify the violation. This is a universally recognized rule of law and has been upheld in case after case with no exceptions found.

Police officers are often confronted by an angry motorist who says, "I was just keeping pace with all the other cars. Why don't you give them a ticket too?" Often is heard the sound of the surprised offender who says, "That law has never been enforced before. Why now? Why me?" All of these complaints have no effect on the ultimate liability of the one accused of a violation or crime, for if the police officer made a proper arrest for a valid offense, the custom of not enforcing the law or refusal in the past to prosecute for such violations will not be a defense. A violator may not successfully claim ignorance of the law because of past failure to enforce the law. Ignorance of the law is generally no defense.

6.12 Religious Belief

The First Amendment to the United States Constitution guarantees religious freedom. The right to believe anything one wants to believe is unassailable. However, can one use this right to avoid criminal liability when the practice of his beliefs causes him to do an otherwise criminal act? The answer in most instances is no. Religious practices which violate positive criminal law cannot be used to justify or excuse any criminal conduct.

It is essential that public peace and moral order be maintained. If this were not the rule, each man could, under the First Amendment, start his own religion in order to evade the law. In other words, by conceding the right to practice certain religious beliefs in violation of positive criminal law, society would be open to fraud and subject to the possibility of chaos.

6.13   Victim's Guilt

The fact that the victim of a crime may himself have committed a criminal act is no defense for the accused. When Andy steals property from Bob, Andy cannot base his defense on the fact that Bob had previously stolen the property from Chris. In this case, both may be punished for their crimes. Even though neither Andy nor Bob had better rights in the property than Chris, the actual owner, Bob had a better right to it than Andy did, for Bob was the first thief.

6.14   The Use of Force as a Defense

A.   General Comments

All too often policemen encounter situations that require them to decide whether or not to take the life of another human being. Law enforcement agencies tend to train their personnel how to use firearms properly but fail to give proper instructions on the legal ramifications of the use of both deadly and nonfatal force. Without having the knowledge as to when deadly force may be used under state law and without proper policy guidance from law enforcement administrators, policemen patrol their beats often wondering what they may legally do if the unfortunate choice should ever present itself.

Many states do not specifically provide by law when a policeman may use deadly force. Some do, but without policy formulation by police executives, the statutes exist in letter only and the interpretation of those laws made by court decisions leave many questions unanswered. The decision when to use his weapon is, without doubt, the most difficult decision a policeman ever has to make, and often he must make that decision within a few seconds.

It is both unfair and impossible to expect the law to have an answer for every conceivable situation that a police officer may encounter in which the use of force may be necessary and justified. But if general principles regarding the use of force can be instilled in the minds of policemen so that these decisions become second nature, they will obviously be more confident that their conduct is legally and morally proper when they do act.

In deciding when. to use deadly force, police officers are expected to use common sense. Too often, however, instinct governs conduct, and instinct may not be compatible with common sense unless adequate training is received. Common sense must be guided by some legal interpretation and policy guidelines. What is required of an officer when he faces a situation in which deadly force may be operative is his reasonable belief that deadly force is necessary. This does not mean that the use of deadly force must actually *be* necessary. It is essential that police officers recognize that they may use deadly force when acting under circumstances that would lead an ordinary and cautious man of ordinary intelligence to believe that the only way he can prevent further harm to his own or another's life or safety would be to use deadly force. When an officer understands this principle, common sense becomes his most important asset.

The fact that the law permits an officer to use deadly force in a particular situation does not necessarily mean that this type of action is required. The words, *as a last resort,* must guide the policeman's use of common sense. It must not be forgotten that in our advanced twentieth century, density of population and technical and scientific advances not only cause unfortunate situations, but also can help prevent those situations. So it is with the use of deadly force. Even if deadly force is permissible in a given situation, it does not mean that it must be used. On the contrary, where safety, duty, and common sense demand, it is preferable that means other than deadly force be used to enforce the laws. Mobility, communications, and the assistance of other personnel should govern the decision when to use deadly force. In addition, the officer must assess the risk he. is taking when he endangers the lives and safety of innocent bystanders by firing his weapon.

Deadly force is that amount of force which is likely to cause, or does cause, death. In all cases, the facts of the particular case govern the amount of force a person may legally use. Most situations warrant the use of nonfatal force, while only a few actually justify the use of deadly force. Whenever force is justified, the law only allows a reasonable amount of force necessary to accomplish a legal objective. The reasonableness of the force used will be a matter for ultimate determination by administrative and judicial procedures. When a police officer uses deadly force, whether he intended to kill or only wound will never be questioned. If an officer is justified in using deadly force, it will be presumed that he intended it to be fatal.

If reasonable force is used, by either police officers or private citizens, to accomplish a legal purpose, any unintended death that results is excusable homicide. For instance, if Art attacks Ben and Ben, in order to defend himself, shoves Art aside, Ben will not be criminally liable for homicide if Art accidentally trips, hits his head on the floor, and dies. The initial force used by Ben to defend himself was reasonable and lawful under the circumstances and the result was unintended.

B. Warning Shots

The practice of, or the prohibition against, firing warning shots is generally one of policy only, not governed by statute. Although firing warning shots is authorized by some departmental policies, the majority of agencies prohibit this, and those courts that have treated the subject have by in large condemned the practice.

Following the definition of deadly force given above, which includes force likely to cause death, the firing of warning shots can constitute deadly force if death results unintentionally. Therefore, warning shots must never be fired unless the police officer would have the right to use deadly force in that particular case and would be justified in killing.

The two most urgent problems arising from the use of warning shots are the danger imposed upon innocent bystanders and the criminal civil liability of the officer. These two factors must govern the choice of whether to fire warning shots. A corporal injury or fatality resulting from an unreasonable use of force will subject a police officer to civil, and perhaps criminal, liability.

C. Homicide to Prevent the Commission of a Crime

As a general rule, one may commit a homicide to prevent the commission of a felony. This statement should not go unchallenged because interpretations of this rule have placed some limits on its application. Before deadly force is justified in such situations, the felony must be an atrocious one involving force, surprise, danger, or death to a person. A good question to ask in these situations is whether reasonably apparent harm is being imminently threatened to someone's life or safety. If so, deadly force would be justified in preventing the felony.

The fact that the person killed was actually committing a felony at the time he was killed will not be a defense if the slayer did not know this fact. In this case, the slayer would have acted with a criminal intent.

The rule is somewhat different for misdemeanor cases. Deadly force is never justified to prevent commission of a misdemeanor. Only reasonable force short of deadly force is allowed. If, however, during the commission of the misdemeanor, the misdemeanant repels the prevention attempt with force that threatens death or serious bodily harm, deadly force may be used. It is allowed on the grounds of self-defense, not on the ground of preventing the misdemeanor.

The following examples are illustrative of situations which arise within the confines of the principles discussed in this section. In these instances, the problems faced by officers are quite common. The solutions we pose should be recognized for what they are—commonsense approaches to very uncomplicated illustrations. In fact, most situations may not be this clear-cut and additional factors must be taken into consideration. Suppose that Officer Jones comes upon a man who has thrown a woman to the ground and is apparently about to rape her forcibly. Based only on these facts, the officer's justification for using deadly force would depend on whether his presence and his threat to use force were to no avail in preventing the commission of the felony. However, he must consider whether deadly force is necessary, and to what degree he will endanger the victim or innocent bystanders if he shoots. In addition, he must consider whether the situation is an actual attempt to commit rape or some other act not necessarily as serious or even criminal. By exercising restraint, the officer may be able to find out more about the facts of the situation.

In the second situation, Officer Smith observes one person robbing another. The question of Smith's right to use deadly force to prevent the commission of this crime depends upon whether the robber appears to be armed or unarmed. If it appears that the robber is armed or somehow capable of using deadly force himself, then the officer would be justified, since this would be an atrocious felony. An unarmed robbery would not fall into this category. As in other cases, the officer should make all reasonable attempts to prevent the felony by means other than using deadly force.

A third simplified problem often encountered involves a policeman who observes a man entering a second story window of a house in the early hours of the morning. Based on just these facts, the officer definitely would not be justified in using deadly force. There are insufficient facts present. The officer must have additional knowledge concerning the circumstances before taking such drastic action. In any event, a burglary is not ordinarily classified as an atrocious felony unless the burglar is threatening to use physical force against an occupant of the dwelling. Consequently, there would be very few occasions where an officer, observing such a scene from the outside, would be justified in shooting. Further investigation is warranted.

D. The Use of Deadly Force to Effect an Arrest or Prevent Escape

A homicide committed while attempting to make an arrest or to prevent an escape can only be justified in felony cases as an absolute last resort if there are no other means of apprehending the felon. This rule covers not only the right to use deadly force to making a felony arrest, but also includes what is commonly referred to as the "fleeing felon" rule. The states are not in absolute agreement about whether the right to use deadly force to effect an arrest is applicable to all felony cases. Some states hold that it is, while others allow deadly force to be used only in cases where the felony is an atrocious one, involving threat of death or serious bodily harm to persons.

Deadly force is out of the question in misdemeanor cases, except in a few states which consider some misdemeanors to be dangerous to the welfare of society. Among those states are Arkansas, Iowa, New Jersey, and North Carolina. This theory of law is based on the proposition that it is better to allow a misdemeanant to escape than to take a life for a petty offense.

There is some disagreement among the states about the justification for the use of deadly force if the officer or private citizen did not know with certainty whether the person actually committed a felony. Most states hold that a reasonable belief justifies the use of deadly force, but a few states say that the officer must *know* that a felony was committed. In those states, the officer acts at his own peril, and if he is wrong in believing that a felony has been committed, he must be prepared to suffer any attendant legal consequences.

To justify a homicide while effecting an arrest, it is necessary that the arrest be lawful. A lawful arrest is not governed by the ultimate determination of the guilt or innocence of the accused; rather, it is determined by the procedures followed to bring him within the custody of the law, such as the issuance of a warrant, the existence of probable cause, or the commission of a crime in the presence of the arresting officer. If the arrest is lawful, the arrestee has no right to resist, and if he does resist to the point of using deadly force, then the officer may counter with such force as is reasonably necessary to affect the arrest up to and including deadly force. If a person resists a lawful arrest with deadly force so as to warrant the use of deadly force in return to protect the life or safety of the person making the arrest, self-defense, not the arrest itself, justifies the use of such force.

If, on the other hand, the arrest is unlawful, the person being "arrested" has the right to use such force as is reasonably necessary to avoid the arrest, up to and including deadly force. Several states have restricted or prohibited by statute the right of one unlawfully arrested to resist with deadly force even where there is a threat to use deadly force to affect the "arrest." The theory is to allow this dispute to be settled in court. However, if it reasonably appears that surrender will not stop the use of deadly force against the arrestee, he may respond with force reasonably necessary to defend himself.

In the case of a felon who is escaping or eluding the custody of a police officer, deadly force should be used only as a last resort, taking into consideration whether the felon himself is using deadly force to effect his escape and whether his escape means that he is likely to inflict serious bodily harm or death to persons unless he is apprehended immediately. As in all other instances involving the possible use of deadly force, common sense, based on adequate training, must guide the officer's actions. He must reasonably believe that deadly force is necessary to make the arrest or prevent the escape; he must consider his own safety, the safety of the victim, the safety of bystanders; and he must be dealing with the type of offense that justifies the use of deadly force.

The use of deadly force against an escaping prisoner, although generally guided by the rules described above, has additional ramifications in some states. A few jurisdictions classify the escape itself as either a felony or a misdemeanor, depending upon the charge for which the accused was arrested. Thus, the authority to use deadly force on an escapee in these states depends upon the charges for which the officer arrested him originally. If the escapee was arrested for a felony, his escape is a felony; if he was arrested and charged with a misdemeanor, his escape is a misdemeanor and deadly force would not be justified. At least one state has changed the common law by making the escape itself a felony so that the injury as to the status of the prisoner's detention need not be involved. As a result, the escaping prisoner would be committing a felony in the presence of the person having custody, and would thus be a fleeing felon. Local law should be consulted.

Again, some examples may serve as useful illustrations of the basic principles involved. A policeman sees a man crawling out of a window of a home that the officer knows is temporarily vacant. The residents are out of town. It is night, and the man is carrying something. Here again, the officer has insufficient facts to warrant the use of deadly force. Certainly he has good reason to suspect that a burglary has just been committed, but he may not use deadly force until he is in a better position to ascertain the facts.

In another case, an officer sees a man commit an armed robbery. While the robber is running from the scene, he throws his gun away. At that time the officer recognizes him. Obviously, since the officer can identify the suspect, an arrest may follow with a warrant at a later time. The use of deadly force is unnecessary and unwarranted in this situation. On the other hand, if the officer cannot identify the suspect and has no chance of catching him, the situation changes a little. If the officer reasonably believes that apprehension will be impossible even with the use of modern methods of communications and transportation, deadly force may be justified as a last resort. Here again, if bystanders or others are likely to be in the line of fire, it is better to let the felon escape than risk shooting. Of course, the felon must always be first given the opportunity to surrender.

In another case, a man has gone berserk on a public street. He has already shot three people when the officer arrives on the scene, and he is standing on the sidewalk waving a gun. In this case, if no other means appear to be reasonably adequate or safe to the officer, he may resort to deadly force. The situation, if allowed to continue uninterrupted, is extremely likely to endanger the lives and safety of innocent persons. The utmost care must be taken.

In a final illustration, a policeman comes upon a scene where a man is running down the street followed by a shopkeeper yelling, "Stop thief!" Situations like this often present the most frustrating and confusing circumstances in which an officer must decide whether to use deadly force. The facts as presented here do not warrant the officer shooting at the fleeing man. He is not sufficiently informed. He does not know whether a felony has been committed, or if there is a danger to persons that warrants the use of deadly force.

E. Self-Defense

One may use as much reasonable force as is necessary to defend one's self. Deadly force is justified only where death or serious bodily harm is threatened. Before deadly force may be used, the danger to life or safety must be imminent. An assault not threatening death or great bodily harm does not justify the use of deadly force. The reasonableness of the force used is based on an objective test: How much force would a reasonable and prudent man be justified in using under the same circumstances?

The right of self-defense implies one has the right to defend himself. When the threat against the person ceases, the right of self-defense ceases. If the person attacked then pursues the attacker to revenge his injuries, he becomes the attacker and cannot justify his actions on the grounds of self-defense. Revenge is not synonymous with self-defense. Suppose Andrews verbally insulted Brown. In anger Brown kicked Andrews lightly, and then turned and started to walk away. Andrews' anger was aroused by being kicked and he went after Brown with the intent to injure Brown seriously. Brown killed Andrews to preserve his own life. Will the fact that Brown struck the first blow affect his claim of self-defense in his trial for murder? No.

This rule is qualified under one set of circumstances. When the initial attack renders the victim so insensible that he is unaware the attack has ceased and thereafter pursues the attacker believing the attack against him is continuing, self-defense may be used as a defense. The attacker's injuries in a case like this are caused by his own initial action. To illustrate, if Andrews assaults Brown and then retreats, but Brown is rendered so insensible from the attack by Andrews that he thinks Andrews is still attacking, or he does not realize what is happening and pursues Andrews and assaults Andrews, Brown will be held to have acted in self-defense.

One need not wait until he is struck by his attacker before the right of self-defense arises. Defense also implies the right to prevent. If the attack is imminent, an individual may, in fact, strike the first blow, and still justify his action on the ground of self-defense. John, with his back against a wall, sees Bill preparing to lunge at him with a knife. John instantaneously picks up a rock and throws it at Bill, striking Bill in the head. If John is prosecuted for causing this injury, he may successfully claim self-defense.

At common law, one was required to retreat as far as possible before he was justified in taking another's life in self-defense. This doctrine is obsolete in most jurisdictions, and the modern rule is that where one is feloniously assaulted in his home, office, place of business, or on property owned or lawfully occupied by him, he is not bound to retreat but may stand his ground and defend himself with such reasonable force as is necessary up to and including deadly force in cases where such force is justified in self-defense. Consequently, if one is in a place where he has a lawful right to be, he is not required to retreat as long as his right is at least equal to, if not greater than, the rights of his attacker. The exercise of a legal right is not ample provocation for the other party to attack and does not deprive the victim of his right of self-defense.

Homicides committed in self-defense are of two types. Justifiable homicide in self-defense is committed when one kills to defend himself from death or serious bodily harm resulting from a felonious attack on his person. Excusable homicide in self-defense implies that the slayer was to some degree at fault for getting into a situation where he had to kill to preserve his own life, but nevertheless did kill in self-defense. The distinction between these two types of homicide was important at common law, but today it is a distinction without a difference. Some jurisdictions, however, still maintain the distinction by statute. Section 7.1 deals with the difference between justifiable and excusable homicide in more detail.

F. Defense of Others

The right to defend others is, according to most authorities, limited to the same right that one would have to defend himself in the same situation. Thus, anyone who uses this defense "stands in the shoes of the victim," and may use the same amount of force the victim could have used in defending himself. One who comes to the defense of another, however, is held to act at his own peril if he has no knowledge of the surrounding facts. Before defending others, particularly with deadly force, one should learn the facts. If the "good Samaritan" chooses the wrong side and aids the aggressor, he will be liable for his actions.

Some states have modified this rule where the defender seeks to help a blood relative. By statute, these states recognize the emotional ties between relatives. Basically, the statutes allow defense of the relative even though the relative was the attacker, as long as it reasonably appears to the defender that his kin needed help or that at the time of the defense it was impossible to determine which party was at fault.

Other states have modified the common law by allowing the defender to act under a reasonable belief that the facts justify his coming to the defense whether the defended person was the assailant or not. This is an application of the objective, or "reasonable man," test.

G. Defense of Property and Habitation

Deadly force is never justified for the defense of property even if it is one's home. Reasonable force, short of deadly force, may be used. Only when an atrocious felony, threatening life or serious bodily harm, is being committed in conjunction with the attack on property may deadly force be used as a last resort. Then that amount of force is justified as self-defense. Again, one need not retreat before he is allowed to use reasonable force to defend his home or property. Consequently, the setting of a spring-loaded gun to injure intruding thieves in a business establishment is not a justifiable use of deadly force.

Questions for Discussion

1. A statute, under which John is prosecuted, forbids and punishes anyone who knowingly and intentionally takes books from a public library within this jurisdiction. John admits taking the book knowing it belongs to the public library. At his trial, John raises the following defenses. Discuss the validity of each.

A. John claims that he was not aware that his act was prohibited by law and therefore contends that he should be acquitted.
B. John also claims he consulted his attorney about his right to take the book and was advised by his attorney that it was all right.
C. Further, John says he just could not help himself, that he saw the book and had to take it. A medical examination discloses that John is a kleptomaniac.
D. Finally, John says that when he took the book, the librarian on duty nodded his head in an up-and-down motion.

2. Mrs. Policewoman, in an attempt to gain evidence, approaches Dr. Jones in quest of an illegal abortion. The doctor, after stating the fee to Mrs. Policewoman and after she accepts, agrees to perform the abortion. As he begins his "operation," Mrs. Policewoman identifies herself and places Dr. Jones under arrest for attempted abortion. At the trial of Dr. Jones, he stands up in court and yells, "I was trapped." Assuming this defense was raised by his attorney in a proper manner, what defense is the doctor raising and how successful should this claim be?

3. Assume that Officer Smith, while off duty, is just arriving home from a picnic with his family. He is carrying his off-duty revolver as required by departmental regulations. As he approaches his home that evening, Smith sees someone climb out a side window of his house and run in the opposite direction. The figure is carrying a sack of some kind and it appears to Smith that it is rather cumbersome. The thought also passes through Smith's mind that the figure appears to be a teen-age boy. Smith realizes he cannot catch the fleeing figure and knows nobody was rightfully in his home. Should Smith shoot? Would he be justified in doing so, if he killed the fleeing figure?

4. Jones verbally insulted Brown. In anger, Brown kicked Jones lightly, and then turned and started to walk away. Jones' anger was aroused by being kicked and he went after Brown intending to injure Brown seriously. Brown killed Jones to preserve his own life. Will the fact that Brown struck the first blow affect his claim of self-defense in his trial for murder?

Chapter 7

HOMICIDE

7.0 Homicide In General

Police officials and members of the public often incorrectly use the terms *homicide* and *murder* interchangeably. Murder is only a part of the broad criminal law category of homicide.

Homicide is the killing of a human being by another human being. This broad definition covers many forms of conduct, only some of which are criminal. It encompasses all deaths either directly or indirectly due to causes other than natural. It also includes death from natural causes resulting from the act of another human being. For example: Tom threatens Jerry with a gun and scares Jerry so badly that he has a heart attack and dies. This is a homicide (4.6).

As discussed previously (4.5), a homicide may be committed by failing to perform a legal duty—a crime by omission, or negative act.

At common law, if the victim did not die within a year and a day after the injury was inflicted, but died after that time, the perpetrator could not be charged with homicide. The reason for this rule was that there could have been too many other factors contributing to death during that intervening period, making the cause and effect relationship too remote to satisfy the legal requirement of causation (4.6). The fact that there were no other intervening causes was immaterial since this was a rule of law, not a determination of fact. The year and a day rule is part of the common law of the United States and, unless changed by statute, will remain so.

7.1 Nonfelonious Homicides

Not all homicides are criminal. Some homicides are specifically deemed to be noncriminal in the eyes of the law. These homicides fall into two categories: justifiable homicide and excusable homicide. At common law, the distinction between justifiable and excusable homicide was important for more than purposes of definition. Although noncriminal in nature, excusable homicide was not entirely free from penalty. A person who committed excusable homicide forfeited certain lands or goods according to the circumstances surrounding the homicide. This is no longer true, but statutes in the various jurisdictions continue to distinguish these nonfelonious homicides.

A. Justifiable Homicide

The common law defined justifiable homicide as the necessary killing of another in the performance of a legal duty or the exercise of a legal right where the slayer was not at fault. This classification includes execution of convicted capital offenders, homicides by police officers in the performance of a legal duty, and so forth. Also included are slayings in self-defense when the slayer is feloniously attacked and has to kill to preserve his own life, provided he is not in any way at fault for the attack on his person. Justifiable homicide carried with it no penalty because the slayer was not at fault.

B. Excusable Homicide

Excusable homicide differs from justifiable homicide in that one who commits an excusable homicide is to some degree at fault but the degree of fault is not enough to constitute a felonious homicide. Excusable homicide covers two fundamental situations resulting in homicide. First, when death results from misadventure. This is similar to what may be termed "accidental" death at the hands of another. Misadventure is death occurring during commission of a lawful act, or a *mala prohibita* unlawful act, committed without any intent to hurt and without criminal negligence.

Examples of misadventure include the death of a child who is being lawfully punished, or the death of a person who runs in front of a moving automobile when the driver is unable to avoid the collision.

The second type of excusable homicide involves self-defense when the slayer is not totally without fault. For example, someone gets involved in a sudden brawl and has to kill to preserve his life.

Note that self-defense may be considered either justifiable or excusable homicide. However, it is more properly treated as a matter affecting criminal responsibility, and for that reason was discussed in Chapter 6.

7.2 Felonious Homicides in General

Felonious homicides are those treated and punished as crimes. They fall into two basic categories—murder and manslaughter.

A. Murder

The common law defined murder as the felonious killing of any human being by another with malice aforethought. Murder was a general intent crime. Specific intent to kill any particular person was not required although a specific intent was sufficient to satisfy this requirement. The difficulties in proving a case of murder at common law basically involved the interpretations given the words "malice" and "aforethought" and the interpretation given both words together as a phrase.

The word malice in legal usage connotes something different than it does in the popular sense. Malice in the popular sense is often used as a synonym for hate, ill will, bad feelings, and the like. For purposes of the law of homicide, malice means the intentional doing of a wrongful act in such a way and under such circumstances that the death of a human being may result.

Malice may be either express or implied. To prove this element satisfactorily, it was necessary to show that the perpetrator either actually intended to kill (express malice) or killed while committing a deliberate and cruel act likely to cause death (implied malice). There are basically four situations in which the law would imply malice at common law. These instances involve, in effect, unintentional killings. The first was intentional infliction of great bodily harm on someone, unintentionally resulting in death. This would warrant a murder charge at common law. John hits Bill on the head with a tree branch, intending to injure Bill seriously but not intending to kill him. If Bill dies from the blows, malice will be implied.

The second situation in which the law would imply malice involved no actual intent to kill on the part of the perpetrator. Instead, it involved an act or omission, deliberately done, of such a nature that it tended to cause death or serious bodily harm. If Sam deliberately drove his automobile in excess of one hundred miles an hour through a crowded city intersection to see how fast it would go, and killed somebody as a result, the law would infer malice.

The law would also imply malice when death resulted during the commission of a felony under the felony-murder rule discussed in detail in the next section.

Finally, when death was caused by one resisting a lawful arrest, the common law would imply malice. The law requires a person to submit to a lawful arrest but permits him to resist an unlawful arrest with necessary reasonable force. If the jury finds deadly force was reasonably necessary to resist an unlawful arrest, the defendant will be found to have committed excusable homicide.

The term "aforethought" conveys the meaning of planning ahead. It means substantially the same thing as the words "premeditated design" commonly found in modern murder statutes.

Although the time lapse between planning and doing the act which causes death is immaterial, there must be a deliberate design. This design may be formed seconds, minutes, or days before the act is performed and may be implied by the courts and juries from the circumstances surrounding the homicide, but it must be proved. Premeditated design or aforethought was the prime element that distinguished murder from manslaughter or "accidental" homicide at common law. It distinguishes the various degrees of murder under present statutory law in many jurisdictions.

The phrase "malice aforethought" can thus be defined as the intentional killing of one human being by another without legal justification or excuse under circumstances insufficient to reduce the crime to manslaughter or a lesser degree of murder.

The malice and the aforethought must exist simultaneously with each other and with the act. For example, Smith says on Tuesday that he will kill Jones. On Wednesday, by accident and misfortune, Smith kills Jones. In this case the forethought may still have existed but under the circumstances, there was no malice. Thus, murder would be an improper charge.

1. The Felony-Murder Rule

The common law courts held that the felony-murder rule applied to deaths occurring during the commission of, or an attempt to commit, arson, burglary, larceny, rape, or robbery. In essence, under this rule any death resulting from commission of any of those enumerated felonies was murder. For a killing to be murder, there had to be malice aforethought. This element was satisfied by treating such a case as one involving implied malice. Whoever committed a felony acted in a deliberate and cruel manner and he was held responsible for the natural and probable consequences of his act. One of the probable consequences of the commission of a felony is that someone might get killed. This is true even though the killing is unintentional and accidental.

The common law felony-murder rule applied only to certain enumerated felonies. Some modern statutes have changed this and allow the rule to operate in cases of homicides committed during the course of committing, or while attempting to commit, *any* felony. Others continue to specify only certain felonies to which the rule applies but some of the felonies may be different from those enumerated at common law. Even in states that follow the latter course, killings in the course of other felonies, not enumerated in the felony-murder rule, are generally covered by a statute making them lesser degrees of murder. Even modern statutes will not answer the practical questions that arise in applying this rule to the facts of a given case. Some important questions which arise include: does the rule cover all homicides during commission of, or while attempting to commit, one of these felonies, or does it have to be a homicide actually committed by one of the perpetrators of the felony? What does "during the commission of a felony" mean? Does it include fleeing from the scene? If so, is the time and distance factor important? What types of causation factors apply to this rule? These and several other questions can only be explained by referring to the cases that have been decided by the appellate courts.

As to whether the rule applies to all homicides committed in the perpetration of, or in attempting to perpetrate, the enumerated felonies, it has been said that there are at least sixteen possible combinations to which the rule may apply. Included in these combinations are: (1) victim killing cofelon, (2) cofelon killing victim, (3) cofelon killing a bystander or police officer, (4) victim killing a bystander or police officer, (5) police officer killing victim, bystander, other police officer, or cofelon, and so on. Among the courts that have struggled with the problem of whether the rule should apply to all these possible combinations is the Supreme Court of Pennsylvania. In the 1940s and 1950s this court was faced with a series of four cases involving the felony-murder rule. The court changed its mind several times before deciding on the scope of felony-murder under Pennsylvania law.

In *Commonwealth* v. *Almeida,* 362 Pa. 596, 68 A. 2d 595 (1949), a police officer was killed during an exchange of shots between police and robbers. The defendant was convicted of first degree murder committed in the course of the robbery. The Supreme Court of Pennsylvania, in affirming the conviction, said, ". . . Their acts were 'the cause of the cause' of the murder. They 'set in motion the physical power' which resulted in Ingling's death and they are criminally responsible for that result. Whether the fatal bullet was fired by one of the bandits or by one of the policemen who were performing their duty in repelling the bandit's assault and defending themselves and endeavoring to prevent the escape of the felons is immaterial."

Six years later, the same court ruled on another felony-murder case. In *Commonwealth v. Thomas*, 382 Pa. 639, 117 A. 2d 204 (1955), the facts disclosed that Thomas and a confederate committed a robbery, and while fleeing from the scene, the confederate was shot and killed by the store owner. Thomas was indicted for the murder of his cofelon. The court granted the defendant's motion to dismiss and the state appealed. The supreme court reversed the judgment. In answer to the question: can a cofelon be found guilty of murder where the victim of an armed robbery justifiably kills the other felon as they flee from the scene of the crime, the court said: "The felon's robbery set in motion a chain of events which were or should have been within his contemplation when the motion was initiated. He therefore should be held responsible for any death which by direct and almost inevitable sequence results from the initial act." It is interesting to note that after this decision, the district attorney *nolle prossed* the murder charge against Thomas.

In 1958, the Pennsylvania Supreme Court repudiated its earlier decision in the *Thomas* case. In *Commonwealth v. Redline*, 391 Pa. 486, 137 A. 2d 472 (1958), involving facts similar to the *Thomas* case, the court said: "In adjudging a felony-murder, it must be remembered at all times that the thing which is imputed to a felon for killing incidental to a felony is malice and not the act of killing. The mere coincidence of a homicide and a felony is not enough to satisfy the requirements of the felony-murder doctrine. It is necessary . . . to show that the conduct causing death was done in the furtherance of the design to commit the felony. Death must be a consequence of the felony . . . and not merely coincidence . . . ." The court also stated that its research has found no cases either in this country or under the English common law in accord with the *Thomas* decision.

Oddly enough, on the same day the *Redline* case was decided, the court also handed down a decision in *Commonwealth v. Bolish*, 391 Pa. 550, 138 A. 2d 447 (1958). Bolish and an accomplice, Flynn, planned an arson. In carrying out the plan, Flynn was fatally injured by an explosion which occurred when he placed a jar of gasoline on an electric hot plate. Bolish was convicted of first degree murder. The judgment was affirmed on appeal. The court held that the defendant "was actively participating in the felony which resulted in death. The element of malice, present in the design of the defendant, necessarily must be imputed to the resulting killing, and made him responsible for the death . . . The fact that the victim was an accomplice does not alter the situation, since his own act which caused the death was in furtherance of the felony."

A review of these cases reveals the confusion that exists as to the scope of the felony-murder rule. Pennsylvania's initial attempt to apply a blanket rule to homicides occurring during the commission of a felony was later rejected because of lack of support from any other American jurisdiction or from English law. Applying the felony-murder rule to all homicides, regardless of by whom committed, fails to take the rules of proximate causation into account (4.6). By following the rules of causation, courts would find it difficult to hold a felon liable for murder in the highest degree when, unrelated to the actual conduct of the felon, one innocent bystander happens to kill another innocent bystander while attempting to help apprehend the felon. Consequently, courts in most jurisdictions where this problem has arisen have extended the felony-murder rule only as far as the rules of proximate causation can justify.

The remaining unanswered questions involve an overall understanding of when the commission of a crime begins and when it ends. Because of the requirement that the homicide occur during commission of or while attempting to commit the felony, time, distance, and escape all become important matters.

Most courts have agreed that the time and distance separating the killing and the felony are not the sole determining factors in deciding when commission of the felony ends. Each case must be judged on its own facts. It is agreed that escape from a crime scene is to be considered as part of the commission of a felony for purposes of the felony-murder rule. The rationale for this rule is simply that one does not intend to commit a crime and be caught.

The problem is best summed up by the Florida Supreme Court, which said,

It is a sound principle of law which inheres in common reason that where two or more persons engage in a conspiracy to commit robbery and an officer or citizen is murdered while in immediate pursuit of one of their number who is fleeing from the scene of the crime with the fruits thereof in his possession, or in the possession of a coconspirator, the crime is not complete in the purview of the law, inasmuch as said conspirators have not won their way even momentarily to a place of temporary safety and the possession of the plunder is nothing more than a scrambling possession. In such a case the continuation of the use of arms which was necessary to aid the felon in reducing the property to possession is necessary to protect him in his possession and in making good his escape. (*Hornbeck* v. *State,* 77 So. 2d 876 (Fla. 1955))

Although the court indicates it is laying down a rule for robbery cases, it is safe to assume that any homicide committed during an escape or flight from the scene of one of the enumerated felonies will fall within the rule if the felons have not yet reached a point of reasonable safety and freedom from immediate pursuit by law enforcement officers. The time separating actual perpetration of the felony and the commission of the homicide, as well as the distance from the scene of the felony where the homicide occurs, are factors to be considered in each case to decide the appropriateness of the felony-murder rule but, in themselves, they are not the sole determining factors.

The felony and the homicide do not merge and it is proper to charge the perpetrators with both the felony and the murder either in separate counts of a single indictment or with separate indictments.

2. Degrees of Murder

Unlike modern law, the common law did not recognize degrees of murder. If a homicide failed to contain the necessary elements of malice aforethought, the proper charge was some other crime and not murder. Modern statutes have modified this rule in most jurisdictions. Thirty-three states and the District of Columbia now divide murder into degrees. Only three of those states, however, have more than two degrees of murder. They are Florida, Minnesota, and Wisconsin. The aim of this legislative action was to limit the use of capital punishment without reducing the seriousness of the crime.

B. Manslaughter

Manslaughter is the second major category of felonious homicide. Manslaughter is charged when a homicide is committed under circumstances not severe enough to constitute murder, yet not mild enough to be either justifiable or excusable homicide.

At common law, manslaughter was divided into voluntary and involuntary manslaughter, each containing certain elements to be proved before a conviction could be obtained.

1. Voluntary Manslaughter

Voluntary manslaughter is an intentional killing but does not contain the elements of malice or premeditated design. Its essential elements include: a legally adequate provocation resulting in a killing done in the heat of passion, before cooling. The law recognizes the weakness of men and regards this type of killing as less severe than killing in cold blood. This is the only justification for the difference between murder and voluntary manslaughter.

a. Adequate Provocation. Incidents that would or do happen to provoke a person are not necessarily legally adequate to reduce the crime from murder to manslaughter. The types of provocation and the degree to which they must exist in order to be legally recognized are questions that are left to the jury to decide. In making this determination, however, the jury must be guided by certain legal principles. The jury must decide, not whether the facts of the particular case provoked the defendant, but rather, whether those same facts would have provoked a reasonable and prudent man under similar circumstances to such an extent that he would kill. This is known as the objective test. As a general rule, a simple assault or a mere technical battery will not be sufficient to constitute provocation adequate to reduce a homicide charge from murder to manslaughter. Words alone, unaccompanied by any conduct, are never sufficient to constitute provocation. If certain types of conduct accompany the words, adequate provocation may exist. Insulting gestures (not identical to assaults) are not adequate. With these guidelines to work by, the jury determines the adequacy of the provocation. For example, juries have found the following to be legally adequate provocation: seduction of a man's wife, knowledge of the rape of a man's wife acquired within a few minutes after the rape, and adultery.

b. Heat of Passion. Heat of passion does not mean the same thing as insanity, but mere anger is not enough. All that must be shown is that the adequate provocation described above was of such a nature that the defendant's mind became so inflamed that he did not know what he was doing. No cold-blooded killing can ever be mitigated to manslaughter. The jury must be convinced that the provocation prevented thought and reflection and the formation of a deliberate purpose. Perhaps the most common case arises where the defendant discovers that someone is having, or has had, unlawful sexual intercourse with a female relative.

c. Cooling. At the time the homicide occurs, the accused must still be acting under heat of passion. If he has cooled to the point where he knows what he is doing, the homicide is in cold blood and will be considered murder. Just as in determining legally adequate provocation, the jury must apply an objective test to determine whether a reasonable man would have cooled under the facts of the particular case. This is not governed by whether the accused had actually cooled or not. All the circumstances must be taken into account. Although a lapse of time between the provocation and the actual killing is important in determining whether a reasonable man would have cooled, this is not the sole determining factor. There is no definite rule for determining when cooling has taken place, but, generally, the greater the passion, the longer the cooling period. On January 1, Mr. Smith had shot and killed the son of Mr. Jones. Smith was tried for that homicide and was acquitted in March. Nothing further happened until November 29. On that date, while walking down the street Mr. Jones observed Smith standing on the corner talking to Parker. Jones walked up to Smith and said, "Hello, Dan," and without further warning fired two shots into Smith in quick succession. As Smith was falling to the ground, Jones fired two more shots into Smith, and then turned and walked away. After going some distance, Jones turned and came back. He put his pistol close to the head of Smith, pulled the trigger two more times (the gun was empty by this time), and said, "You damn son of a bitch, I told you I would kill you; you killed my boy."

Murder would appear to be the proper charge since the time lapse would ordinarily be sufficient for the reasonable man to cool. In addition, the deliberate act of repeatedly firing at the victim evinced a determination to commit cold-blooded killing.

d. Causal Connection. Even where the three prime elements of voluntary manslaughter exist, it must be shown that there is a causal connection between all three elements. In other words, the provocation must cause the heat of passion, which causes the homicide (4.6).

2. Involuntary Manslaughter

Involuntary manslaughter is an unintentional killing. Death resulting from the commission of a *malum in se* unlawful act, or from culpable negligence, is involuntary manslaughter. This definition of involuntary manslaughter contains several essential elements discussed in detail in the following paragraphs.

a. Unlawful Act. The death must result during the commission of an unlawful act. However, if the unlawful act is a felony covered by the felony-murder rule, murder will generally be charged since it is more serious than involuntary manslaughter. In those jurisdictions where all homicides occurring during commission of a felony are, in some degree, classified as murder, involuntary manslaughter can only apply to misdemeanor cases.

b. The Nature of the Act Must Be Malum In Se. The unlawful act must be *malum in se;* that is, the act must be one which is wrong in itself as opposed to *malum prohibitum,* wrong merely because it is prohibited. For example, a motor vehicle operator who unintentionally strikes a pedestrian while exceeding the speed limit by five miles per hour would probably not be charged with involuntary manslaughter if the pedestrian dies. But a motorist who strikes a pedestrian while driving under the influence of intoxicants might very well be charged with involuntary manslaughter if the pedestrian dies, since driving while intoxicated is an act which is wrong in itself.

c. There Must Be a Proximate Causal Connection Between the Unlawful Act and the Homicide. In order to charge involuntary manslaughter properly, it must be shown that the unlawful act was the direct or proximate cause of the homicide. For example, if a child runs out in front of a car and is unavoidably struck and killed, it cannot be said that the intoxicated condition of the driver was the cause of death when even a sober man could not have avoided striking the child. In such a case, despite the fact that a *malum in se* unlawful act occurred, there was no proximate causal connection between the act and the homicide, so involuntary manslaughter would be an improper charge.

d. Culpable Negligence. Involuntary manslaughter may occur either through commission of an unlawful act or through culpable negligence. Simple or ordinary negligence is not sufficient to justify a charge of involuntary manslaughter. The negligence must reach such a degree of blameworthiness that a jury could say it was culpable or criminal in nature. Only then, will it suffice to support a charge of involuntary manslaughter.

A few jurisdictions have a negligent homicide, or fourth degree manslaughter statute, on which a conviction can be obtained for a death resulting from ordinary negligence.

One may then ask the question, "If I investigate a case, a traffic fatality for example, in which there occurred an unlawful act but it was neither *malum in se* nor culpable negligence, what do I charge?" The answer, of course, is that you can charge for the unlawful act itself. The death will be ruled an excusable homicide. This is a common occurrence for it is well understood that not all traffic fatalities result in someone being charged with manslaughter. When manslaughter is not charged, the officer, in effect, and possibly without knowing it, is saying, "There is not enough evidence here, or there is no indication of manslaughter." By not charging manslaughter, he is ruling that the incident was an excusable homicide.

C. Statutory Extension of Manslaughter

Statutes throughout the jurisdictions in the United States label many types of prohibited conduct as manslaughter. Many of these offenses do not fit into the definitions of either voluntary or involuntary manslaughter as described above. Legislatures have created new crimes whose elements do not conform to the traditional categorization of manslaughter but which are not serious enough to be punished as murder. This factor has produced a third category of manslaughter violations not known to the common law. The most common example of this type of legislation is that which makes it manslaughter to kill an unborn child.

D. Infanticide and Feticide

The ever continuing debate over when an infant falls under the protection of the criminal law began early in the common law. Many arguments, moral, legal, ethical, and religious, have all contributed somewhat to the confusion. There are those that insist that from a legal point of view, the law cannot protect an unborn child for it is not yet a human being. Others argue that an infant is a human being from the moment of conception and therefore should be protected by the criminal law from that point forward. Many others propound theories which hold that an infant becomes a human being at some point between conception and birth.

The courts generally agree that killing an infant before its mother starts giving birth is not a common law homicide. These same courts do not agree, however, as to the point where protection does start once delivery has begun. Some contend the infant is a human being at the beginning of the delivery process. A second group holds that the child must be fully born before its death can be a common law homicide. A third group of courts holds that the child must first breathe before its death can be infanticide. Still others say that not until the umbilical cord is severed is the criminal law applicable. A large segment of the courts seems to follow the more widely accepted view that death at the hands of another person is infanticide only after the child has established an independent circulation, separate and apart from its mother.

Whichever of these views is followed by the courts, the required event must occur before killing of the infant can be treated as either common law murder or manslaughter depending on the punishment provided in the various jurisdictions for infanticide. This is not to say that the injury which produces death must occur after delivery. The injury may be inflicted while the child is still in the womb, but if it is born alive and later dies, infanticide has occurred. If, on the other hand, the child was born dead, the common law courts did not recognize this as a common law homicide.

The need for legislation in this area was recognized by most legislatures. They have enacted statutes making it criminal homicide to kill

dont read

an unborn child. These statutes have taken a variety of forms but they all have one thing in common. They all have accomplished the goal of placing the unborn child within the protection of the criminal law. These statutes use different names but the crime may be commonly called feticide, the killing of a fetus.

Although under these statutes killing an unborn child is almost a universally punishable crime, the statutes disagree as to when in the development of the unborn child its destruction is criminal. Nonmedical legislatures have used medical terms which must be interpreted by the courts. The statutes fall into these categories: (1) killing an unborn child "in a pregnant woman," (2) killing an unborn child in a "woman with a quick child," (3) killing an unborn child in a "woman with child," and (4) killing an unborn "vitalized embryo or fetus."

Medically there are three stages of intrauterine development. The first two weeks are known as the ovum stage. The second through eighth weeks constitute the embryonal stage. From that point to birth the unborn child is said to be in the fetal stage. The difficulty that arises with the first two types of statutes is in deciding at what point killing the unborn child is criminal—at the ovum, embryonal, or fetal stages.

Georgia, Illinois, Maine, Maryland, Massachusetts, New Jersey, Oregon, Vermont, and Wisconsin, which recognize feticide with regard to killing an unborn child in a "pregnant woman," disagree. Some say the unborn child must be "quick;" that is, the motion of the unborn child must have become perceptible to the mother. Some of the others indicate that any stage of pregnancy is sufficient for criminal liability to arise.

The "pregnant with a quick child" states, including Florida, Kansas, Missouri, New York, and North Dakota, attempt to avoid the problem by using "quickness" as the turning point. As long as the definition of "quickness" is uniform, there will be no problem in knowing what that turning point will be. However, each child quickens at a different time which, for the prosecutor, presents problems of proof.

The third group of states which requires a "woman with child" have by decision merely required proof of pregnancy at any stage. Arkansas, Colorado, and Hawaii are among this group.

Nebraska alone has adopted the fourth possibility, and, by spelling out embryonal and fetal stages, has eliminated the ovum stage.

If one refers to local statutes it may be difficult to find the crime labeled feticide. States which have extended criminal law protection to the unborn child through these statutes have attached varying labels to them. In one state you may find it specifically punishable as manslaughter. In another it might be found in the abortion laws. In still

another state it may be intermingled with the homicide statutes, but not assigned a specific traditional homicide label.

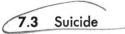 7.3   Suicide

Suicide was a common law felony for which forfeiture of lands and goods could be imposed if the suicide was successful. Suicide is, strictly speaking, outside the scope of homicide since it is not death caused by another human being but it is often discussed as a related subject.

Under modern legislation, suicide has been maintained as a felony in some states, has been completely abrogated by statues in others, and remains as a holdover from common law as a misdemeanor in a third group of states.

Nobody has yet found a means of directly punishing the successful suicide but attempted suicides are punishable. It would seem that applying the criminal law to attempted suicides would have little significance in a day when medical treatment would have a much more lasting value. However, collateral problems surrounding a successful or attempted suicide do involve significant legal questions.

The most common question concerns the liability of one who helps another commit self-murder. Several alternatives are available to solve this problem. In those states where suicide is still a crime, it is possible that one may be guilty as an accessory before the fact or a principal in the second degree. Some states have even gone so far as to create a specific statute punishing separately the person who assists in a suicide. It is still possible in these states that a chargeable murder or manslaughter may exist because of the direct effect of the help given. The rules of proximate causation play an important role.

In those states which have abolished suicide as a crime, there can be no liability as an accessory before the fact or principal in the second degree. However, if the person who aids the suicide does so in such a direct manner as to be the proximate cause of the death, he can, of course, be charged with murder or manslaughter.

An often cited situation involves the "suicide compact," two people agreeing to commit suicide. If, in the attempt, one of the participants dies and the other survives, the survivor can be charged with murder unless he abandoned the compact and urged the other also to abandon the compact.

What happens if, while a man is attempting to kill himself, he kills another? Is there a chargeable homicide? Yes. The degree of liability will be judged by the traditional elements of the various homicide laws including the ever essential intent element.

Questions for Discussion

1. Dan was the proprietor of a small retail grocery store. One day while Dan was alone in the store, John, a stranger to Dan, entered the store and suddenly drew a revolver, pointed it at Dan, and commanded him to march to the rear of the store and open the safe. Dan, believing John's revolver to be loaded, made as if to obey. After taking several paces, Dan whirled suddenly, drew a revolver from under his coat, and fired twice in rapid succession at John. One of the bullets killed John and the other, missing John, killed Xavier, a passerby who was lawfully proceeding along the street in front of the store. In fact, Dan was carrying his revolver in violation of a state statute making it a misdemeanor for any person to carry a concealed weapon without first obtaining a permit. A subsequent examination of John's revolver disclosed the fact that it was unloaded.

   On the foregoing facts, Dan is separately indicted for the murder of John and the murder of Xavier. Is Dan guilty of the crimes charged, or of either of them? Why?

2. Gamblers were threatening Don about debts he owed. Don decided to resort to robbery to get money to pay the gamblers. He concealed himself at about 11:30 p.m. in a dark alley and sprang on Alan, manager of a theater, on his way to a night bank depository with the evening receipts. Don struck Alan on the head with a section of lead pipe, seized the bag containing the money, and fled. Alan died about two hours later as a result of the attack. Don arrived home about thirty minutes after committing the robbery. He heard a man's voice in the bedroom used by himself and his wife. Don peeped through the keyhole and saw Fred, partially disrobed, in conversation with Don's wife. Don waited until Fred left and then discussed the situation with his wife. A bitter argument ensued. About three hours later, Don armed himself with a gun and proceeded to Fred's home. Don shot and killed Fred without saying a word when Fred opened the door in response to Don's knocks at the door. What liability, if any, does Don have for the deaths of Alan and Fred? Why?

Chapter 8

ASSAULT AND OTHER RELATED CRIMES

8.0 Assaults In General

At common law there were no recognized categories of assault. All assaults were misdemeanors. Aggravated cases of assault differed only in the severity of punishment imposed by the judge. Legislation has reclassified the more severe types of assault as distinct offenses. Even though they often occur together, assault should be distinguished from battery since they are separate crimes. Assault is an attempt or offer to do harm while a battery is the doing of the harm. A completed battery, like any other crime, includes an attempt (in this case an assault). Under the doctrine of merger, if the battery is completed there is no assault, yet statutes and courts continue to refer to the completed crime as assault and battery. Properly, it should be called simply a battery.

The remainder of the chapter will discuss simple assaults, assault and battery, aggravated assaults, assault with a deadly weapon, assault with intent to commit a felony, and other related offenses.

8.1 Simple Assault

Simple assault is an attempt or offer, with unlawful force or violence, to do nonfatal injury to another. This definition is not self-explanatory and requires some interpretation. By definition, alternative methods of accomplishing an assault are available.

Under the first alternative, an assault may be committed by an attempt in the strict sense. In this instance, assault is identical to an attempt to commit any crime, the sole difference being that the target crime of assault must be battery. In such a case, all the elements of an attempt must be present(4.7.) Suppose Fred strikes at Bill with his fist, but misses. Fred can be charged with a simple assault or with an attempted battery since the facts satisfy the elements of either charge.

An assault may also be committed when there has been an offer to do violence. The term offer denotes the attempt of many courts to adopt the civil law definition of assault and include it in the body of criminal law as a second alternative for committing simple assault. This approach holds that assault may be committed by placing the victim in fear of immediate injury. When Fred draws back his fist threatening to strike Bill, but does no more, courts would find it difficult to support a charge of assault under the attempted battery theory. However, under the civil law theory, a chargeable simple assault would exist if Bill were reasonably apprehensive of imminent bodily harm.

The act must be done with unlawful force or violence. This means that the accused must act in some unlawful manner nonfatally to harm the victim by an act which is forceful or violent to some degree. "Unlawful" in this sense implies that the accused had no right or privilege to offer or attempt the violence. There are occasions when one is entitled, within reason, to use force. If such a right or privilege does exist, force is not unlawful. Thus, parents may discipline their children, teachers may (subject to statutes) exercise discipline privileges. Individuals may defend themselves or others and people may defend their homes.

Numerous elements must be shown to exist for the crime of simple assault. First, there must be some overt conduct on the part of the accused which would indicate he was about to commit battery. The overt act may be of any nature and need not go so far as would be required to charge an attempt, although assault must also go beyond mere preparation. Words alone will not satisfy this requirement. A raised fist, a pointed gun, and the like are the types of act required.

The second element deals with the *mens rea,* or state of mind, with which the accused acts. If he actually intends to injure and if he comes dangerously close to completing battery, assault is complete. But there is an additional manner in which this element can be satisfied. Many courts, including those of Alabama, Florida, Georgia, Iowa, Massachusetts, Michigan, Montana, New Hampshire, New York, North Carolina, Tennessee, and Texas, recognize that an assault should be looked at from the point of view of the victim as well as the defendant. They require only *apparent* present intent to injure, as determined by the victim. These courts hold that if the accused acts in a way likely to create apprehension (fear of being harmed) on the part of the victim, assault has been committed regardless of the actual intent of the accused.

The intent or apparent intent must be to inflict injury at the time the threat is made. Threat to inflict harm in the future will not constitute an assault. For example, if Joe doubled up his fist and said to Bob: "If we weren't in mixed company, I'd knock your block off," there is no assault. Since they *were* in mixed company, Joe did not have the present intent nor could Bob be apprehensive of imminent harm. Joe's remarks clearly indicated his lack of intent to inflict harm at the present time.

A conditional threat will not negate an assault if the condition is unlawful. This refers to situations where the accused does the necessary overt act to constitute an assault but his intent shows that he is giving the victim an opportunity to avoid the battery by complying with a condition. If the condition imposed by the accused is one which he has a lawful right to make, there is no assault. If, however, the condition is unlawful, the assault is complete once the overt act is done. For example, if Alan says to Ben, "If you don't pay me the money you owe me, I will kill you," while pointing a pistol at Ben, Alan is imposing a condition on Ben by which Ben could avoid the attack. However, the condition is one which Alan has no right to impose and therefore the assault is complete. On the other hand, if Alan after warning Ben that he is trespassing shakes his fist and says: "If you don't get off my property, I will knock your block off," the condition is a lawful one and no assault has occurred.

The last element of simple assault pertains to the accused's ability to commit battery. At common law and in some jurisdictions today, it must be shown that the accused was actually able to commit battery when he made the threat. One who pointed an unloaded gun at another and threatened to use it could not be guilty of assault. The majority view today holds that this element is satisfied if it appears to the victim that the accused was presently able to inflict injury. In the above example, if the victim was not aware the gun was unloaded, the assault was complete. If the victim knew the gun was empty, there could be no assault since there was no present ability to hurt nor was there an apparent present ability to inflict battery.

Another aspect of the ability problem involves what is commonly referred to as the "striking distance" doctrine. Even though the force threatened is unlawful and the means threatened will actually do harm, the accused must be close enough actually to harm the victim. Otherwise there can be no real apprehension in the victim's mind under any rule. Suppose Art, with an offer of unlawful force, threatens to cut Bill's throat with a Bowie knife. If Art is 300 yards from Bill at the time, there can be no assault. But if the means used is a loaded M-1 rifle and the distance is 300 yards, there is an assault when Art unlawfully threatens to shoot Bill.

8.2 Assault and Battery (Battery)

The completed act, when the injury threatened by the assault actually occurs, is the crime of battery, or, as it is called in most jurisdictions, assault and battery.

A battery is defined as an unlawful injury, however slight, done to another person, directly or indirectly, in an angry, revengeful, rude, or insolent manner. The injury inflicted need not be serious. The least touching, done in any manner described above, will be enough. The force used to commit the injury need not be inflicted directly by the hand of the accused. For example, if Smith assaults Jones in a manner which makes Jones apprehensive so that he jumps out a window to avoid the imminent battery, the injury resulting is a battery for which Smith may be held liable.

Criminal intent is a necessary element of battery, but the intent may be implied from the seriousness of the circumstances. An unlawful arrest constitutes an assault and battery and reasonable force necessary to avoid an unlawful arrest is justified, but an excessive amount of force used to avoid unlawful arrest will also constitute a battery.

Since the offense of battery requires the accused to have acted with an intentional state of mind, injury inflicted as a result of culpable, criminal, or gross negligence will not support a charge of battery. To fill this gap, some states have enacted statutes providing punishment for injuries inflicted in a criminally negligent manner.

Consent is a valid defense to an assault and battery charge, but all elements of this defense must be satisfied (6.9).

8.3 Statutory Assaults

As mentioned earlier, legislatures have divided assaults according to the degree of severity. Simple assaults remain misdemeanors. The more serious assault cases have been defined as distinct offenses.

Perhaps the most common legislative assault is aggravated assault —a felony in most states. An aggravated assault in general encompasses all cases of assault which are vicious in nature, including assaults with a specific intent to commit a felony and assaults with a deadly weapon. Since aggravated assaults are creatures of legislation, many states have further subdivided aggravated assaults into separate offenses called assaults with intent to commit felonies and assaults with deadly or dangerous weapons.

As a general rule assaults with intent to commit felonies require specific intent. Assaults with deadly or dangerous weapons are general intent crimes requiring no proof of intent to kill.

The major difficulty with the assault with a deadly weapon statutes involves defining a deadly weapon. A deadly weapon is anything capable of causing death depending on how it is used and with what intent it is used in any particular case. The fact that a weapon is capable of causing death is not the determining factor in declaring it a deadly weapon. This determination depends on the manner and intent with which the weapon is used in addition to its natural capability.

8.4 Mayhem

One form of battery was given separate treatment at common law because the act deprived the victim of the ability to defend himself. This common law crime, called mayhem, included any act against the person which violently deprived him of the use of any members so as to make him less able to defend himself. The character of the member was the key to determining the existence of this crime and not the seriousness of the injury. Likewise, the fact that an injury disfigured the victim did not constitute mayhem unless that same injury would weaken the individual to a point where he was less able to defend himself. Oddly enough, the common law courts held that cutting off another's ear or nose was not mayhem under the above definition, for this only disfigured and did not weaken. Modern statutes alter the rule and include intentionally inflicted acts of disfigurement within the purview of mayhem.

The injury must be inflicted willfully and maliciously and must be of a permanent nature to constitute mayhem although premeditation is not a required element. The commission of one of these prohibited acts in necessary self-defense is not criminal.

Mayhem is among those crimes for which consent may not be given by the victim. As previously discussed (6.9), consent in such a case is not a valid defense to this crime.

Questions for Discussion

1. A statute of the State of Excelsior allows a person to trespass on another's land for the purpose of recapturing his cattle which have strayed onto such other person's land. Johnson is a farmer

in a small rural community in Excelsior. He makes his livelihood by raising cattle. One day he noticed that four cows had wandered out of his pasture and onto the property of his neighbor, Green. Johnson entered onto Green's property for the purpose of retrieving his cattle. Just as Johnson approached the property, Green rushed out of the house and, in no uncertain terms, ordered Johnson off his property. An argument ensued and ended in Johnson knocking Green to the ground. Johnson took his cattle and left. Shortly afterward, Green reported the incident to the police who arrested Johnson for assault and battery. In light of the statute mentioned above, would a conviction be proper?

2. Brown was to be a witness in a trial against Howard. The day before the trial as Brown was crossing a street, he observed a vehicle approaching at high speed. Brown hurried toward the curb but the car veered off its path and headed straight toward him. Brown was observant enough to see and remember the license number. The following day, the police arrested a suspect who admitted driving the car. The state, however, was unable to prove any intent on the part of the suspect to murder Brown. Does the state have an alternative charge on which to proceed against the suspect?

Chapter 9

SEX OFFENSES

9.0 Introductory Remarks

One need only glance through a daily newspaper to see how much sex is in the limelight in contemporary societies throughout the world. Nevertheless, certain segments of many societies still hold the view that sex is not a proper subject for public display or discussion. It is not our purpose to debate the pros and cons of such arguments, nor is it our function to comment on the effect that the changing attitudes of society will ultimately have on the laws regarding sex offenses and related areas. Suffice it to say that the law must change to conform to the desires of society. Any major laws which are contrary to the desires of society will not, as our experience shows, exist for long. This point was classically illustrated in the early part of this century with prohibition.

In the public spotlight today are the laws concerning narcotics and dangerous drugs. A movement is afoot to legalize the use of certain previously prohibited drugs. Whether such steps should or should not be taken is a subject we will not discuss now, but this trend illustrates the effect of society's attitudes on the laws of the day.

Closer to the subject matter in this chapter is the ever growing debate over liberalization of abortion laws. The past and present status of abortion laws will be fully discussed later in this chapter. What will happen in the future depends on the ability of the various factions in society to convince the lawmakers of the rightness of their separate views on the issue.

There is one further controversial issue in the forefront of today's news. Are the X-rated movie films, becoming so prevalent in this country, effecting the sex crime statistics in any way? To our knowledge, no statistical proof has been presented to show either an increase or decrease in sex crimes as a result of the more liberal attitude of society toward films like these. Recently released statistics from Sweden, where pornography laws have been liberalized or eliminated except where juveniles are concerned, show some variations in the figures regarding sex offenses, but officials caution against assuming any direct correlation between these statistics and the new laws. The status of pornography laws will also be discussed in this chapter.

9.1   Forcible Rape

Forcible rape is defined as having unlawful carnal knowledge of a female by force and against her will. The following paragraphs will discuss each of the elements involved. This crime was recognized at common law.

A.   Unlawful

The unlawfulness of the carnal knowledge requires no great amount of legal discussion. "Unlawful" implies that intercourse takes place without the consent of the victim and against her will. The significance of the word unlawful as used in defining this crime, however, does raise one interesting question. Can a man rape his wife? Sexual intercourse is an integral and essential part of the marital relationship. Such conduct is not only expected but is wholeheartedly sanctioned by all segments of society. As a consequence, it is a universally accepted rule that a man cannot rape his wife even though he may, on occasion, need to resort to physical force to accomplish his purpose. Subject to this exception, any female may be the victim of forcible rape. In connection with this point, the authors have often heard the comment that a prostitute cannot be raped. This statement, of course, is completely without merit. If the elements of the crime of rape are present in a particular case, it makes no difference what the victim's background happens to be.

One qualifying statement about the man and wife situation should be made. Although a man may not rape his wife, this does not mean that a man may not be found guilty of the crime of rape with his wife as the victim. As we have pointed out (4.11), aiding and abetting another to commit a crime makes one liable as a principal in the second degree. This rule applies to the man and wife situation. If a man aids and abets in the rape of his wife, he is liable for rape as a principal in the second degree or simply as a principal in states which have abolished the degrees of principals.

B. Carnal Knowledge

Carnal knowledge is a legal term for sexual intercourse. In a rape case, it must be shown that there has been sexual intercourse. The law defines sexual intercourse as penetration of the vagina by the penis. Consequently, this requirement can be satisfied if the slightest penetration can be shown. It is not essential for the completion of this crime that there be any emission of sperm.

C. Of a Female

There is little need for discussion on this point except to raise a few questions. Can a man be the victim of a forcible rape? Many cases have arisen where a man has been sexually assaulted. To our knowledge there is no case on record where such facts have supported a forcible rape charge. All the elements of the crime clearly indicate that it would be inconsistent to call such acts forcible rapes.

Nevertheless, it should be remembered that even though a female cannot actually rape a man, a female can be just as easily convicted of rape as a male can. If the female acts either as an accessory before the fact or as a principal in the second degree, her liability is no less than that of the man she procured or aided in committing the rape (4. 11).

An interesting question in this area of the law is raised by the modern medical phenomenon of sex change. Will a person who has had a sex alteration from male to female be considered a female for purposes of the law of forcible rape? The authors make no attempt even to guess at the possible answer to this perplexing question. To our knowledge the case has never yet come before the courts. There was an interesting divorce case in England not too long ago in which the court held that the "female" was a "man," and as a result the marriage was declared void.

D. By Force

The law requires that force be used to establish the crime of forcible rape. How much and what type of force will satisfy this requirement are discussed in a number of court opinions. Today, it is rarely held that actual physical violence must be shown. Of course, if there is physical violence, the element is satisfied. Most modern courts also recognize threats of force or violence as a sufficient alternative, however. If a woman were threatened to the point where she justifiably feared immediate death or great personal injury to herself or to an immediate member of her family who was present, the requirement would be met. Notice that the threat has to involve immediate personal injury rather than future injury. Threat to property will not supply this element.

No discussion of force can be complete without an inquiry into the amount of resistance the victim must offer. If the victim offers no resistance, it cannot properly be said that intercourse was forced. Formerly, the majority rule was that the victim must have resisted to the utmost of her ability. Today, this view has become fairly obsolete and the majority of courts now only require that the victim resist as much as her age, strength, and all the other circumstances surrounding the event allow. If the victim has a knife at her throat and death is threatened, there is little point in physically resisting. If the victim does resist, as required by the law, and is still overcome, there is no further requirement that she continue to resist. Once there has been the slightest penetration, the crime is complete.

E. And Against Her Will

The element requiring that carnal knowledge occur against the will of the victim also conveys the idea that it be without her consent. This may seem like a distinction without a difference, but we will see that there are situations in which these two phrases may, if construed literally, convey separate and inconsistent meanings. There is some overlapping between this element and the one discussed previously. If, in fact, physical violence does accompany the attack, lack of consent will be implied.

As a general rule, lack of consent will be implied in forcible rape cases. If, however, the defendant raises consent as a defense to the charge, the state must prove that there was no consent and that intercourse was against the will of the victim. This is true because lack of consent, being an essential element of the crime, is a part of the burden of proof that the state must carry in order to convict. Therefore, let us reexamine the elements of the defense of consent (6.9), and determine how they apply to the law of forcible rape.

First of all, rape is the type of crime for which consent can be given. Second, the victim is giving consent for herself and not for a third party, so she would have the authority. The last two elements, however, present some problems. Even though the victim has the authority to give consent, she may not be legally capable of giving consent. This lack of capacity may arise either as a matter of law or as a matter of fact. Let us examine a few problems in this area. The most obvious situation that comes to mind concerns the young female. In all states, a child under a certain age is, by law, treated as incapable of giving consent. Thus, her "consent," if she did give it, would not be recognized and would not be a valid defense. Because of the nature and frequency of such occurrences, state legislatures have enacted separate statutes dealing with these cases. The penalties for this offense are usually less severe than for forcible rape because the victim was, in fact, a willing partner. If force is used to have intercourse with a child under the statutory age, however, forcible rape is a proper charge.

There is an exception to this exception. A child under the age of ten years was, and still is, considered totally incapable of consenting or even being a willing partner to sexual intercourse. Consequently, intercourse with a female child under ten years is forcible rape, regardless of any surrounding circumstances.

Capacity to give consent also brings up the question of intercourse with an unconscious woman. It is here that the semantic difference between the phrases "against her will" and "without her consent" could be disastrous were it not for the interchangeable interpretations given these phrases by the courts. It is difficult to say that intercourse with an unconscious woman is against her will for, in fact, her will is not being exercised at the time. However, there is little difficulty in holding that the act would be without her consent if she were unconscious. This is the interpretation given in cases like this and courts uniformly hold that this constitutes forcible rape. The problem is similar when the victim, although conscious, is so drunk that she does not understand the nature of the act to which she is "consenting." Here again, courts hold that if the victim is so drunk, a forcible rape charge will stand.

A similar question is raised when a man has intercourse with a female idiot. Many legislatures have enacted statutes specifically covering this situation. If the victim's mentality is so low that agreement to the act of intercourse is really beyond her ability to comprehend, her agreement will not be recognized as legal consent.

The last problem with consent involves consent obtained by fraud. As mentioned previously (6.9), fraud in consent may take either of two forms, only one of which will invalidate the defense. If the fraud concerns the very nature of the act as where the victim consents to have an operation and the doctor has intercourse with her while she is anesthetized, there is no consent. The victim did not consent to intercourse. On the other hand, if the victim agrees to intercourse, knowing full well the nature of the act, but is fraudulently induced to consent for whatever reason, her consent is valid and will be a defense to a charge of forcible rape.

At common law, a male under the age of fourteen was held incapable of committing forcible rape. This followed the arbitrary common law classification of infants and their capacity to form the necessary mental element to commit crimes. As stated in 6.3, a child under the age of seven years was conclusively presumed incapable of criminal intent and a child between seven and fourteen years was rebuttably presumed incapable. In the case of rape, this rebuttable presumption was made conclusive. Some modern legislatures have recognized the impracticality of this common law rule and have either modified it so as to make it a rebuttable presumption again or eliminated the rule completely from their statutes.

If all the elements of forcible rape are present, the victim's subsequent forgiveness of the act will not bar prosecution for the crime. Upon satisfaction of all the elements, the crime is complete. Likewise, a subsequent marriage between the accused and the victim is no defense. Admittedly, there are some practical problems created by either of these situations, especially if the victim refuses to testify, but legally such circumstances do not bar prosecution.

9.2 Statutory Rape

The reader will note that throughout the entire preceding section, the crime of rape was always referred to as forcible rape. This was done deliberately to avoid using a broad term to cover all types of rape. Statutory rape is a label given to a type of crime which was unknown at common law and which was created by statute. However, even at common law, a female under the age of ten years was considered incapable of consenting to sexual intercourse. This was true even if she knew the nature of the act. Her consent in such a case was no defense to a charge of forcible rape. The key difference between forcible and statutory rape is that in the latter, force and consent are immaterial. At common law, it was not rape to have intercourse with a female over ten years of age if she consented. Legislatures took the view, however, that a child under a certain age limit was not mature enough to understand the full implications of consenting to sexual intercourse. As a result, the statutory rape statutes were enacted. Under these statutes the adult partner is held liable for the underage partner's lack of responsibility.

As mentioned in the previous section, consent by the underage partner is not a valid defense to the crime of statutory rape. Similarly, absence of force in these cases is immaterial. The mere doing of the act is all that is necessary to convict. However, if the victim does not consent to intercourse and if force or the threat of force is used, all the elements of forcible rape have been satisfied and the age of the victim is immaterial. The prosecution may very well choose to prosecute for forcible rape, which carries a much more severe penalty than statutory rape.

Some jurisdictions may not recognize statutory rape by that name. There is some misconception fostered by this name since the elimination of force and consent really takes this offense out of the rape classification. But, however the equivalent statute reads, it is still designed for the purposes set forth above.

Some further qualifying remarks are needed to cover this offense fully. Many of these statutes require that a victim of statutory rape be unmarried. Further, many states require that the victim be of previous chaste character. This requirement is designed to prevent fraud on the courts by young persons of promiscuous habits. In a statutory rape case, if it can be shown that the victim was of previous unchaste character, the statutory rape charge will not stand. If, however, it can be shown that whenever the victim has had intercourse it has been with the defendant, the courts will not allow his prior misdeeds to bar his conviction.

A defense often raised in statutory rape cases is mistake of fact. The defendant claims that his underage female partner looked older than her actual age, misrepresented her actual age (sometimes to the point of producing falsified identification), and was physically endowed beyond the norm for her actual age. Since statutory rape is a crime requiring no intent, there is nothing for the defense of mistake of fact to operate on, and these attempts at justification will be to no avail. The defendant is held to act at his peril. Likewise, a claim that the defendant is going to or has married the victim after committing the offense is not a defense.

In recent years considerable controversy has arisen concerning current rape statutes, law enforcement, and prosecutorial practices in rape cases. Television productions have attempted to point out that often both the supposed victim and alleged ravisher are on trial. The main themes of these attacks come from equal rights for women advocates, who state, with some justification, that most male law enforcement officers and prosecutors do not believe a woman can be raped. Police and prosecutors have experienced cases of alleged rape where defense counsels have shown that the cry of rape has come from victims trying to cover unwanted pregnancies, voluntarily induced, and desiring revenge against an errant lover. Rape is often a better explanation for illicit sex than is infidelity. These and other motives have been successfully demonstrated in court, only to leave the prosecutor embarrassed at his own investigatory techniques. Along these lines are a number of instances where the victim, although not having consented to the rape, conducted herself in a provocative manner prior to the attack. Cases have revealed that the victim answered her door in a see-through negligee and made no attempt at modesty when permitting the ravisher-to-be salesman or repairman to enter the house. Finally, there are some erroneous feelings on the part of some officials that no woman could even be raped.

In response to growing criticism of current practices, some states have enacted new statutes. Many are designed to remove some of the ordeal for the victim at trial by keeping the mind of the jury from side issues not relevant to the conduct in question. In California and Iowa, for example, statutes now prohibit inquiry into the past sexual conduct of the rape victim. Iowa and Connecticut repealed their statutes requiring corroborative evidence. Massachusetts has enacted a statute that the victim no longer is required to show that she was physically forced to submit. The *threat* of physical force will be enough to bring a conviction. Several other states have enacted or are about to enact such amendments to their pre-existing laws. The student is urged to determine the current status of such statutes.

Although in most states a man cannot be raped, at least one state by statute recognizes a forcible homosexual attack as rape.

9.3   Seduction

Seduction was not a recognizable common law offense but has developed by statute. Definitions and elements of this offense vary from jurisdiction to jurisdiction but several basic requirements are common. The gist of the offense is enticing or luring an unmarried female of previous chaste character to engage in sexual intercourse by fraudulently promising to marry her or by some other false promise. Reliance must be placed on the promise as the reason for submitting to intercourse. If the female consents solely for the purpose of engaging in the sexual activity without relying on the promise, the crime is not complete. Many statutes which make seduction a criminal offense provide that if, in fact, the promise is kept—when the parties subsequently marry, for example—the crime may not be charged.

9.4 Fornication and Adultery

Although fornication and adultery are found in the statute books of most jurisdictions, these laws are rarely enforced. The State of Florida, for example, has prosecuted only one case in the last hundred years for violation of the adultery statute. Perhaps the reason for this lack of enforcement is the fact that normally these violations occur under conditions not generally public in the sense that they are injurious to the people of the state. Notwithstanding the enforcement practicalities, both offenses are criminal if declared so by statute, and deserve mention at least by way of definition. Yet, even the definitions of these offenses are not settled and they may vary from state to state.

Fornication is sexual intercourse between unmarried persons. Adultery is generally sexual intercourse between a male and female, at least one of whom is married to someone else. In the definition of adultery, there is considerable variation. Some states require both parties to be married to other people before the crime is satisfied. Other states direct that only one of the parties need to be married but disagree as to which one. In many of these latter jurisdictions, the law may still hold the unmarried partner liable for fornication. There is no universally accepted rule as to what constitutes these crimes, and local statutes must be consulted.

9.5 Incest

Incest is a crime in all states. It involves sexual intercourse between persons who are related to each other by blood. The closeness of the relationship varies from state to state and is spelled out in the statutes. Sexual relationships between father and daughter, or mother and son, or brother and sister are uniformly prohibited throughout this country. Sexual intercourse is an essential element of this crime. In some states, marriage between close blood relatives is included in the criminal statute if accompanied by proof of sexual intercourse. Marriage alone between close blood relatives will, of course, be grounds for divorce in a civil action but will not, of itself, necessarily constitute the crime of incest.

9.6 Abortion

As noted in the introductory remarks to this chapter, abortion laws have become the subject of much concern with members of the public at large and particularly with legislators throughout the country. Bill upon bill has been introduced seeking to liberalize abortion laws. It may very well be that the number of situations in which a legalized abortion may be obtained will increase in a number of states within the next few years.

Abortion was a recognized common law offense classified as a misdemeanor. It was defined as causing the miscarriage of a woman quick with child, with or without her consent, when it was not necessary to so do in order to preserve the life of the mother.

The common law did not protect an unborn child. As to the death of the fetus, no crime was committed. Legislatures have changed this situation, but what of the death of the mother during an abortion? The common law courts held that if the mother died during commission of an abortion, it was criminal homicide. The degree of the homicide depended on the manner in which the abortion was performed. If the abortion was performed by means likely to inflict serious injury or death, the crime was murder if the mother died. On the other hand, if done in a manner not likely to cause death or serious injury to the mother, an abortion which did cause the death of the mother would result only in a charge of manslaughter.

The common law definition of abortion required that the woman be quick with child. Quickness is defined as the stage in development when the fetus first starts to move in the mother's womb. This occurs around the middle of the term of pregnancy—four and one-half months after conception. This is a matter to be proved in a trial of a person charged with abortion.

Despite modern legislation concerning feticide (7.2), the homicide laws still leave a gap in the criminal law when a miscarriage is procured before the fetus has quickened. It was basically for this reason that the abortion laws were established. In many jurisdictions, the scope of abortion laws has been extended to include the aborting of any pregnant woman, eliminating the necessity that the fetus be developed to the quickened stage. In still other jurisdictions, the crime is complete if the accused commits some overt act toward abortion, such as using an instrument or administering a drug intending to commit an abortion. In these states, the statute does not require that the victim even be pregnant. Thus, criminal intent becomes the crucial factor in determining whether the crime has been committed. Usually, in these states the act must go further than what is required to charge an attempt.

At common law and today in most jurisdictions, there are situations in which a legal abortion may be performed. Under common law abortion was allowed only if it was reasonably necessary to preserve the life of the mother. The problem created by this rule was in deciding whether or not abortion was reasonably necessary to preserve the life of the mother. If this is a medical decision, as it obviously should be, why permit judicial review of a medical decision? The two professions are often at variance, as we saw earlier in the case of insanity (6.1). Some states have extended the common law rule to permit abortion if, on the advice of two or more doctors, abortion seems necessary to preserve the life of the mother.

In those states where acting with intent to procure a miscarriage is all that is essential to commission of the crime, intent is an indispensable element and must, of course, be affirmatively proved by the prosecution. See Chapter 5 for a complete discussion of the intent element in criminal law.

Some jurisdictions have gone a little further and legalized abortion if it appears reasonably necessary to preserve either the life *or the health* of the mother.

The cry for liberalization of abortion laws in this country became much louder with the advent of widespread use of contraceptive devices such as the birth control pill. Fuel was added to the fire when the news broke concerning deformed babies being born to mothers who had consumed the drug Thalidomide. Still more controversy arose when reports of the effects of LSD on pregnant women were released.

In 1973 the United States Supreme Court rendered two opinions regarding the constitutionality of abortion statutes. In *Roe* v. *Wade*, 410 U.S. 113 (1973), an unmarried, pregnant woman challenged the Texas statute which allowed abortions only when the life of the mother was threatened. The case contains a fine brief history of the law and attitudes surrounding the issue of abortion.

The court said that the state has a legitimate interest in seeing to it that safe and proper medical procedures are followed. But, the court went on to say, that the right of personal privacy includes the abortion decision. This right is not unqualified, however, and must be considered against important state interests. The state's important and legitimate interest in the health of the mother, the "compelling" point in the light of present medical knowledge, is at approximately the end of the first trimester. Prior to this the physician in consultation with his patient is free to determine, without regulation by the state, that the pregnancy should be terminated. After the first trimester, or ninety days, the state may regulate the abortion procedure. After viability, the court concluded the state may promote the potentiality of human life and prevent abortion except where necessary to preserve the life or health of the mother. The courts define viability as the capability of the fetus to have a meaningful life outside the mother's womb. The courts say that after viability the state's interest has both logical and biological justification.

The second case, *Doe* v. *Bolton*, 410 U.S. 179 (1973), challenged the Georgia statute which provided for a committee to approve all abortions. The court said this was not constitutionally justifiable. Likewise, the court declared the practice of requiring that the patient be a resident of Georgia to be invalid.

Thus, the court paved the way for the liberalization of abortion practices. However, the state can still require some medical expertise by the one performing the abortion.

In 1972 the American Bar Association gave its approval to the Uniform Abortion Act. Under this act the decision is left to the doctor and the patient through the first nineteen weeks. After that the abortion must be justified on the well-being of the mother. If her life is endangered, or if her health or mental condition would be gravely impaired, or if the child would be born with a grave physical or mental defect, or if the pregnancy were the result of rape or illicit sex, then an abortion could be performed after twenty weeks. This statute requires an abortion by a licensed physician, performed in the doctor's office, a hospital, or clinic. This act is based on the New York Abortion Act.

A number of states had revised their abortion statutes along the lines of the Model Penal Code. In that code the abortion must be justified, but it is more liberal than older statutes. States adopting this law are Arkansas, California, Colorado, Delaware, Florida, Georgia, Kansas, Maryland, Mississippi, New Mexico, North Carolina, Oregon, South Carolina, and Virginia.

By 1970 four states had repealed criminal penalties for abortions performed in early pregnancy by a licensed physician subject to certain procedural and health requirements. Those states are Alaska, Hawaii, New York, and Washington. Since then other states have liberalized their laws, and the student should consult the statutes to see if the Uniform Act or Model Act version has been adopted.

9.7 Sodomy

Sodomy was a felony at common law and included such sexual acts as intercourse between a human and an animal or anal intercourse between human beings. The acts prohibited by this law are still violations in most jurisdictions today and are often entitled "crimes against nature" or the like. Homosexuality is usually encompassed under these laws and in no state does homosexuality appear in the statute books as a separate offense.

9.8 Indecent Exposure

The act of exposing one's self in a public place or in a place where the public could view such conduct was a common law misdemeanor. This offense has been included in the statutes of most jurisdictions and remains a misdemeanor.

9.9 Obscenity

Much emotion has been aroused in the 1970s over the relationship between the law and matters of pornography and obscenity, particularly
concerning written materials and motion pictures. In the light of court
decisions which seem continually to expand the scope of lawful subjects
for public consumption and narrow the scope of those fitting the ever
changing definitions of obscenity and pornography, police officers and
other members of the public are showing some concern over the status
of these laws in today's society. A brief review of the historical developments of the laws of obscenity and pornography may help explain the
reasons for the confusion and concern that exist today and will lead to a
discussion of the current law.

In 1957 the Supreme Court of the United States was confronted
with an important constitutional test. In *Roth* v. *United States,* 354 U.S.
476 (1957), the defendant, who published and sold books, was charged
with violation of the federal obscenity statute. In a companion case, *Alberts* v. *California,* 354 U.S. 476 (1957), the defendant, Alberts, conducted a mail order business in the State of California. He was charged
with violation of that state's obscenity laws for lewdly keeping obscene
and indecent books for sale. The question presented to the Court in both
these cases was whether the statutes under which these defendants were
charged and convicted (the federal statute in the *Roth* case and the California statute in the *Alberts* case) were constitutional. The decision
turned on whether these obscenity laws violated the First Amendment's
guarantee of freedom of speech and the due process clause of the Fourteenth Amendment. The defendants argued that the wording of the respective statutes did not provide reasonably definite standards of guilt so
that people could understand and conform their conduct to the requirements of the laws. The Court held that the statutes were constitutional,
that not every form of speech or expression is protected by the Constitution, and that obscenity laws, designed to protect the morals of the
people, do not infringe on the area of protected speech or expression
under the First Amendment, and that the wording of the statutes gave
adequate warning of the types of conduct prohibited. The Court went
on to say that the test of obscenity is whether, to the average person applying contemporary community standards, the material appeals to prurient interest.

Thus, the Court established the broad rule that obscenity was not
constitutionally protected. This view has been reaffirmed in case after
case since 1957. The problem then becomes one of defining the term
obscenity. The test propounded in the *Roth* and *Alberts* cases appears

rather subjective since it takes a court to determine whether the material at issue in a particular case is, in fact, obscene.

Since 1957 several state statutes prohibiting the use, sale, or possession of obscene material have been ruled unconstitutional by the courts. In general, these decisions have not held that obscenity is lawful and fully protected by the First Amendment and the Fourteenth Amendment. What they have said is that although obscenity is still not protected, the statutes that were attacked did not adequately define obscenity or provide reasonably ascertainable standards of guilt. The statutes were too vague to be understood by the people of the state who must conform their conduct to the requirements of the law. If these states were to draft new laws prohibiting obscenity and word them in such a way as to define clearly the prohibited conduct, the statutes would be constitutional.

From 1959 to 1973 the courts had utilized a test for obscenity based upon the social value of the work. If a book, film, or other material had some redeeming social value, it was not obscene. It was up to the courts to determine whether a particular item had redeeming social importance. This test was applied along with the test propounded in the *Roth* and *Alberts* cases, under which the courts had to look to contemporary community standards.

But what community? The nation? The county? The state? The city? Much debate arose as to the scope of the community. A good many people said that a national standard should be applied.

In 1973 the Supreme Court of the United States defined the community and redefined obscenity. In a series of cases the court made major revisions concerning the right of the community to protect itself from allegedly obscene materials.

The first and most important case dealing with the definition of obscenity is *Miller* v. *California*, 413 U.S. 15 (1973). The Court here defined obscenity and the community, pointing out that obscene material is not protected by the First Amendment. The newer definition, as the Court saw it, is that any work that depicts or describes sexual conduct which taken as a whole appeals to the prurient interest in sex and portrays sexual conduct in a patently offensive way and which taken as a whole does not have serious literary, artistic, political, or scientific value is obscene. The Court rejected the utterly without redeeming social value test.

The Supreme Court defined what patently offensive meant in two parts. First, patently offensive are representations or descriptions of ultimate sexual acts, normal or perverted, actual or simulated. Second, patently offensive are representations or descriptions of masturbation, excretory functions, and lewd exhibition of the genitals.

As to what community should be looked to with regard to the

standard of offensiveness, the Court said, "It is neither realistic nor constitutionally sound to read the First Amendment as requiring that the people of Maine or Mississippi accept public depiction of conduct found tolerable in Las Vegas or New York City." The Court recognized the differences in people and was unwilling to impose uniformity. Therefore, a state, through individual courts and by the decisions of individual juries, is permitted to determine whether any work is patently offensive.

In a companion case, *Paris Adult Theater* v. *Slaton*, 413 U.S. 49 (1973), the Court said that even though obscene materials are shown only to consenting adults the state has a right to challenge such materials and, if found to be offensive, to prevent their sale and distribution.

In yet another case decided on the same day, *U.S.* v. *Orito*, 413 U.S. 139 (1973), the Supreme Court held that Congress has the power to prevent obscene material from entering the stream of commerce. The Court therefore held that the *Stanley* case, which protected the right of people to keep obscene materials in the privacy of their homes, did not extend beyond the home. Therefore, although a person can have such material at home, it appears he or she could have difficulty transporting it there.

The final case dealing with the definition of obscenity is *Kaplan* v. *California*, 413 U.S. 115 (1973). The Court here simply said that books without pictures can be obscene.

With these definitions in mind, the law enforcement officer will naturally ask the question: How can I determine if the crime of selling or distributing obscene materials has been committed? Since a book, film, or other material is not obscene until so declared in the proper forum and since the police officer has to make a guess at whether the community standards are offended, the Supreme Court is reluctant to allow seizure of such materials without some kind of neutral magistrate intervening.

At the same time that the definitional decisions came down, the Court rendered two opinions dealing with the seizure of films. In the case of *Roaden* v. *Kentucky*, 413 U.S. 496 (1973), the court found these facts: A sheriff saw the film at a local drive-in theater. At the conclusion of the film he arrested the theater manager and seized a copy of the film. This was done without a warrant. The Court said this was unreasonable and violated the Fourth and Fourteenth Amendments. The Court said because the First Amendment is also involved, a higher hurdle of reasonableness must be met. The Supreme Court prefers the method followed in the companion case of *Heller* v. *New York*, 413 U.S. 483 (1973). In the *Heller* case the police went to the theater and viewed the film. After that, accompanied by a state prosecutor and a judge, the police went back and viewed the film. They had already prepared affidavits and warrants which needed only the judge's signature. The judge viewed the film, agreed that it was obscene, and signed the arrest and search warrants. The Court upheld this action.

What it comes down to is simply this: Without a prior determination of obscenity and without absolute knowledge of what a community will think is obscene, there is no way for the police to know if a crime has been or is being committed. Unlike other crimes as discussed throughout this book, the crime involving obscenity does not have clear-cut elements about which, when observed, one can say, "I just saw a crime."

Despite the fact that the United States Supreme Court in *Miller* severely limited what could be found to be "hard core" pornography, some prosecutors and police still brought borderline cases to the courts. The Court reemphasized that only "hard core" materials are obscene. *Jenkins* v. *Georgia*, 15 Crim. Law. Rep. 3259 (June 26, 1974). The Court said, "It would be a serious misreading of *Miller* to conclude that juries have unbridled discretion in determining what is 'patently offensive.'" Occasional scenes of nudity are not enough to make material legally obscene under the *Miller* standards. Only the public portrayal of hard core sexual conduct for its own sake and for ensuing commercial gain is punishable.

9.10   Prostitution and Related Offenses

Prostitution is defined as the offering by a female of her body for intercourse with men for monetary or other gain. Prostitution is an offense in most states but is not criminal in England anymore. Most American jurisdictions follow the common law definition and require that the sexual activity be for hire, implying some gain, usually money. A small number of states have eliminated this element of the offense and define the crime as any indiscriminate sexual activity whereby a female offers her body to a number of men for sexual intercourse whether for gain or not.

The crime of pandering, also generally prohibited in the prostitution statutes, is the offense commonly called "pimping." This offense, usually carrying even more severe penalties than prostitution because of its social degradation, consists of procuring a female to work in a house of prostitution or procuring a house of prostitution in which the female may work.

Bawdy houses, also called houses of ill fame and houses of prostitution, were prohibited at common law as nuisances. Today, of course, it is still unlawful to maintain such a place. However, proof of this offense generally requires more than an isolated incident or two. It must be shown that the "house" is regularly used for prostitution. Likewise, one who leases a premises for the purposes of, or knowing that it will be used for, prostitution is guilty of an offense.

The word *house* as used to describe a house of prostitution is not confined to its meaning as a residence. The court have treated such other structures as a tent, boat, or even an automobile as coming within the definition of a house of prostitution, provided all other elements of the offense are satisfied.

There is a federal statute on this topic that deserves mention. The White Slave Traffic Act, or Mann Act as it is called, was enacted by Congress in the exercise of its powers over interstate commerce. The federal law prohibits interstate transportation of a female for the purpose of prostitution or for other immoral purposes. Prosecutions for violation of this statute are held in federal court. Although the legislative history of this statute indicates that the intent of Congress was to attempt to close an avenue of revenue for organized crime, time after time courts have held that the statute applies to isolated cases in no way connected with organized crime. To prove this offense, interstate travel must be shown to bring the case under federal jurisdiction as well as the accused's intention of traveling for immoral purposes, such as prostitution.

9.11 Bigamy and Polygamy

Bigamy was not a common law offense but was first created by statute in England. All American jurisdictions have enacted statutes to prohibit marriage between two people when one of them is legally married to someone else. Bigamy is not a specific intent crime. The elements are satisfied by showing that the accused married again, did so intentionally, and knew, at the time, that he or she was already legally married to another. Such defenses as mistake of fact (6.6) and mistake of law (6.7) will be taken into consideration in a bigamy trial.

Polygamy is the act of being married to several spouses at the same time. This too is prohibited by the laws of the United States. In one respect, however, the outlawing of polygamy is a rather recent innovation. The religious beliefs of certain groups allowed and sanctioned the practice of polygamy in the United States. This led to a court case in which the United States Supreme Court declared polygamy to be unlawful. The decision hinged on the First and Fourteenth Amendments to the United States Constitution. The argument for allowing polygamy as a religious practice was based on the First Amendment guarantee of separation between church and state, prohibiting the state from intervening or interfering with religious practices. The argument for outlawing ployg- amy was that it would be a denial of due process and equal protection

to allow one portion of society to practice polygamy and subject someone outside the particular religious group to criminal penalties for doing
the same thing. The second argument won out, and polygamy is now
uniformly prohibited in this country.

9.12   Child Molesting

Child molesting is prohibited by statute in most jurisdictions. This offense is broadly defined to include most sex offenses committed against
children. All other areas of sex offenses are drawn from and come within
the purview of this statute, including handling and fondling. In a number of states, special procedural rules for the treatment of persons convicted of child molesting are established.

9.13   Criminal Sexual Psychopath Laws

In many states, legislatures have enacted laws to provide for committing
and treating persons with a background or history of deviant sexual behavior. These statutes are called criminal sexual psychopath laws, or
mentally disordered sex offender laws. The statutes usually identify the
types of individuals the law applies to and the procedure by which the
state may commit and treat these individuals. These laws do not define
another substantive criminal offense. They are merely tools by which the
state seeks to prevent further deviant sexual behavior.

Questions for Discussion

1. Smith has intercourse with Alice, a prostitute, who says she is
    19 years old. Actually, she is only 17 years, 10 months. Assume
    that the state law sets 18 years as the age of consent. What is
    Smith's legal position?

2. John and Marsha, husband and wife, owned a farm in the State
    of Central. Jim was a hired hand who worked for them. After
    several months, Jim realized he was in love with Marsha. He
    decided to try to have sexual intercourse with Marsha but he
    was well aware that she was deeply devoted to her husband. Jim
    looked somewhat like John and was of approximately the same
    build and appearance. One night, while John was working out-

side the house and Marsha had just gone to bed, Jim entered the house and walked into the bedroom. He got into bed with Marsha and made love to her. Marsha, thinking Jim was her husband, made no objection. After Jim had had sexual intercourse with Marsha he started to leave. Marsha turned on the light and discovered Jim's identity. Jim was arrested for rape. What should be the outcome of Jim's trial?

Chapter 10

THEFT OFFENSES

10.0 Theft in General

I. LARCENY
10.1 Larceny in General
10.2 Degrees of Larceny
10.3 Lost, Mislaid, and Abandoned Property

II. EMBEZZLEMENT
10.4 Introductory Remarks
10.5 Embezzlement Defined

III. THEFT BY FRAUD
10.6 Introductory Comments
10.7 False Pretenses
10.8 Confidence Games—The Swindle
10.9 Larceny by Trick

IV. RECEIVING OR CONCEALING STOLEN PROPERTY
10.10 General Comments
10.11 Elements

10.0 Theft in General

The word theft in its broadest sense describes many forms of criminal conduct. In this chapter we will discuss four basic types of theft offenses: larceny, embezzlement, obtaining property by false pretenses, and receiving, concealing, and possessing stolen property. In fact, this list does not cover all the possibilities. The crime of robbery discussed in the following chapter is a theft offense of sorts since it involves the stealing of property. Because of the force or fear element in robbery, it is usually classified as a crime against the person rather than a theft offense.

Also, forgery and uttering and publishing worthless checks are theft offenses. Because of their frequency and importance, however, we treat them separately, as do most statutes. Many other crimes also involve theft, for example, a majority of burglary cases. Of the more serious offenses, theft is probably the most frequent.

Before we discuss specific theft offenses, certain terms should be defined. Throughout the chapter, we will refer to possession, custody and control, and ownership. The presence or absence of any or all of these factors will largely control the type of offense committed, if any.

Possession is a word thrown around loosely in everyday life. The phrase "Possession is nine-tenths of the law," has become a cliché. Although few laymen really understand the meaning of this expression, from a legal standpoint it contains more truth than falsity.

A man has possession of property when he may exercise his discretion in the use and handling of that property. The scope of this discretion may or may not be limited by other factors. Possession must thus be distinguished from mere custody and control over an item. One may be physically in control of an article without necessarily having possession of it. If he has no right to exercise discretion as to its use or handling, he has only custody and control, not possession. If Sam says to Bill, "Hold my coat while I change this flat tire," Bill has custody and control of the coat but not possession. If Sam says to Bill, "You may borrow my coat for your date tonight," Bill has discretionary use of the coat during that time so he has possession. Similarly, a shopper in a store who picks up an item from the counter to examine it has only custody and control. If the shopper takes the item home on approval with permission of the store before purchasing it, he has possession of the item.

It is not very difficult in the average case to distinguish between possession and custody and control. When an employee steals from his employer, however, it becomes necessary to determine whether the goods stolen were in the possession of the employee or whether he only had custody and control. Determination of this issue will govern the charge to be placed against the thief. As a general rule, employees only have custody of the property of their employers, and possession remains with the employer. If the property is entrusted to the employee in a position of trust and confidence, however, he is considered to be in possession of the goods. The classic illustration of an employee in such a capacity is the bank teller. Although his discretion is limited, he is permitted to distribute monies given by one person to another.

Possession may be obtained either lawfully or unlawfully. If other elements of a particular theft offense are satisfied, the fact that one gained possession lawfully does not mean he has committed no crime. The lawfulness or unlawfulness of his possession only governs the type of crime for which he may be held liable.

Ownership confers complete and unlimited discretion. Legal title is the essence of ownership. An owner is always entitled to possession, but he may give up possessory rights in property, either temporarily or permanently, and still retain ownership. A leased automobile is owned by the leasing company but is possessed by the lessee. When property is owned and possessed by the same person, few problems will arise, but the distinction is important because larceny and embezzlement are crimes against the possessor of property, not necessarily the owner of the property. Legal title will be important to our discussion of the crime of obtaining property by false pretenses.

I. LARCENY

10.1 Larceny in General

The legal definition of larceny contains five essential elements. These are: (1) the taking, (2) and carrying away, (3) the personal property, (4) of another, (5) with the intent to permanently deprive. Each of these elements is subject to various interpretations. For this reason, we must look to the decisions of courts for their true meaning. It would be unwise to rely solely on the wording of the larceny statutes for an understanding of this offense.

A. Taking

To accomplish a larceny, property must first be taken. The taker must have no right to possession of the property. This is called trespassory taking. One cannot commit a larceny against property he lawfully possesses since larceny is a crime against possession. All that is necessary to satisfy this element is to show that the taker has gotten possession of the property and that his possession is wrongful. This can be established by showing he exercised discretionary control over the object without being entitled to do so.

The trespassory taking usually occurs in a manner that presents little difficulty. For instance, Fred picks up an item of merchandise from a store counter and walks out with it concealed under his coat. This example obviously satisfied the element of trespassory taking. There may be variations on this theme, however, such as the cases covered by the rule of continuing trespass. Every crime generally requires an act and a simultaneous intent. This rule presents some difficulty in the law of larceny. Suppose, for example, that Al wrongfully and without Bill's consent takes some property belonging to Bill. When he takes the property Al does not intend to steal it but he later forms that intent. This case presents a dilemma since the property was taken at one time and the criminal intent was formed at a different time. Act and intent are not simultaneous. This problem is solved through a legal fiction—the widely accepted rule called continuous trespass. In essence, this rule provides that if the initial taking involves trespass, the trespass continues until the criminal intent required for larceny is formed. At this point, the act and intent become simultaneous and, if all other elements are satisfied, the crime of larceny occurs.

The distinctions between possession and custody and control discussed previously play an important part in determining whether the trespassory taking element is satisfied. If someone possesses but does not own property, his later conversion of that property in a way that permanently deprives the owner of his rights to that property will not be larceny. This situation does not fulfill the requisite taking element of larceny. If one merely has custody and control of an article, his conversion of that article deprives someone else of their possessory rights and does constitute a trespassory taking.

Suppose Sam asks Bill to keep a sealed carton for him. Bill agrees. Bill then has possession of that carton. Bill does not, however, have possession of the contents of the carton. He only has custody and control. Under the doctrine of breaking bulk, if Bill steals the carton, it is not larceny. If he breaks open the carton and steals the contents, he has committed larceny.

A further complication of the taking element involves delivery by mistake. Suppose property is given to the accused by mistake and he is not aware of the error. He later discovers the mistake and decides to keep the property. This is not larceny since he was in possession of the property at the time the intent was formed. If, however, he knows about the mistake at the time of the delivery and decides to keep the property, his acceptance of delivery will be considered a trespassory taking. For example, John goes to a bank to cash a check for $1.27. By mistake, the new teller reads the date line instead of the amount. The date is 1/27/69. She pays John $127.69. If John is unaware of the mistake and takes the money but later learns of the error and decides to keep the extra money, he has not committed larceny. On the other hand, if at the time of the transaction, John knows about the mistake and decides to keep the money, he has committed a trespassory taking and may be liable for larceny.

Consent may be a defense to larceny if it is given by someone who has authority to give it. But consent is no defense if the amount taken is more than the amount consented to. If John allows Bill to take a one-dollar bill out of his wallet and Bill takes ten dollars instead, the taking of the extra nine dollars is trespassory. All the elements of consent must be present to support this defense (6.9).

B. Carrying Away (Asportation)

Once the property has been taken, it must be carried away. The Latin-derived term for this element is asportation. The general rule of asportation is that the article taken must be entirely removed from the place it formerly occupied. The article does not have to be carried any great distance as long as it is entirely removed from the place it occupied just before being taken. Although this element usually presents no significant difficulty, in some cases it may become an issue. For example, an accused pickpocket is caught in the act. The wallet he was removing from the victim's back pocket was only partially removed when he was caught. Since there is not much room in a pocket, the wallet would have to be completely removed before asportation is complete. If it is not completely removed, there is no larceny, only an attempt.

The means of accomplishing asportation are immaterial. The act may be accomplished either by the hand of the accused, through an innocent human agent, an inanimate object, or an animate nonhuman agent such as a monkey or dog (4.4).

C. Personal Property

Personal property is anything capable of ownership, except land or things permanently affixed to land. Things like cars, animals, furniture, and money are all classed as personal property. Trees and houses are generally considered real property but once they are detached from the land, as when a tree is cut down or a house is torn down, they take on the characteristics of personal property and may be the subject of larceny. Courts have held that minerals, once they are mined, become personal property.

Personal property may or may not be tangible. In a number of cases, it has been held that water, gas, electricity, and oil may be subject to larceny. This is frequently done by tapping electric or telephone lines or tapping water or oil lines. The identity of the victim may depend on whether the tap is made before or after the electricity or water has gone through a householder's meter.

D. Of Another

Since larceny is a crime against possession, one cannot commit larceny against goods he already possesses. The identity of the person who has possession is important, not after the theft has occurred, but immediately before the theft. It is obvious that the thief has possession afterward. Theft must be committed by one who does not have possession against one who does have possession in order to constitute larceny. A person who has only custody and control of goods may commit larceny of those goods since he does not have possession immediately before the theft. An owner may commit larceny against goods he owns if someone else has possession. The classic example of this involves the innkeeper who keeps the luggage until the bill is paid of a guest who refuses to pay for his previous night's lodging. If the owner of the luggage takes the property back without paying the bill, he is guilty of larceny. The law permits the innkeeper to retain possession of the luggage under these circumstances even though he does not own it.

E. With the Intent to Permanently Deprive (Animus furandi)

Larceny is a specific intent crime. The thief must intend to permanently deprive the rightful or previous possessor of his discretionary use of the property. This intent in larceny is referred to as *animus furandi*. The intent must be to permanently rather than temporarily deprive. This intent may be shown from the facts and circumstances surrounding the incident. It is provable just like the intent for any crime is provable—by what is said and done. In many cases, where it is difficult to prove intent to permanently deprive, legislatures have created separate offenses. Even temporary deprivation, if it is done wrongfully, should not go unpunished. If an automobile is stolen and the intent cannot be shown to support an auto theft or larceny charge, legislatures have created statutory offenses, such as driving away an automobile without the owner's consent. Statutes of this kind do not require that intent to permanently deprive be shown.

If property is taken with the intent to permanently deprive, it is immaterial whether it is subsequently returned even if the thief does so voluntarily. This may affect the severity of the sentence but the crime is complete when the property is taken. If the thief holds property until the rightful possessor agrees to pay a reward for its return, he is considered to have intended permanent deprivation.

It is not necessary that the thief keep the property or gain any benefit from it as long as the rightful possessor has been permanently deprived of his property.

10.2   Degrees of Larceny

The common law knew no degrees of larceny. All such crimes were felonies. Most modern statutes divide larceny into two degrees: grand larceny and petit larceny. The distinction hinges on the value of the article stolen. Each state establishes its own arbitrary line between the two degrees. In some states it is fifty dollars. Others define the theft of property valued at one hundred dollars or more as grand larceny. The important thing for law enforcement officers to remember is that the value of the property must be provable in court. Since law enforcement generally investigates on behalf of the prosecutor, it is imperative in investigating larceny cases to determine the value of the property stolen. Determining value may present problems. There are many different measures of value; for example, fair market value, cost value, replacement value, reasonable value, sentimental value, and so forth.

As a general rule, courts base their decisions on fair market value if one is available. Otherwise cost value as opposed to resale value or replacement value is preferred. Sentimental value is not a consideration in the criminal law because this might be subject to exaggeration. Local requirements should be studied to determine the rules for evaluating stolen property.

No matter which rule is followed in a particular jurisdiction, there is usually little problem in determining the degree of larceny committed when the theft involves a single transaction. There may be a problem when a series of small thefts are committed by an individual over a period of time. If the circumstances are right, two alternatives may be open to the prosecution. Several petit larceny offenses may be charged, or all the transactions may be combined into one grand larceny charge. In order to have this option, the prosecution must show that the accused committed a series of separate small thefts with a single felonious intent according to a common scheme or plan to accomplish a single overall objective. Suppose grand larceny in State A is the theft of property worth fifty dollars or more. John, a resident of State A, finds out his wife is going to have a baby some time in July. John begins to worry about how he will pay the doctor and hospital bills after the baby is born. John recalls that there is a certain parking meter downtown which has a faulty lock and that the meter can be opened by simply tapping it in the right place. Nightly, John empties the meter of its contents. At no time does he take more than three or four dollars. By July, John has accumulated over four hundred dollars from this single meter. What degree of larceny has John committed? Of course, he could be charged with each of the separate petit larceny offenses. But in this instance, it can be shown that John acted with a single felonious intent to get enough money to pay the doctor and hospital bills, taking each time from the same victim under an overall general plan. This would give the prosecution the choice of combining all the separate offenses into one grand larceny charge.

Would the result be the same if John committed several small thefts against different people under different circumstances to achieve the same objective? The answer is no. The prosecution would only be permitted to charge the separate counts of petit larceny (hoping the sentences will run consecutively if John is convicted). Although John's motive was the same, his intent was to steal from different victims by different means.

10.3   Lost, Mislaid, and Abandoned Property

When lost, mislaid, or abandoned property is found, some interesting problems in the law of theft are presented. Property is said to be lost when the possessor unintentionally parts with it under such circumstances that he is unaware it is missing. For example, a man gets on a bus and, unknown to him, his wallet falls out of his pocket.

Property is mislaid when the possessor intentionally places the property in a certain location but forgets to retrieve it. For example, John takes out his wallet to pay his dinner bill and sets it on the cashier's counter. After receiving his change he fails to pick up the wallet and walks off, leaving it there. In each case, the possessor did not give up possession. The original possessors retain possession until the property is discovered and taken by the finder. Whether the taking is legal or illegal depends upon the intent of the finder and other circumstances at the time of the taking.

Abandoned property, unlike mislaid or lost property, cannot be subject to larceny. A person abandons property when he intentionally decides to give up his possessory and ownership rights. Only an owner can abandon property. The intent of the owner determines whether property is abandoned, not the circumstances under which the property is found. If John takes possession of an apparently abandoned automobile, which has been left unattended for a period of many months, he acts at his peril. If, in fact, the true owner did not, and does not, intend to disclaim ownership, John may be guilty of theft. He should make every effort to determine whether the car is truly abandoned or not.

The finder of lost property takes possession either rightfully or wrongfully depending on the nature of the article found and the place and circumstances under which it is found. If because of the nature of the property it would be impossible to locate the former possessor, the finder takes rightful possession. If Sam finds a ten-dollar bill in a crowded parking lot without seeing who dropped it, he may take it. His possession is rightful. Because of the nature of the article and the place where it was found, it is highly improbable that the original possessor will be identified or will return for the money. The fact that Sam intended to convert money to his own use at the time he found it would not make his conduct criminal because his possession is legal.

Suppose Sam finds a wallet in that same crowded parking lot under circumstances that indicate the wallet is obviously lost. Can Sam claim rightful possession when he takes it intending to convert it to his own use? No. Sam has found an article that normally contains items which would identify either the true owner or possessor or would give hints as to the identity. Therefore, the law says it is wrong to take the wallet except for the purpose of returning it to the rightful possessor. Sam's act of taking the wallet combined with his unlawful intention of keeping it constitute larceny. If, however, Sam took the wallet intending to return it to its true possessor, but some time later decided to keep it and its contents for himself, there would be no larceny because his original taking was lawful.

Lost property may be the subject of larceny if, at the time it is found, there is a reasonable apparent possibility of identifying the true possessor and yet the finder instead intends to keep the found property permanently. The criminal nature of the act depends on the nature of the property, the place where it is found, and the intent of the finder.

Mislaid property may also be subject to larceny. If someone discovers a box of new clothes on the seat of a bus, he may not take the property unless he intends to return it to the rightful possessor or owner. Because of the nature of mislaid property and because of the probability that the true possessor will remember where he left it and will return for it, any other intent is wrongful. The fact that the owner cannot be identified by examining the mislaid article is immaterial to a charge of larceny, provided the finder takes it intending to permanently deprive the rightful possessor of his property.

Abandoned property, as already indicated, can never be subject to larceny. The first finder who takes possession becomes the owner of the property. This is true, however, only when the property has been completely abandoned by the previous owner. The intent of the finder when he takes the property is unimportant. It is up to him when he takes the property to find out what the previous owner's intention was. The intent of the taker is unimportant because takers of apparently abandoned property usually take such property for their own use and benefit.

II. EMBEZZLEMENT

10.4 Introductory Remarks

Although embezzlement was not one of the common law crimes, it was defined as a crime in England early in the history of Parliament. It is a statutory crime throughout the United States today. Often called a white collar crime, embezzlement as a statutory crime was created to fill the gaps in the common law left by the law of larceny.

Conversion of property completely depriving the true owner, committed by one who has rightful possession, is not larceny. Here the distinctions between possession and custody and control become important. If a trespassory taking could not be shown, there was no crime at common law. To alleviate this situation, the crime of embezzlement was created.

10.5 Embezzlement Defined

Even though all the statutes are not exactly alike, embezzlement can be generally found in the laws of all states. It may be called larceny by a bailee, larceny by embezzlement, or larceny after trust, or by some other name. Essentially, however, the offense is composed of certain standard elements.

Embezzlement is a crime against ownership. The essence of the crime is conversion of property by someone to whom it has been entrusted. Possession is obtained rightfully, and the thief later decides to steal it. The key distinction between larceny and embezzlement is that embezzlement involves no trespassory taking. In all other respects, the elements of embezzlement and larceny are identical.

What is meant by entrusting property to another? Entrustment involves possession given by an employer to his employee, by a master to his servant, or by a principal to his agent. An agent is someone who represents the interests of another (his principal) and who can act for and bind the principal to contracts and the like. Entrustment is also characteristic of the bailor-bailee relationship created by leases, or by leaving property with someone to be repaired or cleaned. A bailment can also be created in a number of ways when property is given to another for safe-keeping.

Under some circumstances, rightful possession may be obtained without entrustment. This may happen when lost property is found. If the finder later decides to permanently deprive the previous possessor of his property, this is not generally considered embezzlement because no entrustment is involved. Usually, there is no crime in a situation like this except in a few jurisdictions which have stretched their embezzlement statutes.

Many embezzlement statutes tend to restrict the offense to those who hold special positions of trust, such as public officials, stockbrokers, bank personnel, and others in similar positions. A thorough reading and proper interpretation of these statutes will generally show that they cover most situations not covered by larceny laws.

III. THEFT BY FRAUD

10.6 Introductory Comments

Under this subheading we will discuss three additional theft-related of-fenses created by legislation. Because obtaining property by false pretenses, larceny by trick, and confidence games involve fraudulent means used to obtain ownership, these crimes are set apart from larceny and embezzlement and discussed here. Each of these offenses involves ob-taining ownership by some fraudulent means. But the fraudulent method used in each differs so that the *corpus delicti* of each crime requires dif-ferent types of proof. In each of these crimes, the objective is to gain dominion and control over the property for the converter's sole use.

10.7 False Pretenses

The crime of obtaining property by false pretenses always involves mis-representation by the accused of a past or present fact. The accused must be aware that his statement is false while the victim believes it to be true. The property must be delivered in reliance on the misrepresenta-tion to the detriment of the victim and the benefit of the accused. Each of these elements will be discussed separately.

The accused must misrepresent a past or present fact. He must misrepresent fact—not opinion. Opinion may play a part in the confidence game but not in this crime. The fact misrepresented must be a present or past fact and not conjecture about the future. This problem becomes complicated when the accused says that his "representations were merely dealers' talk or puffing," as it is known in the law.

The misrepresentation must have been false when it was made. If it was true at that time, the accused did not obtain property under false pretenses even if it later turns out the accused did not know it was true at the time. This means it must be proven that the accused knew the representation was false. It is also essential that the victim not know the claim was false. If the victim knew it was false, the accused cannot be convicted, for no one was deceived. The victim, however, is not under any obligation to verify the accused's statements. It is no defense that the victim was negligent or even stupid not to check.

The victim must part with his property in reliance on his belief in the misstatement of fact. If he gave his property to the accused for some other reason, there is no crime. However, if the victim parts with the property partially in reliance on the misrepresentation and for other reasons as well, the crime will still have been committed. The misrepresentation need not be the sole factor compelling delivery.

Since this is a statutory, not a common law, crime the property obtained must be of the kind and value described by the statute. In general, modern statutes recognize the same subject matter in the offense of obtaining property by false pretenses as in larceny.

As in larceny, the accused must intend to permanently deprive the true owner of his property.

The misrepresentation can be communicated by any method. It can be written or oral. As a matter of fact, it can be communicated by conduct indicating that some fact is true. Failure to disclose facts, however, even when directly asked, will not make the accused liable.

Let us illustrate this crime by examining the following situations. Bill wishes to sell his zircon ring for a considerable sum in order to pay off a gambling debt. He knows that Mary, a wealthy widow, always has ready cash and likes rings and other precious baubles. Bill calls Mary and tells her that he has a diamond ring for sale. She tells him to bring it over. Bill shows her the ring and says it is a two-carat diamond worth $20,000, which he will sell for $5,000. Mary buys the ring believing it to be a diamond. She has it appraised some weeks later and learns for the first time that it is worth only $25. Bill's statement to Mary about the ring's worth will not support a criminal charge. A statement of worth is merely an expression of opinion. But as to the nature of the article, Bill misrepresented a known fact and Mary relied on this statement to her detriment and to Bill's benefit. Therefore, the charge of obtaining money or other property under false pretense would be proper.

Suppose, however, Smith went to a car dealer and bargained over the purchase of a new car. Smith and the dealer settled on the price of a new convertible. By doing some fancy talking, Smith convinced the dealer to sign the title at that time, agreeing to return within the hour with the full cash purchase price. Smith left with the car, fully intending to return to pay for it. Smith later changed his mind and ran off with the automobile to which he had title. Since Smith did not misrepresent any fact at the time the car was delivered, his failure to return and pay the purchase price would not support a charge of false pretenses. In fact, under these peculiar circumstances, it is difficult to identify any chargeable criminal conduct under present law. Would the result be any different if Smith had not intended to pay for the car when he obtained the title? Was the promise to return, which the dealer relied on, a misrepresentation of a present fact or a misrepresentation of a future fact? At first glance it would seem to be a misrepresentation of a future fact—a promise to pay later—which would not constitute a criminal false pretense. Some courts follow this logic. Others would say that the promise itself was a present fact which was misrepresented and which would satisfy this element of the crime.

10.8   Confidence Games—The Swindle

Related to the crime of false pretenses is a series of statutory offenses commonly known as obtaining property by means of confidence games. The gist of these crimes differs from false pretenses in one important aspect. False pretenses involves reliance by the victim on a misrepresented fact. The personality of the accused has nothing to do with the crime. Under the confidence game statutes, reliance is placed on the accused more than on his representations. The con man sells himself to the victim. The victim is often out to get something for nothing. The facts represented may even be true. But where the accused has no intention of applying the property for the reason obtained, the crime is complete and chargeable.

10.9   Larceny by Trick

One further offense related to obtaining property by false pretenses is the offense of larceny by trick. Basically the same as false pretense, this crime differs only in one respect. Under false pretense, title is intentionally passed to the accused by the victim in reliance on the misrepresented fact. In larceny by trick, only possession is surrendered because of some artifice, trick, deception, or fraud. The victim expects to get his property back. For instance, a man intending to convert a rental car to cash goes into a car rental office and says he will use the car for a day. He pays the deposit required and signs the contract with a false name and address. When he gets the car, he sells it to the underworld for cash as he intended. The car rental agency merely intended to give up its possessory interest for a short period of time.

IV. RECEIVING OR CONCEALING STOLEN PROPERTY

10.10 General Comments

The reader may, at one time or another, have heard the words "possession of stolen property" used to describe a criminal offense. This is a popular misnomer. The crime referred to by this phrase is accurately known as receiving or concealing stolen property. Statutes rarely, if ever, punish a person for merely possessing stolen property. Perhaps the reason for this, as discussed in 4.1, is that possession is a weak act and cannot be made criminal unless accompanied by a readily provable intent. The terms *receiving* and *concealing* include, by implication, possession with knowledge. Receiving and concealing also imply some overt physical activity on the part of the accused to satisfy the criminal law requirement that every crime consist of an act.

Although some jurisdictions label this crime receiving *and* concealing stolen property and others call it receiving *or* concealing stolen property, the distinction is without a difference. There is no legal significance to using the different conjunctions. By almost unanimous decisions of the courts, the words receiving and concealing are treated as separate and distinct types of conduct, either of which may apply to any given case. This does not mean that in a particular case the accused may not both receive and conceal stolen property. It means only that one or the other is essential to every case.

There is some evidence that the crime of receiving or concealing stolen property did not exist at early common law—at least not by this name. At early common law, persons who committed acts like these were usually charged with either compounding a felony, a misdemeanor committed by agreeing not to report a felony or to withhold evidence (4.11), or misprision of felony, a misdemeanor committed by failure to report a felony without agreeing to do so (4.11). The obvious shortcoming of these two offenses was that they were misdemeanors carrying light penalties even though the receiving or concealing may have been a severe offense and the value of the property may have been great. In light of these and other reasons, many modern statutes have made the crime of receiving or concealing stolen property a felony. Some states classify it as either a felony or a misdemeanor depending on the value of the property involved.

Some common law courts apparently did hold that receiving or concealing stolen property could also make one liable as an accessory after the fact. This, however, conflicts with the generally accepted view at common law and with the universally held view today that an accessory after the fact must render aid and comfort to the felon personally (4.11). The acts of receiving or concealing stolen property do not constitute personal aid. Of course, an accused could render personal aid to a felon and also render nonpersonal aid by receiving or concealing stolen property. In such an instance, the person may be liable for several different types of criminal conduct.

Although not all the statutes on receiving and concealing stolen property are identical, all contain essentially the same elements. These elements include: (1) the receiving or concealing; (2) of stolen property; (3) knowing the property to be stolen; and (4) with the intent either to gain personally from the act or to prevent the rightful possessor from enjoying his property. The remaining sections of this chapter will deal with each of these elements individually.

10.11 Elements

A. Receiving

The word *receiving* does not necessarily mean the receiver must have manual and actual control over the property. He need not hold the property in his hands any length of time. All that is necessary is that the accused exercise dominion and discretionary control over the property. How does a person gain dominion over property without actually touching it? He can direct the property to be delivered to a certain place over which he has control. If this is done, he has received. For example, Sam tells Joe to put the stolen radios in Sam's garage. Sam never sees or touches the radios before his arrest for receiving stolen property. He has received.

The accused may direct that the property be delivered to a third person who works for him. In such a case, the accused has received through his agent. Obviously, if he (the receiver) takes manual custody of the property this element is satisfied.

Although often the receiver of stolen property may give something in exchange for the goods, payment of any type of consideration is not a necessary part of receiving. One who does pay for stolen property is commonly known as a "fence." The fact that one accused of receiving stolen property only intended to retain the goods temporarily will not affect the character of the receiver. He has received just the same as if he had intended to keep the goods permanently.

Under most modern statutes, husbands and wives may be criminally liable for receiving stolen property from each other. This differs to some extent from the common law rule that the wife could not receive stolen property from her husband because the common law considered husband and wife to be one person. Even at common law, however, a husband could receive stolen property from his wife. One further exception recognized at common law and still recognized in most states today is that one who steals property may not be charged as a receiver or concealer of that same property. This rule was interpreted by the common law courts to include all principals in either the first or second degree. However, the rule did not and does not extend to accessories before the fact. This exception creates a dilemma. Consider those states that have abolished the distinction between principals and accessories before the fact and now classify them all as principals (4.11). Suppose John procures and counsels Bill to steal certain goods from Sam. Bill steals the goods and gives them to John, who receives them. Although John would have been an accessory before the fact at common law he is now a principal. Can he be charged with receiving stolen property or can he be tried only for the actual theft as a principal? Actually, the prosecution may do either. The prosecution can elect to charge him with receiving or they can charge him as a principal, but the prosecution cannot do both. The choice will be made on very practical grounds. Which will be the easiest charge on which to convict him? If the prosecution chooses to charge him with receiving, can John raise the defense that he is a principal and thus not subject to prosecution for receiving stolen property? The answer, of course, is yes. But by raising this defense, John is admitting his guilt as a principal, and he can then be tried on this charge. The converse is also true. If John were charged as a principal in the theft and based his defense on the rule that the thief may not be the receiver of property he stole, he would be confessing to a charge of receiving. A few states have avoided this problem by a finding that the assimilation of an accessory before the fact should be disregarded in cases like this. In those states, the accused may be convicted of both receiving stolen property and the original theft.

The receiver of stolen property need not receive goods directly from the thief. Under early common law, this issue presented some problems. Today, it is fairly generally recognized that one may receive stolen property from another who was also a receiver rather than from the thief. Can a person be charged with the crime of receiving if he received the property from a person who did not know it was stolen? For example, John has heard that the Hope Diamond has been stolen. Billy, a seven-year-old child, finds the diamond but thinks it is a piece of glass, which he shows to his friend John. John immediately recognizes it as the stolen diamond and gives Billy a nickel for it. John is guilty as a receiver of stolen property because he knew the property was stolen. The fact that he received it from an innocent intermediary is immaterial. John does not even have to know the identity of the thief nor who the rightful owner of the property is.

B. Concealing

Most state statutes, at least by implication, make receiving and concealing alternatives to satisfy the elements of this crime. Consequently, one may be guilty of concealing stolen property without ever having received it under any of the rules just discussed. At first blush, it might appear inconceivable that one could conceal property without having at least some limited dominion or control over it. Liberal interpretation of the statutes prohibiting concealment of stolen property have avoided this logical overlap by treating cases of aiding another in concealing stolen property as violations of the statute. This is true also because the courts have tended to construe strictly the word *receiving* within the context set out in the previous section. It must be remembered that one may be guilty of both receiving *and* concealing stolen property, but such conduct will be considered a single offense. There is some authority to the effect that even though the thief cannot be guilty of receiving stolen property, he can be guilty of concealing property he stole. The distinction can be justified on the basis that receiving is inherently a part of stealing, while concealing is not necessary when the theft takes place. Nor is concealment necessary later on even though it is the natural thing to do. If, however, the thief does conceal the property, he usually does so as a separate and distinct act. In any case, if a particular jurisdiction allows a thief to be charged with concealing property he stole in a separate indictment or information, the authority will be based on the statutes of that jurisdiction.

A person doesn't have to hide stolen property under his bed to be convicted of concealing. Neither the statutes nor the courts have required a manual hiding of the property. Naturally, if someone does hide stolen property from view he will be guilty. All that is really required to satisfy this element of the crime is that the accused actively help the thief do something with the property which will either secure the goods to the benefit of the thief or in some other way prevent the true owner from using and enjoying his property. Perhaps the most notorious method of concealing stolen property is connected with auto theft. Persons who had no connection with actual theft of the vehicles spend a great deal of time distinguishing the stolen property by changing the color of the car, removing identification numbers, switching engines, and more.

To illustrate the principles discussed in this section, let us consider the following situation. John steals a color television set. Bill, a friend of John's, knows that the set was stolen by John. Bill suggests a plan to John to help prevent the police from discovering the location of the set. Bill tells John to deliver the set to Bob's E-Z Pay Repair Emporium, pretending it needs service. Bill explains to John that this gimmick will put the set right under the noses of the cops and anyone else for that matter. John delivers the set to Bob's and places it on a counter in the front of the store where it can be seen by anyone passing the repair shop. This situation illustrates the two basic rules discussed above. The fact that Bill never exercised any physical control of the color television set does not prevent him from being charged with the crime of concealing stolen property. His active participation in helping John satisfied this element of the crime. Neither does the fact that the property was not hidden from the view of the public lessen his criminal liability. Bob may have a problem also. If a police investigation shows Bob was aware of the fact that the color television was stolen, he could be guilty as a receiver of stolen property. This would be true even though he did not communicate this knowledge to John when the set was brought into his place of business. If Bob knew the property was stolen, he could also be guilty of concealing the stolen color television set. His act of allowing the set to remain in his shop for the purpose of depriving the true owner of his rights in the set would constitute actively helping the thief conceal the stolen television.

C. Stolen Property

At common law, stolen property, for the purposes of this crime, could only be property taken through larceny. If the property in question was taken during commission of some other theft offense, such as false pretenses, or embezzlement, or was taken during the commission of any number of closely related offenses such as burglary or robbery, receiving stolen property could not be charged. Recognizing the illogic of this situation, state legislatures and state courts expanded the scope of the definition of stolen property by statutes and judicial decision. In most states today, there are either statutes or court decisions holding that property taken during commission of any offense that would justify call-ing the property "stolen" is treated as stolen property for purposes of the receiving and concealing statutes. '

Once property is stolen, does it always remain stolen? Can the property ever lose its character as stolen property? Can it lose its charac-ter as stolen property and still be possessed by the original thief? These and other questions are important to an investigating officer in cases in-volving receiving or concealing stolen property.

Although it is possible for property to remain stolen forever, it can lose its stolen character. There are any number of ways this can occur. If the rightful owner of the property decides, after the theft, that he wants to relinquish his rights to the thief voluntarily, he may do so. At that point, the thief obtains rightful possession and the property is no longer stolen. Of course, this does not cancel the original theft. He is still liable for larceny or some other theft offense but now he may rightfully exercise discretionary control over the goods. Any person receiving goods from this thief or helping him conceal the property would not be liable unless he received or concealed before the possessor relinquished his possessory rights to the thief.

The same rule would apply if the true owner relinquished posses-sory rights to someone who had knowingly received stolen property. His liability for receiving would not be affected but he would become the rightful possessor of the property.

One further way property may lose its "stolen" character is by re-capture. Once the victim regains control of his property, anyone he gives it to could not be convicted of receiving or concealing stolen property. Upon recapture by the victim, the property loses its character as stolen property. Recapture also includes voluntary return by the thief.

For someone to be liable for receiving or concealing stolen prop-erty, the property must be "stolen" as defined by the particular jurisdic-tion when it is received. If the property is not stolen when received, either because it has lost its character as stolen property or because it was never stolen in the first place, the accused can not be convicted of the offense. This is true even if the accused thinks the property is stolen at the time and intends to receive stolen property. If the property is not, in fact, stolen, the crime has not been committed.

D. Knowledge

One of the most controversial elements of the crime of receiving or concealing stolen property is knowledge. There is no doubt that the in-dividual who actually knows property is stolen is guilty of receiving or concealing stolen property. However, would a person be guilty of this crime if he believes or suspects that the property is stolen but does not actually know it? This is perhaps the most argued point. In answering this question, reference must be made to the wording of the statutes of the various jurisdictions. If the statute is worded to require the existence of actual knowledge, the accused may not be convicted unless it is proven he had actual knowledge. No mental status short of positive and affirmative knowledge will satisfy the requirements of such a statute. If the statute specifically requires "knowledge" on the part of the accused, there is little room for interpretation. However, some statutes are worded in such a way that it is unclear whether positive knowledge is required or whether mere suspicion or belief will suffice. Usually, statutes which require that the property be received "knowing" it to be stolen are the ones which create confusion. In states which use the word *knowing* as an element of the crime, some have interpreted this to mean actual knowledge while others hold that a strong belief that the property is stolen will suffice to convict if, in fact, the property is stolen. Still others go so far as to say that if a person receives property under circumstances which made him reasonably suspicious that the property might be stolen, he may be found guilty of receiving stolen property. Again, the property must, in fact, be stolen. The suspicion may arise in many ways. For instance, the suspicion may arise from the nature of the property itself, the appearance of the seller, the time of day the proposition is made, the price, the location at which it is offered, and perhaps more. One might suspect he is buying stolen goods if he is offered a color television set at 3:00 A.M. in an alleyway, by a grubby looking wino, at the unheard of price of $25 with no state sales tax.

E. Intent

The intent required in the crime of receiving or concealing stolen property is the same as that required in larceny and the other theft offenses. The accused must intend to benefit personally by his act or must intend to permanently deprive the true owner of his property. Even though the person receiving stolen property knows it to be stolen, if he takes it intending to return it to the true owner or rightful possessor, he will not be guilty of the crime. An investigator should not assume merely because an accused has received stolen property with knowledge of its stolen character that he is automatically guilty. Intent must be proved.

Questions for Discussion

1. A member of a private security patrol was assigned to guard a store which has been partially burned in a blaze of suspicious origin. He had keys to the store and was supposed to check both

the inside and outside. During the night, the guard entered the store, took a couple of transistor radios, and put them in his car. The owner of the store discovered the loss shortly after the guard completed his tour of duty. The guard could be properly charged with what crime(s), if any, and why?

2. The defendant agreed to buy some apples from Smith for cash. Relying on the defendant's fraudulent promise that the cash would soon be paid, Smith let the defendant have the apples. Why would the defendant not properly be chargeable with larceny? What crime, if any, has the defendant committed?

3. Hotel X left a box of matches at the registration desk as a service to the patrons. A guest took the whole box of matches to his room. The hotel management had the house detective visit the guest in his room and inform him that the management did not regard the act in a kindly spirit and asked the guest to return the box of matches. The guest refused. An argument commenced, ending with many harsh words on the part of both parties. The manager directed the house detective to obtain a warrant for the arrest of the guest. Would a charge of larceny be proper here?

4. If a diamond ring is lost and a person finds it and there is no clue as to the owner, it is not larceny if it is kept, although at the time he found it, he intended to appropriate it to his own use. Why is this true?

5. Smith goes to Johnson's Bar and gives the bartender a $10 bill by mistake for a $1 bill. The bartender, believing it to be a $1 bill, rang it up. Smith soon thereafter discovers his error and the mistake in the change given to him. He asked the bartender to correct to mistake. The bartender refused and an argument ensued, resulting in Smith's being forcibly ejected from the bar. Smith summons a deputy sheriff and demands that the bartender be arrested for larceny. Would the charge be correct?

ROBBERY

11.0   Introductory Comments

One of the first crimes we hear about as children is robbery. The "cops and robbers" game involves shootouts, wild chases, and "you'll never take me alive" scenes played with great gusto. Of course, a bank is always held up by gun-brandishing desperados. How surprised first-time students of the law are when they find out that robbery can be committed by other than gun-wielding thugs and in places other than a bank. We will examine this common law crime and its statutory modifications element by element throughout this chapter.

11.1   Definition of Robbery

Robbery, a specific intent crime, is one of the hybrid or combination type common law crimes. As a combination type crime it involves all the aspects of assault as well as a larceny. Although personal property is taken, robbery is not classified as a crime against property but rather as a crime against the person. Any number of legislatures still put robbery in the midst of their crimes-against-property section. Whether this is done intentionally or not the authors do not know. When one illegally takes property with some value from another person or in his presence, by using force or by threatening to use force, the common law crime of robbery has been committed.

11.2 The Taking in Robbery

There must be a larcenous taking along with force or threat of force for there to be a robbery. Larceny, as was seen in Chapter 10, involves taking and carrying away the personal property of another intending to permanently deprive the owner of his property. If a man takes a gun and points it at his victim and says, "your money or your life," and nothing more happens, there is no robbery. This is assault and attempted robbery. Until the money has actually been taken and carried away, there can be no robbery. As in larceny, however, once the taker slightly removes property from the place it once occupied, he has done enough taking to commit robbery. If the gun-pointing accused removes a wallet from his victim's pocket but is caught before he can even take a step, he is guilty of robbery. It is not necessary that the robber actually take the property from his victim. There is sufficient taking if the victim delivers property to the robber under force or threat of force.

The property taken must belong to another and not to the accused. Although he may have committed aggravated or merely simple assault, a man has not committed robbery when he takes his own property from another by force or threat of force. This raises some interesting questions. Can a man who, in good faith, forcibly takes property he thinks is his own be convicted of robbery?

Suppose Fred loaned John his lawn mower two years ago. John claims he does not have the mower. Fred sees his neighbor Sam using a mower identical with his own and he decides to get his mower back. Fred walks up to Sam with a hoe and tells Sam that he will hit Sam with the hoe if Sam does not give the mower to him right away. Sam complies and lets Fred take the mower home. Sam then reports the incident to the police. Fred is arrested, charged with robbery and brought to trial. It is proved that the mower was, in fact, Sam's. Fred's defense is that he honestly thought the mower was his.

If the jury believes Fred's story, he should be acquitted of robbery. Mistaken identity is a commonplace thing that the law takes into account. Since robbery is a specific intent crime, the defense of mistake of fact may apply (6.6).

Another problem involves a repossessor of property or other zealous creditor-taker. Suppose John owes Fred $700, which John has failed to pay. Can Fred forcibly take $100 from John as part payment of the debt and escape liability for robbery? Most states say yes as long as Fred had a clear-cut right to the money. When does a man have a clear-cut right to money? Basically, when there is a valid written contract which fixes the obligations and rights of the parties. What if Fred and John are involved in an automobile accident through Fred's fault? Can John go over to Fred and forcibly take money from Fred in settlement of the claim? No. The amount of Fred's liability has not yet been settled by a court judgment, nor have the parties entered into an enforceable settlement agreement. Therefore John has no clear-cut right to the money.

These two situations undoubtedly raise some interesting questions in the mind of the reader. The first question which should arise is, "Do you mean to tell me a man can forcibly or by threat of force take property from another man and escape liability for the crime of robbery?" Yes. As illogical as this may sound, particularly to police officers, there are volumes of case law which support this view, with very few cases to the contrary. Basically, both situations involve what is known as the self-help doctrine. One is entitled to self-help when he has a claim or rightful entitlement to property. This was the second situation. The $100 clearly belonged to Fred. The first situation also involved self-help, when Fred mistakenly believed he had a claim of right to the lawn mower. The third example, the auto accident, involved self-help with no claim of right. However, this does not mean that no crime has been committed in the first two situations. The law will not permit one to use violence or threat of violence to regain possession of property by self-help. In each of the first two examples, even though there was no larcenous taking to satisfy the elements of robbery, there was definitely an assault for which the taker would be criminally liable.

As in the case of all theft-related offenses, when consent is given or a claim of right exists, there is robbery if the accused takes more than he is entitled to under a claim of right or more than he has permission to take. If Fred were to take $800 from John instead of the $700 he was entitled to, Fred would be liable for robbery.

Property must be taken from the person *or* in his presence. What constitutes taking from the presence of the victim? The property does not have to be physically held by the victim or be on his person. It merely has to be under his control. Control in this sense means the right or privilege to use the property as the victim sees fit. Although the property has to be under the control of the victim, it is not essential that the property be visible to the victim when the crime is committed. Remember that robbery is primarily a crime against persons. John is guilty of robbery if he secures the keys to Fred's car by force or threat of force and makes off with the car even though Fred couldn't see the car at the time. The most important aspect is not the location of the property but the reality of the force or threat of force, which we will discuss later in this chapter.

With this in mind, let us consider the following problem. John wants Fred's valuable paintings which hang in Fred's home. John points a gun at Fred, forces him into a closet, and locks it. John then removes the paintings and drives off. Is John guilty of robbery? Yes. The fact that Fred could no longer see John is immaterial since Fred was threatened by John. It isn't essential that the victim and robber be side by side throughout the transaction.

Since the victim must have only control or the means of controlling the property, it is not essential that the victim have possession of the property. It is essential that the victim have custody of the property but no more. (The legal distinctions between possession, and custody and control are fully discussed in Chapter 10.) It is possible for someone to be guilty of robbery even though he forcibly took stolen property from the original thief or from any other bare custodian of the property, such as a bus driver.

11.3 The Force or Threat of Force in Robbery

We mentioned in the beginning of this chapter that robbery is a crime against persons. For an act to be a crime against persons, it must involve some physical or social force or threat of physical or social force directed at the victim, his family, or his property. Robbery must, however, involve physical force or the threat of physical force, not social force. Social force or intimidation is found in such crimes as extortion, blackmail, and criminal libel, for example, a threat to expose someone as a homosexual. This is a threat against ones' social standing in the community rather than one's personal physical safety.

Taking of property without force is merely larceny. The force used to separate the victim from his property need not be great in robbery, however. Whether or not force was used is not a difficult question in most cases. Shooting a man to get his property; hitting him over the head to get it; or pushing the man down to get the property would all make the taker subject to prosecution for robbery. But is a "purse-snatcher" guilty of robbery? This depends on a factor known as resistance. Suppose a woman puts her purse next to her on her bus seat but does not keep her hand on it. If someone quickly grabs the purse and runs, is he guilty of robbery? No. Neither the object nor the woman resisted. Would the result be the same if she had been tightly clutching her bag? No, because the victim resisted. Resistance does not have to be a fight to the death. Even slight resistance indicates that some force, greater than needed normally to take the article by simple larceny, was used.

Is the average, run-of-the-mill pickpocket guilty of robbery? Unless more force than is normally necessary to remove the article is used, the pickpocket would not be guilty of robbery. Taking property from a person by stealth is larceny not robbery.

When must the force be used? If John takes Bill's wallet stealthily and then hits Bill over the head, is John guilty of robbery? No. Force must precede or accompany the taking. Force applied after the taking does not make the taker guilty of robbery. He is, however, guilty of the separate crimes of larceny and assault.

Suppose property is taken by stealth, without force. The victim sees the thief making his escape and he chases the thief, trying to recover his property. Force used by the thief in the struggle that follows does not make this a case of robbery. Larceny and assault may be charged. This illustrates the principle of concurrence of act and intent. (See Chapters 4 and 5.)

Without using actual physical force, someone may be guilty of robbery if he threatens force against his victim to secure the victim's property. To repeat, force must be threatened against the victim or his family's physical well-being, not against his social position. If Taker tells Fred that he will tell everyone Fred is a bigamist unless Fred gives Taker money, there is no robbery even if Fred gives money to Taker. This is a threat to social position and not to physical well-being. If Taker points a loaded gun at Fred and says, "your money or your life," Taker has threatened force so that if Fred parts with his money, there is a robbery.

Must the person threatened with physical harm be actually frightened to the point of panic? No. It is enough if the victim is reasonably apprehensive of harm—aware of the potential for injury. A person can be apprehensive about harm to himself, his family, or his property without actually being scared.

According to some authorities, the threat may be directed against the physical well-being of the victim's property. If John threatens to blow up Bill's business building unless Bill turns over all his money, the force or threat of force element is satisfied according to these authorities.

11.4 Modern Robbery—Statutory Modifications

Like most other common law crimes, robbery has been affected by most of our state legislatures. A few legislatures have put the common law crime in statutory form without any modification whatsoever. This is called codifying the common law.

Let us look at some of the changes made by a few states which illustrate the more common modifications found in all states. Illinois imposes a penalty of up to twenty years for common law robbery. A sentence longer than twenty years can be imposed for violent or armed robbery. Illinois' neighbor, Indiana, also adopts the common law, but if a wound is inflicted a life sentence may be imposed instead of the ten to twenty-five imposed for ordinary robbery.

Michigan classifies robberies by names. It recognizes armed robbery, unarmed robbery, and bank safe and vault robbery. New York, although recognizing somewhat similar offenses, divides robbery by degree. North Carolina, a common law state, recognizes these separate offenses with greater penalties: armed robbery, train robbery, safe cracking, and safe robbery.

Pennsylvania has ordinary general robbery, armed or violent robbery, robbery of bank vaults, and train robbery. A more severe penalty is imposed for robbery with an accomplice.

Although Wisconsin abolished the common law crimes, it adopted the common law definition of robbery and provided an additional penalty for armed robbery.

These have been the most common changes in the definition of robbery made by most state legislatures. Their primary purpose has been to increase the penalty for certain acts of robbery which seem more serious or pose more of a threat to society.

Questions for Discussion

1. Smith, Jones, and Walker approach Millie and falsely identify themselves as police officers. They claim that they have come to Millie's house under legal authority to repossess her furniture. They threaten to arrest her, handcuff her, and throw her in to jail if she does not let them take the furniture. Millie submits and lets them take the furniture. Has a robbery been committed?

2. Lester was traveling through the country in his automobile. The engine became hot and he stopped his car to allow it time to cool. While waiting in his car he fell asleep behind the wheel. Al and Sam saw that Lester was asleep and went over to the car. Al grabbed Lester and shook him and ordered Lester to get out of the car. Sam took the key from the switch. They told Lester that he was under arrest and that Al would take Lester before the judge unless Lester gave Al $100. Sam stood before Lester with clenched fists. Lester gave Al the $100. Can Al and Sam be charged with robbery?

3. Andy went to the Flea Bag Hotel and approached his good friend John, who was the desk clerk of that hotel, with a plan

for a fake robbery of the hotel safe. Andy was to come in late one night and point a gun at John, whereupon John would hand over the keys to the safe. On the appointed night Andy shows up, walks up to John, and points the gun saying, "This is a stickup—hand over the keys to the safe." At the same time, some ten feet away there stood a hotel guest whose watch was in the safe. John handed over the keys and Andy cleaned out the safe. Has a robbery been committed? Why or why not?

Chapter 12

BURGLARY AND RELATED OFFENSES

12.0 Burglary Defined
12.1 Statutory Modifications

12.0 Burglary Defined

The common law offense of burglary was defined as breaking and entering the dwelling house of another, in the nighttime, with intent to commit a felony therein. Each element of the offense is discussed in the following paragraphs.

A. Breaking

The element of breaking originally conveyed the idea that there had to be some type of forcible entry as the term, in its common usage, implies. Modern court decisions have somewhat extended this concept. Of course, if an accused breaks open a window or door of a dwelling house, this will satisfy the element, as it would if he merely had to turn a knob or twist a handle. There was some disagreement in the earlier cases as to whether pushing open a door that was already slightly ajar was sufficient to meet this requirement. Most later cases hold this is a sufficient breaking. The opening of a closed door or window will suffice regardless of whether it is locked. The modern test seems to be that if force is used to remove or put aside something material that constitutes a part of the dwelling house, which is relied on to prevent intrusion, there has been a breaking. Pushing open a door that is ajar or tearing a screen over a window or opening a screen door all would constitute breaking within the legal definition.

Breaking, as required in the crime of burglary, must be trespassory;

that is, it must be unlawful. If one breaks into a dwelling he has a lawful right to break into, he cannot be charged with burglary regardless of his intent at the time. If Fred breaks into the house where his estranged wife lives, but which he owns, in order to take a color television set his wife purchased in her own name, this is not burglary.

The breaking must involve some part of the dwelling or of a building within the curtilage (building attached to or adjacent to the dwelling house used in support of the dwelling house). Burglary may not be charged when the intruder opens only a fence gate or other structure solely to enter the property where the dwelling is situated.

The courts have not limited the element of breaking solely to breaking an outer portion of the dwelling. There are occasions when an accused may enter a dwelling house without breaking in, when a door is left completely open, for example. If, however, an inner door or window must be opened to reach another room or other part of the house, and the accused proceeds to open the inner door, his act will constitute a breaking within the meaning of the offense. This should not be confused with a statutory crime called entering without breaking discussed later in this chapter. Breaking an inner door is considered breaking within the meaning of common law burglary.

When breaking *out* of the dwelling house will satisfy this element depends on the wording of the statutes in the various jurisdictions. Under the common law definition of burglary, breaking out of a dwelling was not a breaking for it was not done with intent to commit a felony. Breaking out was done for the purpose of escaping. Under the interpretations of most modern statutes, breaking is also limited to breaking in. There are, however, a few cases on record where the statute does not specify or imply the necessity of breaking in, where it has been held that breaking out will suffice to charge a breaking.

The rules so far discussed have referred to an actual breaking where the accused acts with his own hand. Another means of breaking is recognized in most jurisdictions. This is called constructive breaking. When an accused manages to have the occupant of a dwelling open a door by using some trick or device and then forces his way into the dwelling, the law holds this to be a breaking within the meaning of this element. This does not mean that if the accused enters with the owner's consent, he has broken in. If the occupant of the dwelling consents to the entry, there is no breaking. If the defendant forces another to break into the house or to open a door which the other has a right to open in order to gain access to the interior of the dwelling, there is a breaking. It is a constructive breaking if the accused has a confederate employed inside the house and the confederate allows the accused to enter without the consent of the occupant.

B. Entering

For an act to constitute the crime of burglary, there must be an entry as well as a breaking. The entry need not involve entry of the entire person through the break that was made. The slightest entry is sufficient to satisfy this element. The entry of a finger, hand, foot, or head is enough. This does not mean that only the entry of a part of the human body will constitute an entry. As in the commission of other crimes, the method used may also be a nonhuman agency, such as an animal or stick, or another innocent human agent. If an instrument is used to gain entry, it must be an instrument which is capable of helping the accused accomplish his felonious intent. It is not sufficient if the instrument is merely one that helps him break into the dwelling. If, in order to break into Steve's house to commit larceny, John throws a brick through a glass window, he has broken but there is no entry into the house. The brick is not an entry within the definition of burglary. There is no way the brick can help John accomplish his intended purpose. It merely served as a tool to help him break in.

Both the breaking and the entering must occur in order to warrant a burglary charge, and the entry must be a consequence of the breaking. The breaking must be done for the purpose of breeching the security of the house and allowing the perpetrator to enter. If, for example, Sam breaks a window in a dwelling house and then enters through an open door, there is no burglary. It is not necessary, however, that the breaking immediately precede the entry. It is burglary if the breaking occurs on Tuesday and the entry occurs on Wednesday, if it can be shown that this was all part of a single plan with one felonious intent.

C. Dwelling House

Like the crime of arson, described in the next chapter, burglary is a crime against the habitation rather than a crime against the property itself. Therefore, the law is not concerned with the character of the property so much as it is concerned with the fact that it is occupied as a dwelling. A dwelling is defined in law as a place that is habitually used as a place to sleep. It can be seen that this is a rather broad concept and may include many structures that would not ordinarily be considered houses within the broad meaning of that term.

A structure is a dwelling house if it is occupied for the purpose of dwelling therein. An unfinished house which has never and is not presently being occupied as a place where someone habitually sleeps is not a dwelling even though it may be intended for that purpose at a later time.

Until someone moves into the house and uses it as a dwelling, it does not take on that characteristic. It is not necessary, however, that construction be completed before the house will acquire the characteristic as a dwelling.

A building or other structure may serve a dual capacity and still be a dwelling. If Sam owns a store and lives in the back of the store, the premises is treated as a dwelling for purpose of the burglary laws.

A structure that has once acquired the status of a dwelling may lose that status when it is abandoned by the occupants. A permanent abandonment is required. The occupants' temporary absence from the dwelling will not destroy the house's status as a dwelling. This is true even if the absence continues over a long period of time. If the occupant intends to maintain the house as a residence where he will dwell, it is a dwelling house.

A dwelling house must be one that is capable of being occupied by human beings. The question arises as to whether breaking and entering a chicken coop is burglary under the common law definition. The answer has to be an emphatic no. But this leads to a discussion of another common law rule regarding the definition of a dwelling house. It was recognized at common law that more than one structure may serve as the dwelling house. As a result, the common law recognized that any structure within the curtilage may be subject to burglary. The curtilage includes any structures within a common enclosure which serves as part and parcel of the dwelling. This would include outhouses and, in more modern terms, garages. It is not necessary that the other structure be attached to the dwelling house itself as long as it is near enough and used as part of the dwelling situation. A barn may, under certain circumstances, be considered within the curtilage of the dwelling for purposes of common law burglary.

D. Of Another

Occupation rather than ownership is the essence of the subject of burglary. It is not necessary that the owner dwell within the dwelling house. If the owner also occupies the dwelling house, he may not commit burglary against it. On the other hand, if the property is leased to someone else who occupies it, the owner may be liable for burglary if he breaks and enters the dwelling intending to commit a felony. If the lawful tenant—occupant of a dwelling—breaks and enters it for an unlawful purpose, the owner may not complain that burglary has been committed since the tenant is the occupant.

One area of much confusion to law enforcement officials seems to be the status of a hotel room, motel room, or other such living quarters as a dwelling within the meaning of the burglary laws. The rules governing these situations go back to the definition of a dwelling house. It was stated that a dwelling house is a place habitually used as a place to sleep. A transient who stays at a hotel for one night is probably not dwelling in that room since it is not habitually used by him for that purpose. In such a case the landlord would be the victim of the burglary if he resides on the premises, and only he would have the right to complain. If it is the landlord who breaks and enters the room of a transient, burglary would probably be an improper charge. On the other hand, if the guest is not transient, his hotel room is a dwelling if he intends it to be one, and a breaking and entering of the premises with the intent to commit a felony therein against him or his property would be a burglary.

E. In the Nighttime

At common law, the offense of burglary had to be committed at night. This meant that both the initial elements of the offense—the breaking and the entry—had to occur at night, but both elements did not have to be committed on the same night. If Fred broke into John's house on Monday night but did not enter, and returned during daylight on Tuesday to enter, the crime of burglary was not committed regardless of Fred's intent.

The definition of nighttime created problems for the courts. At early common law, nighttime was established as anytime between sunset and sunrise of the following day. Alterations of this rule produced the standard accepted by the later common law which was to the effect that nighttime was when there was not sufficient natural daylight to make out a man's features. The fact that there was moonlight or artificial light available, so that features and identity could be established, was not material to this determination. If there was not sufficient natural daylight for this purpose, it was nighttime.

Some modern jurisdictions have kept this common law rule but many states have changed the definition of nighttime. In some states, nighttime is defined as the period between one half hour after sunset until one half hour before sunrise. In other states, it is one hour after sunset to one hour before sunrise, and so forth. Still other states have resorted to the early common law rule and established the hours between sunset and sunrise as nighttime.

Several states no longer require that the offense be committed in the nighttime in order to charge burglary. Breaking and entering the dwelling house of another with the required intent carries the same penalty regardless of when it occurs. Another group of states has kept the element but has created a separate offense of breaking and entering the dwelling house of another in the daytime with intent to commit a felony therein. Usually, in these states, a daytime burglary carries a less severe penalty than a nighttime burglary. In some states that have eliminated nighttime as a requirement of burglary, a presumption arises if the act did, in fact, occur at night. It is presumed that the intruder entered with a criminal intent but that intent would be to commit only a misdemeanor. This statutory presumption could be used by the prosecution if it was unable to prove the accused intended to commit a felony.

In states that have kept nighttime as an element of the offense, a problem often arises. Burglaries often occur when there is no one present in the dwelling. In such a case, it is often difficult to pinpoint the time when the burglary occurred. Since the element of nighttime must be affirmatively proved by the prosecution in those states, factual situations arise which may very well bar prosecution for this crime. Suppose the Smith family leaves their house for a weekend visit. They depart on Friday afternoon and return early Sunday evening to find their house has been broken into and their furniture is gone. There are no witnesses, but Wilson is arrested for the crime after his fingerprints are found at the scene. The state is unable to establish when, during that weekend, the offense occurred. There is little chance the state could convict Wilson of burglary in the nighttime. There may be some other statutory offense for which he is liable, but it will not be nighttime burglary.

F. With the Intent to Commit a Felony Therein

In order to be chargeable with common law burglary, the intruder must break and enter intending to commit a felony. The intent is a specific intent (5.2), which must be affirmatively proven by the prosecution. In order to prove this element, the specific felony the accused intended to commit must be shown and it must be alleged in the indictment or information. If the prosecution cannot prove the intended felony, burglary is an improper charge. Any felony at common law would have satisfied this requirement. Today, any felony under the statutes of the state will satisfy this requirement. It is not necessary that the felony be larceny. This is a popular misconception due, in part, to the fact that larceny is the most common object of the burglary. If the felony is, in fact, committed after the breaking and entering, there is no merger. No other felony has elements in common with breaking and entering. Consequently, both the committed felony and the burglary are separately chargeable offenses.

The intent to commit a felony must be simultaneous with the elements of breaking and entering. Even if the breaking and entering occur on different dates, the intent to commit a felony must continue to exist along with both acts. This is so because the instant when the breaking and entering occur determines whether the crime of burglary is complete. If the requisite intent exists at that time, the offense is complete despite any further conduct on the part of the accused. If this seems to imply that it is not necessary for the target felony to be completed, that is exactly correct. The fact that the intruder does not commit a felony once he gains entry to the dwelling is immaterial to a charge of burglary. His intent when he breaks and enters completes the crime. If Fred breaks and enters a dwelling to commit rape or larceny but once inside is prevented from accomplishing his objective or changes his mind, he has still committed the crime of burglary. Of course, the fact that he did commit a felony would lend additional weight to the state's contention as to his intent, but it is not an essential ingredient of the prosecutor's case. In fact, it is not even necessary that the accused could have committed a felony upon entry. Suppose Jack enters a dwelling house to commit grand larceny but, upon entering, he finds there is nothing to steal. If he intended to commit the felony when he entered, this unknown fact will not serve as a defense.

Burglary is a specific intent crime. It is often difficult affirmatively to prove intent to commit a felony. As a result, legislatures in some states, in order to prevent this problem from being used as an escape mechanism, have created a presumption that if intent to commit a felony cannot be shown, it will be presumed that the accused intended to commit a misdemeanor when he broke and entered. This, of course, is not common law burglary but it is made a separate offense by these statutes. Like burglary, it is generally a felony.

A similar problem concerns intent to commit larceny. Larceny was not divided into degrees at common law. All larcenies were felonies. The statutory distinctions between grand larceny (a felony) and petit larceny (a misdemeanor) would cause havoc with the burglary laws if no provision were made to eliminate this problem: How to determine whether a burglar who broke in intending to commit larceny intended to commit grand or petit larceny. Whether burglary is a proper charge may depend on the answer to this question. Several alternative solutions to this dilemma are followed by the various states. In some states, the problem has been solved by adding a few words to the burglary statute so that it reads, ". . . with the intent to commit a felony or petit larceny." Other states have eliminated larceny as one of the crimes which can be the object of a burglary. Still others word their statutes so that they read, ". . . with the intent to commit a felony or larceny." Many jurisdictions have reached the same result through court interpretation of the burglary laws. These states have ruled that even if the accused only committed petit larceny, if there had been more property to take or if he could have carried more out, he would have taken more, so he intended to commit a felony.

12.1 Statutory Modifications

A number of statutes have been enacted in each jurisdiction to expand the common law burglary offense. A number of these statutes deal with conduct which would amount to burglary except for the fact that one or more of the elements of burglary are missing. As a result, there are statutes providing criminal penalties for: (1) entering without breaking, (2) breaking and entering the dwelling house of another in the daytime instead of nighttime, (3) breaking and entering a building or structure other than a dwelling house, and (4) breaking and entering with intent to commit a misdemeanor. In each of these statutes, all the elements but one are identical to the common law definition of burglary. For example, in (1), all elements of burglary are satisfied except that there is no breaking. In (2), it is not done in the nighttime. Number (3) does not require that the building be a dwelling house, and in (4), the intent to commit a felony need not be shown. The holes left by the common law definition of burglary are fairly well closed by the enactment of these and other statutes.

To avoid confusing any of these statutory crimes with common law burglary, they are usually classified as "breaking and entering" crimes rather than burglary. Actually, the difference is one of semantics. Most people use the terms *burglary* and *breaking and entering* synonymously to designate the entire group of offenses, including common law burglary. Technically, the distinction between these statutory offenses and the common law crime of burglary should be maintained. For example, the distinction might be important in a felony-murder case. Suppose a state statute provides that a homicide occurring during commission of, or attempt to commit, burglary is murder. Does this mean burglary as the crime was defined at common law, or does it include all the breaking and entering offenses? The answer to this question will depend on whether the courts of each state use the terms *burglary* and *breaking and entering* interchangeably. Some states distinguish the offenses by recognizing different degrees of burglary.

No matter how the courts interpret the statutes, one thing is certain. The interpretations given the elements of each of these crimes are identical to the meaning of the elements of burglary. In the crime of entering without breaking, entering means the same thing as it does in the crime of burglary, and so forth.

Some additional statutory crimes include: breaking and entering an automobile and breaking and entering (or burglary) with the help of explosives or similar devices. The use of explosives generally increases the penalty.

Questions for Discussion

1. Mr. and Mrs. Green have occupied their old homestead for the last fifty years. Last week, their property was condemned by the State Road Department and taken to be used as part of the right-of-way for the new interstate highway. The Greens were to have been out yesterday morning but, unknown to the state officials, they are still sleeping in the house. Last night, Paul Jones broke into the house after seeing the condemnation sign and thinking the house was vacated. Paul's purpose was to steal the plumbing and light fixtures before the house was torn down. Has Jones committed burglary?

2. Smith intends to rob Brown. Smith knows Brown goes for a nightly walk. One night while Brown is out of his house, Smith hides in the bushes near the front door of the house. When Brown returns and puts his key in the door to unlock it, Smith springs from the bushes with a gun in his hand. Without a word, Smith pushes Brown through the partially open door and enters behind him. Smith proceeds to rob Brown of his valuables, which are worth an enormous sum of money. Has Smith committed burglary?

Chapter 13

ARSON

13.0 Arson in General

Arson was considered a very serious common law offense. Today, arson and its modern counterparts are still considered heinous offenses. Arson consisted of willfully and maliciously burning the dwelling house of another. The common law definition of arson contained four essential elements to be proved. The next few sections will analyze each of these elements. Following the discussion of the common law, much of which still applies, we will turn our attention to modern arson laws and other related burning offenses.

13.1 Willful and Malicious

As in other common law crimes, *mens rea*, or intent, was an essential element of arson. Willful and malicious intent had to be proven to support a charge of arson. If someone acted voluntarily and without justifiable excuse, he acted with the necessary mental state. Although it was said to be a general intent crime, arson did not require that the actor have any ill will toward the owner or his property. If the fire was set negligently or accidentally, however, the necessary intent could not be proven. Deliberate conduct was a necessary ingredient.

A rule similar to the felony-murder rule is applied to arson. In fact, it could probably be called the felony-arson rule. If one set fire to or burned a house while committing another felony, he was liable to prosecution for arson. This was true even if the felon-arsonist did not intend to burn the house. His commission of the felony supplied the intent necessary to support an arson charge.

13.2 Burning

The requirement of a burning would seem to present no problem at all. However, it presented, as it still does, one of the more complex problems of arson. A roaring blaze which consumes the entire structure is not needed to complete the crime, although, of course, it would be sufficient to justify a charge of arson. Smoke damage was not enough. The distinctions between a scorch and a char were used to determine whether or not there had been any burning. Scorching only involves discoloration of the surface. There is not enough of a chemical change in scorching to constitute a burning. On the other hand, charring involves ignition of a flammable substance to the point where there is a noticeable chemical change. For the law of arson, it is only essential to show evidence of charring in order to prove burning. The question then is how much charring is essential? Not much. If any part of the house, no matter how little, is consumed by the fire, it is enough. But it must be a part of the house or its fixtures. Burning personal property, such as furniture or drapes inside the house, is not arson unless these items, in turn, ignite and char the house itself.

If a police officer catches someone in the act of setting a fire, the charge cannot be arson unless there is some charring. If there is none, the charge should be attempted arson.

13.3 Dwelling House

Almost as troublesome as burning is the term dwelling house, the second element to be proved. The definition of a dwelling house has two important aspects which must be understood. First, what is a dwelling house? Second, how far does it extend? Does the definition include other buildings and property beside the dwelling house itself?

The first question may come up when an unfinished house has never and is not presently occupied as someone's home. Is this a dwelling house? No. Even if the builder-owner intends to reside permanently on the property, the house has not yet become a dwelling house. On the other hand, an unfinished house which is occupied is a dwelling house even though it is incomplete. Would it be arson to burn a store building which also serves as the storekeeper's home? Yes. The fact that a building has a dual purpose does not mean it is not a dwelling house.

Once a building acquires the status of a dwelling, can it ever lose that status? Yes. Permanent abandonment of a house will cause it to lose its status, but the occupants' temporary absence from their house does not make it lose its dwelling-house status. Suppose John and his family decide to go on a world tour for a year but intend to return to their house once the tour is complete. Will intentional burning of the house make the defendant guilty of arson? The length of the occupants' absence is not the key. Their intent to return or not is the determining factor. This intent is determined as of the time of the burning. It follows, then, that the dwellers need not be present in the house at the time of the burning. The common law crime of arson was a crime against habitation or possession and not against property or, strictly speaking, the person.

The question arises as to whether certain modern structures and some not so modern structures in which people dwell can be classified under the common law as dwelling houses so that it would be arson to burn them. For example, would it be arson for someone to burn the mobile home or trailer of another? Since arson is a crime against habitation and not against property, the burning of such a structure would be arson as long as all other required elements are present. Wouldn't the same be true of a tent? The answer would no doubt be yes if the tent was someone else's dwelling.

Would this be true if the structure burnt is a camper being temporarily used as a dwelling? Permanency of residence is not a key factor. The test is whether the structure is being used as dwelling at the time it is burned.

The second set of problems involves the territorial aspect. The definition of a dwelling house for purposes of the law of arson is identical to the definition of a dwelling house under burglary law. As a general rule, any structure within the curtilage of the home falls within the definition. The other buildings do not have to be attached to the house but they have to be close enough so that it is possible for a fire to spread to the dwelling house if it is set in the other building or buildings.

13.4 Of Another

Since arson is a crime against possession or habitation it is not essential that the owner dwell in the house as long as *someone* dwells there. If the owner was the possessor, he could not, at common law, be guilty of arson against his own dwelling. If the owner rents his house as a dwelling to another person can he be guilty of arson against his own property? Obviously yes. Arson is a crime against habitation. The tenant would be the rightful inhabitant. Can a tenant be guilty of arson against the house he is renting? No, because he is the possessor and inhabitant. The inhabitant need not be rightfully on the premises. Even a building inhabited by a trespasser is protected by the arson laws.

13.5 Statutory Modifications of Arson

Of course, there were obvious shortcomings to such a limited burning crime. Other burnings, since they were only attacks against possession, were criminal trespasses. Unless the fire spread from a nondwelling to a dwelling which then burned, there could be no arson charged. Second, with the advent of fire insurance, there were those who burned for profit. Finally, why should a man escape liability for burning merely because he burned his own dwelling? Responding to these and other problems, many state legislatures have either modified their arson laws by adding to the type of buildings and property which can be burned, by making it a crime to burn with intent to defraud an insurer, or by doing both.

Even though a number of legislatures have in some way extended or modified arson laws, certain common problems and concepts remain constant. Arson statutes that retain the dwelling house element still involve the problems of what constitutes a dwelling house. The problem of what constitutes burning under modern statutes is still settled on the basis of the common law tests.

Some of the common statutory innovations in the law of arson and related offenses will take up the balance of this chapter.

A number of states now label the burning of other buildings besides dwelling houses as arson. Many of these same states label the burning of someone else's personal property as arson. In most of these statutes, the value of the other's personal property is specifically set out.

The common law did not specify the time when the burning had to take place. However, modern statutes in at least twenty states impose a more severe penalty if the burning takes place at night.

A few states, such as Florida, have made it arson to burn one's own property. This represents an extension of the common law.

Maine seems to be the only state which requires a specific intent to commit arson.

Some states have created a specific crime labeled attempted arson. At first, one would not think this was necessary because of the existence of general attempt statutes in all jurisdictions. However, the attempted arson statutes generally impose a more severe and definite penalty including a fine. In most of these states, attempted arson is a felony.

Many jurisdictions have enacted separate statutory punishments for burning schools, churches, or other public buildings. In these statutes, the punishment provided is more severe than for general arson.

13.6 Burning with the Intent to Defraud an Insurer

Perhaps the most innovative change in this field is the enactment of statutes making it a crime to burn or attempt to burn any building or personal property of a certain value in order to defraud an insurer. Unlike arson, this is not a crime against habitation.

Although the statutes are not exactly the same in each state, certain common principles have been developed.

Primarily, the crime is a specific intent crime since the fundamental basis of the offense is intent to defraud. The mere fact that there is an insurance policy on the property does not, of itself, bring the burning under these statutes. If a man burns his own property knowing it to be insured, for the purpose of collecting the insurance, there is no doubt that he has breached this statute. Suppose, however, a man believes he has insurance but, in fact, the policy is not in force. Does his burning of the property to gain the proceeds make him guilty of this crime? Yes. Under most, if not all, of these statutes, the validity of the insurance is not an element as long as the defendant thought he had insurance. Michigan requires, however, a valid and in-force policy for such a conviction.

Some states still recognize the common law classification of parties to crimes as principals in the first and second degree, and accessories before and after the fact. In those states, there can be only one principal in the first degree for this crime. He is the person or persons who will directly, financially benefit from the proceeds of the insurance policy.

Some of the states have made this crime a degree of arson, making it a lesser included offense. The others have maintained the arson statutes separate, so it is possible in some states to be charged with and convicted of both.

Questions for Discussion

1. John owns a home which he decides is no longer of any use. He sets up an elaborate electrical system hooked to an alarm clock. When the alarm clock rings, the electrical current will set off a

spark that will ignite a five-gallon can of gasoline. He sets the alarm and leaves the house. A severe electrical storm moves across the city. Lightning hits the house, ignites the gasoline, and the house burns down. Under the common law could John be charged with arson? Under modern law can he be charged with arson?

2. Fred goes to Ben, the insurance agent, and fills out an application blank for home insurance which covers losses arising from a fire. Fred leaves a check with Ben. Ben forgot to tell Fred that he has no authority to insure the house until the home office approves the policy. That evening Fred returns to his house after going to a movie. Fred sees a wastebasket on fire in the house and decides to let the house burn since he thinks it is insured. The application blank is in the mail and has not yet been received by the company. Could Fred be charged with any crime under common law? Under modern law?

Chapter 14

FORGERY AND RELATED OFFENSES

14.0 General Comments

At early common law, there was a group of misdemeanors called cheats. Among these offenses was the crime of forgery. Counterfeiting and uttering forged instruments were separately recognized common law crimes. The worthless check violations were not known at early common law primarily because checks are a comparatively recent innovation. In this chapter we will discuss each of these crimes, their common law background, if any, and the effect of modern decisional and statutory law.

14.1 Forgery

Forgery is defined as falsely making or materially altering a writing which, if genuine, would be of legal efficacy or the foundation of legal liability intending to defraud or prejudice the rights of another. To illustrate the difference between intent to defraud and intent to injure let us consider this example. John is the registrar of Big University. Fred, a graduate of that institution, wants to take postgraduate work at Small College and writes John asking John to send a transcript of his work to Small College. John does not like Fred and forges a transcript which appears to be Fred's work. The forged transcript shows that Fred barely graduated. Fred was an honor student while at Big University. In this situation, John intended to injure Fred. Using the same basic facts, suppose John was a friend of Fred. John forges a transcript which shows Fred to be a perfect 'A' student even though he was not. Here, John's intent is to defraud Small College. Admittedly there is but a shade of difference between the two, but there is a difference.

A. The Intent to Defraud or to Injure Another

Unless intent to defraud or to injure another is proven there is no crime. People in everyday life write on and change written instruments, many of which are the basis of legal liability. There are times, for instance, when people inadvertently leave blanks on checks. A man cannot be prosecuted for filling in these blanks unless he does so intending to get something he is not entitled to or unless he intends to injure another. Intent, as in other crimes, is proved by the surrounding circumstances. If the blank filled in is the date blank, under what circumstances could a fraudulent purpose be found? It would not be fraud to fill in the correct date. It would not be fraud, in most instances, to fill in any date the parties agreed upon. However, what if the true date of issue would make the check or document "stale" so that it would not have any legal efficacy or force any more? Would it be forgery to fill in a date that would make it "fresh" and negotiable? Unless the maker (the one who wrote the check) agrees, it would be forgery. The same rule would apply to changing a date to make it a good instrument.

Bill writes a check for $25 naming Sam as the payee. The check is written and dated February 1, 1961. Under the laws of the State of Blackacre, "No check shall be honored or paid if it is more than one year old. Such a check is null and void." On January 1, 1970, Sam changes the last number "one" in the year numerals to make it look like a "nine" so that the date line reads February 1, 1969. Sam did this in order to cash the check. This is a forged instrument because Sam changed the date to make a stale check fresh and negotiable. Filling in the amount on a document could also be criminal if it is done with intent to defraud or injure. Whether filling in the payee's name would be forgery depends on the name placed there. Everyday checks are given to people with the payee line blank so that the payee can affix his store's rubber stamp. When this is done with the consent of the maker, there is no forgery. If an employee of the store were to put his own name in the blank instead of the rubber stamp of the store, forgery is likely. The next step would be to inquire whether the intended payee, the store, gave the employee the right to insert his name instead.

Although the accused must intend to defraud or injure another, the law does not require that the fraud or injury intended be successfully concluded. Only the completed act and the necessary intent are required for there to be forgery. As a matter of fact, it is not essential to prove that the forger would have personally benefitted if his scheme had been successful. It is sufficient if someone else is injured or defrauded.

B. Instruments Subject to Forgery

Only a written instrument or document can be forged. But the definition of an instrument or document is as broad or as narrow as the courts and the legislature want it to be. The category of instruments commonly subject to forgery includes: bills rendered upon completion of services; checks, cancelled and uncancelled; bonds; deeds; bank notes; bank account books; bank deposit slips; promissory notes; mortgages and all other commercial paper. Besides these commonly known instruments, there are some that would not normally come to mind. For example, a fraudulent letter of recommendation or character reference would render the maker liable for forgery. A high school or college diploma can be subject to forgery. Tickets to a circus, theater, or other events can be forged.

It is not forgery to imitate a manufacturer's label because labels are not treated as legal documents. For example, Art, a local producer of jams and jellies, is having a hard time selling his products because they are not well known. He decides he would sell more if they bore the same label as that of the leading brand of jams and jellies, called Spanky's. Art buys a printing machine and engraving equipment and prepares labels which are the exact duplicate of the Spanky label. He puts the labels on his jars and offers them for sale. This is not forgery, but it would probably be counterfeiting, as we shall see later in this chapter. Would it be forgery for a man to paint a picture and then sign some great painter's name to it? Generally no. This would be a counterfeit, but paintings, sculpture, and so on are not subject to forgery because they are not documents.

C. Legal Force of the Instrument

The document or writing must have some apparent legal force or efficacy. It must have the potential to be legally binding, to create or destroy legal liability, or be liable to defraud someone. Unless a document has this potential, it can be forged to the hilt without making anyone liable for the crime of forgery.

How is it determined whether the forged writing or document has this potential? If the instrument is invalid on its face, there can be no charge of forgery for the instrument has no legal significance. For example, most states require at least two witnesses to a valid will. Would a charge of forgery be proper if an accused offers a forged will for probate that has no witnesses' signatures? No. No one can be defrauded by this instrument because it is void, without legal effect. The omission of some item without which the instrument would be absolutely void prevents the charge of forgery.

Do mistakes in spelling or mere form prevent the fraudulent maker from being charged with forgery? Formal errors such as these do not relieve the maker of his criminal liability. Sloppiness counts. In the case of signature forgeries, all that is required is that the name bear some resemblance to the actual name sought to be forged. This is not to say that there must be a resemblance in handwriting. This is not necessary. There is one limitation, however. A jury is permitted to consider whether the attempted forgery is so imperfect or inaccurate that it could not possibly deceive a man of ordinary prudence.

If some required stamp or seal is missing from the instrument, can the fraudulent maker be prosecuted for forgery? If the missing item does not make the instrument void, a charge of forgery is proper. However, if the instrument has no legal effect without this missing item, no charge of forgery can be upheld.

D. The Act Required in Forgery

There are any number of ways that an instrument may be forged. By ways we mean either the actual device used to make the forgery or the method employed.

As to devices, forgery can be accomplished by ink or ball-point pen or by pencil or other writing devices. It can also be accomplished by any printing method such as lithographing or mimeographing. One can also forge by engraving.

Alteration of the written instrument is one of the methods which may be employed. An alteration occurs when a material portion of the instrument has been crossed out or erased. One can alter an instrument by adding material terms to the instrument, by writing or typing additional terms on the instrument, or by improperly filling blanks intending to defraud.

Perhaps the most popular method of forgery known involves the use of signatures. It is forgery to sign another person's name to an apparently legally effective instrument, intending to defraud. If Sam somehow secures one of Fred Smith's checks and Sam then signs as Fred Smith with the necessary intent, there has been a forgery.

There are times when a person has the power to sign on behalf of someone else. Corporate officers are agents authorized to sign papers on behalf of their corporations. The corporation is considered a "person" or legal entity under the law. If an officer exceeds his authority in signing something, with intent to defraud, there has been a forgery. If he exceeds his authority without intent to defraud, he may be civilly liable but he has committed no forgery. Other examples of agents with power to sign on someone else's behalf are: partners, those holding powers of attorney, and public officials.

A forgery may be committed when a person signs with a fictitious name. Use of an assumed name or alias with intent to defraud on a document having potential legal efficacy is forgery.

The authorities are split over whether it is forgery to get someone to sign something through fraud. Some states, such as New York, say this is forgery while others say that it is not. If it is not forgery, what crime would it be? (See Chapter 10.)

Would it be forgery if John signs his own name to an instrument which he pretends is a receipt for payment when in fact it is not a receipt at all? Yes. This is a false instrument even though the signature is good. On the other hand, if a man fills in a financial statement with false facts and signs his real signature, would this be forgery? Yes, and the same would be true if he took someone else's financial statement and added his own name or took a financial statement prepared by an accountant and made changes in it to make it look better.

If two men have the same or similar names, under what circumstances could a forgery arise? Suppose Joe is a bank officer with authority to grant loans. Joe knows that a certain businessman in town is a good credit risk but he has never met this man. A man by that name comes into the bank and asks for a loan saying he is the businessman but, in fact, he is not. Joe grants the loan and the man signs his real name to a promissory note. Has there been a forgery? Yes, because he has intentionally created a false instrument by deceptive practices. Could he be charged also with false pretenses? (See Chapter 10.)

14.2   Uttering a Forged Instrument

At common law if anyone gave or attempted to give another person an instrument which he knew to be false, with the intent to defraud, he was guilty of the common law misdemeanor of uttering a forged instrument. The intent required for this crime was the same as required for forgery.

A. An Instrument Known to Be False

The person passing or attempting to pass the instrument must know of its ungenuine character to be charged with the crime. A man who knows the instrument is false can give it to someone innocent of that knowledge to pass it on. In this situation, the innocent man cannot be charged but the one who knows the character of the instrument, using the innocent man, may be charged with the crime of uttering.

B. The Utterer

As stated, uttering was a separate common law offense from forgery. It was not and is still not essential that the utterer be the forger. But a forger was almost always an utterer except when the one doing the forgery passed the forged instrument to another guilty party for use in a fraud scheme. But even in that situation, he could be charged as a principal and was truly an utterer also. So it is a problem of semantics. A number of states have the two offenses, one called forging and a separate offense called uttering a forged instrument. In essence, the utterer need not be the forger.

C. The Act of Uttering

As with other crimes, there must be an act. The act of uttering occurs when a person, who knows an instrument is false, attempts to pass the instrument representing it as the real thing. No one need take the forged instrument. Simply offering the instrument as genuine, by word or conduct, is all that is needed. The key word here is offer. The law considers mere offering of a forged instrument in an attempt to get property or other rights enough of a social harm, and, therefore, does not require that the final object be obtained or accomplished.

Although property does not have to be exchanged for the forged instrument, the person to be defrauded has to receive the forged instrument for there to be a sufficient act. Until there is actual receipt by the intended victim, no uttering has been committed. The word *receipt,* as used here, may appear to contradict the explanation of the term *offer* in the previous paragraph. What is meant is that upon being offered the instrument, the person to whom it is offered must have the option of accepting it or not. If he does have the option, he has received it within the meaning of the uttering laws. For example, suppose John negotiates a loan with a bank on the strength of a promissory note which he says he holds and he gets the loan without ever showing the note. John does, in fact, have a promissory note on his person and it is, in fact, forged. Has John committed the crime of uttering? No. No offer of the instrument has been made and the bank is not in receipt of the instrument. But would the result be the same if John had placed the note on the banker's desk in full view of the banker who read the note and, on the strength of what he saw, made the loan? Would there be an offer within the limits of this crime? Yes.

Bill gets a forged deed from Sam, and Bill knows it is forged. Bill gives the deed to his son Fred to take to the county courthouse to be recorded. Fred does not know the deed is forged. Before Fred can get to the courthouse, he is picked up by the police. Can Bill be charged with uttering a forged instrument? No. The forged document has not been offered to the person intended to be defrauded. Could Bill be charged with uttering if Fred gave the deed to the clerk for recording? Yes, at that point the necessary offer has been made.

14.3 Making and Uttering Worthless Checks

Unknown at common law, the crime of making and uttering worthless checks was created by statute. A person who made out a check on a non-existent account and attempted to pass it as valid could always be charged with forgery at common law. Similarly, a person who made out a check on the existing account of another person could be charged with forgery. But could a man who made out a check on an existing account of his own, knowing there was not enough in the account to cover the check, be charged with forgery? Most authorities said no. Yet there were thousands of merchants throughout the country who each day took such bad checks in good faith. What could be done to help deter this flood of bad checks? The answer was to make it a crime knowingly to draw a check on an account that had insufficient funds to cover the check. This is the gist of most worthless check statutes. However, some states have included within their worthless check statutes the problems raised by the first two examples in this section of the chapter: writing a check on a nonexistent account or on the existing account of another person.

All the statutes require insufficient funds but not all agree as to when the insufficiency must exist for the offense to be chargeable. Some say that if one issues a check and at that time there are insufficient funds, the issuer is liable to prosecution if he has the required intent. Other states say until the check is presented to the bank for payment and there are no funds to cover it, liability does not arise. Suppose John knowingly issues Bill a bad check. Bill, not knowing the check is bad, calls the bank and asks if there is enough money to cover it. The bank says no. Can John be charged? In those states that say mere issuance is enough, the answer is yes. He is chargeable at that point. But in those states which require actual dishonor of the check by the bank, the charge would be premature.

Whether property has to be obtained or not varies from state to state. Some states require that something of value be given in exchange for the check, while others merely require the uttering of a bad check. Suppose a state requires that the victim actually part with something of value in reliance upon the validity of the check. Would there be a violation of the statute in this instance? John borrows money from Fred and promises to pay it back in twelve months. John pays by check with good checks for nine months but, when the tenth payment is due, he knowingly draws a bad check which is dishonored by the bank. The courts of the states which require that the victim part with something of value conflict as to whether the statute has been breached. Some say that since the check was offered or given as payment for a debt already in existence, no crime can be charged. On the other hand some states would pay no attention to the fact that the debt was already in existence and hold John liable for the crime.

Does the issuance of a postdated check render one liable under the worthless check statutes? A postdated check is one that is issued on one day but is dated on the dateline for some later time. For example, John gives his grocer a check for $10 on March 1 but it is dated March 10. This is a postdated check. Here again, the states' decisions vary. Most postdated checks are worthless in the sense that most people give them in the hope of having money in the bank when the check is presented to the bank. Some states flatly prohibit the issuing of postdated checks and make it a crime to issue one when, at the time of issuance, there are not sufficient funds in the bank to cover the check. Other states say that even if given in good faith, if there is no money on deposit the crime has been committed. A few states would not follow this line of reasoning unless the issuer never intended to have the proper amount of funds in the bank on the date the check was to be presented.

The foregoing discussion of bad checks illustrates the confusion which exists in this area of the criminal law. Until such time as a uniform worthless check statute is passed by all legislatures, this confusion will continue. The student is urged to consult local statutes to determine the scope of his state's worthless check statutes.

In some states the amount stated on the worthless check will determine whether the person issuing the worthless check is guilty of a misdemeanor or felony. In a number of these jurisdictions, the prosecution may not bring a single felony charge for the issuance of a number of small checks in the misdemeanor category even though, when added together, they total an amount equal to or greater than the amount required for a felony charge. This is true even though a single intent can be shown. Many law enforcement officials are seeking to have this procedure altered. As it stands now, an individual can "paper" the town all day with worthless checks and escape the stigma of being convicted of a felony.

14.4 Counterfeiting

Since forgery covered only the making of false documents, or the falsification of existing documents, the common law crime of counterfeiting arose to cover instances where something other than a document was falsely made with intent to defraud. One who duplicated a famous statue and sold it as the original could not be guilty of forgery. But he would be guilty of counterfeiting under the common law. Under forgery, there does not have to be a genuine original in existence. The document forged is usually the only one of its kind, or in the case of alteration, it is the original. Although in counterfeiting, there does not have to be a valid or genuine original in existence, there usually is. The existence of a genuine Picasso or Rembrandt or ten-dollar bill is what gives the counterfeit an aura of respectability. In forgery, the victim usually relies on the representations of both the document and the issuer. This is usually true in counterfeiting also. However, in counterfeiting the victim often relies more on the genuineness of the object than he does on the reliability of the person offering it to him.

Practically every item of tangible personal property that cannot be subject to forgery can be subject to counterfeiting. There are areas where counterfeiting overlaps forgery even though forgery does not overlap counterfeiting. Bank stock which can be forged can also be counterfeited. At this point, the two crimes appear to be alike. With which crime should the men in the following example be charged—counterfeiting or forgery? John Jones is the president of the XYZ Bank, a corporation organized under the laws of State B. Bill Smith is the secretary of the bank. These men have the authority to sign stock certificates which the board of directors want issued. All the stock of the bank was properly issued and all the printed certificates were used. John Jones and Bill Smith decide they need more money. They have a printer print up new stock certificates which are identical to the ones that have been issued. They sign the certificates and sell them to people who do not know that they are bogus duplicates. In this situation, the men are chargeable with either counterfeiting or forgery and uttering, since the elements of each of these crimes have been fulfilled.

Counterfeiting is most commonly thought of in the context of bogus money. Only Congress has the power to print money and mint coins under our form of government. Likewise, only Congress has the power to punish those who would print or mint bogus money. But both Congress and the state legislatures have the power to create laws punishing the person who passes or utters counterfeit money.

The states can and do have statutes which punish those who would counterfeit items other than money. Such statutes usually cover the counterfeiting of state and municipal bonds, corporate securities, and so forth. Many states make it a crime to counterfeit labels which are attached to consumer goods. The reader should consult his local statute to see what items may be subject to counterfeiting.

Questions for Discussion

1. Brown enters the First National Bank of Perryville in the State of Roxy. He opens a checking account with a deposit of $500 in cash and receives a checkbook. Brown proceeds from the bank to Ace Television Sales and Service. He purchases a color television set and writes a check for the full amount of $457. He suggests that the salesman call the bank to cover the check. The salesman calls and is advised that there are sufficient funds to cover the check. Brown leaves with the television. Shortly thereafter he enters White's Television Sales Company and repeats the same procedure, purchasing another television for an identical amount. Again the salesman calls the bank and verifies that there are sufficient funds to cover the check. Brown repeats this four more times and each time the check is verified. Brown loads all the televisions into a trailer, stops by the bank and closes his account before any of the checks are presented, and leaves town. Of what crime or crimes is Brown guilty?

2. Smith is arrested for burglary. At the time of his arrest, he is carrying false identification and gives the arresting officers a fictitious name to match the identification. Smith decides that he wants to be bonded out. He calls I. Letugo, a local bail bondsman, who agrees to bond Smith out. Smith gives Letugo the same false name and signs the papers the same way. He later forfeits the bond. Of what crime or crimes is Smith guilty?

Chapter 15

FALSE IMPRISONMENT, KIDNAPPING, ABDUCTION, AND RELATED OFFENSES

15.0 Introductory Comments

The English early recognized the necessity of protecting each individual's freedom of mobility. To prevent interference with this fundamental right, three offenses were created. These were misdemeanors known as false imprisonment, abduction, and kidnapping Each of these crimes still exists today in the United States in one form or another. In this chapter, we will examine each of these crimes and their modern counterparts.

15.1 False Imprisonment

One of man's fundamental rights is freedom to move about, to move from one location to another. The framers of the Constitution, recognizing this right, included it in that document. Of course, as with all other rights, society must impose certain limits on its exercise to prevent chaos. When a man breaks a law, society demands that his freedom of locomotion be restricted through a process called arrest. The law imposes limits on how fast a man may travel and, to some extent, where he may travel.

But since this is a fundamental right, no person may detain, imprison, or arrest another without legal justification. The common law recognized this right early by establishing the crime of false imprisonment, defining it as the unlawful restraint by one person of the physical liberty of another. The key words that spell out the two essential elements of the crime are unlawful and restraint. When a peace officer unlawfully restrains another by arresting him, the offense is usually called false arrest.

A. Illegal Restraint

The victim must be detained against his will, but that is not all. Every man serving time in prison is probably there against his will. This detention is lawful because it is done within the framework of society's processes. Even an innocent man who is mistakenly convicted cannot successfully prosecute a charge of false imprisonment. The law recognizes that this situation is unjust but not unlawful. The victim must be restrained against his will *and* unlawfully.

Unlawful restraint is an act that deprives another of his freedom of locomotion without legal authority. An *invalid* arrest by a peace officer or private citizen without proper authority or in excess of authority is unlawful restraint, in other words, false imprisonment. In fact, any person who decides that someone else should not be allowed to move about and who restrains the other without lawful authority commits the crime of false imprisonment.

There is a corresponding civil action for false imprisonment which requires unlawful restraint. In a criminal action, however, the person accused of false imprisonment may base his defense on a good motive, good faith, or honest belief that he was doing the right thing in view of the facts as he saw them. Although these defenses are permitted, they do not affect the unlawful character of the restraint. These defenses are allowed because a man may intentionally restrain someone, thinking he is doing it lawfully when, in fact, he is doing it unlawfully. Society will not accept these excuses when only civil damages are involved; but mistake of fact is an acceptable defense when a man is faced with the possibility of imprisonment.

Police officers should be aware that they are subject to prosecution for false imprisonment if they unlawfully restrain someone. However, the law treats police officers more liberally because the police are compelled to make quick decisions in many instances and, as a result, they are more susceptible to error. This is not meant as a commentary on the quality of police training and police officers. It is simply a recognition of the complexities of the job.

A police officer may be guilty of unlawful restraint when he makes an arrest using too much force; arrests someone outside his jurisdiction; makes an arrest without a warrant, probable cause, or witnessing the violation; or makes an arrest at an unlawful time. This last point may sound ridiculous, but the common law used to provide that on Sundays and certain holidays there could be no arrests. This does not seem to be the state of the law today. In general, procedural defects in the manner in which an arrest is made may make the restraint involved unlawful. The guilt or innocence of the person arrested has no bearing on this question.

There are other requirements involved in making a lawful arrest under various state laws. Failure to comply with these regulations will invalidate an arrest and may subject the arresting officer to prosecution for false imprisonment. Examples include failure of a plainclothes officer to identify himself as a police officer when making an arrest. The likelihood of prosecution is slim, but it should be realized that most states, by statute, require that a police officer announce his identity and purpose to the person he seeks to arrest.

Restraint that begins as lawful can become unlawful. Suppose Officer Smith arrests a man for driving while intoxicated and decides that the man needs to sober up before he can go before the judge. Officer Smith jails the man on Friday night and goes home expecting to return Saturday morning. Smith forgets about the man for two months. In this situation, the once lawful restraint has become unlawful. Likewise, failure to release a prisoner once he has served his term constitutes unlawful restraint and false imprisonment.

The crime of false imprisonment is most often prosecuted against nonpolice officers. Johnson may decide that his neighbor's son, Art, should not take the usual shortcut through Johnson's yard. Johnson takes aim with his rifle and tells Art to stop where he is and not to move. This is unlawful restraint because Johnson exceeded the amount of force he could lawfully use to prevent trespass. An overzealous store clerk who locks a suspected shoplifter in the rest room may be guilty of false imprisonment if the suspect turns out to be innocent. Another type of unlawful detention might involve a group of escaped convicts who break into John Doe's house and tie up John Doe and his family. This last example is more likely to lead to a conviction than the case of the overzealous store clerk. The type of restraint that involves no good faith motive is what the law seeks to prohibit. In essence, restraint is unlawful if it is done without legal justification or beyond the point of legal justification. But understanding only the nature of unlawful restraint solves only half the problem. The next part of this section will deal with the restraint itself and the elements that constitute detention.

B. The Restraint Itself

As in the immortal words of the poet: "Stone walls do not a prison make nor iron bars a cage." It is not necessary that the victim actually be locked behind bars for a false imprisonment to be committed, although this type of restraint would qualify if it is done unlawfully. It is possible for a person to be confined in an open field. Suppose a very strong man threatens to mutilate a very weak man if the weak man moves. Even if this takes place in the middle of an open field, the weak man is imprisoned. Realistically he would be foolish to move. The limits on his freedom of motion are as real as any four walls could be. This example raises two problems. The first concerns the area in which confinement takes place. Two examples have already been given indicating that confinement with or without a structure such as bars or stone walls may satisfy the element of restraint. In the open area restraint cases, the courts have been presented with situations in which force or threat of force reasonably caused the victim to feel bound not to move. The area to which mobility was limited was immaterial because of the presence of the threat. As in other crimes that involve threats, the threat must be designed to cause reasonable apprehension of immediate bodily harm.

The second problem area involves the element of escape. In the last example, if the weak man had a reasonable way to escape, he could not say he was imprisoned. However, if the only means of escape would expose him to danger or injury, confinement is complete. For example, it would be unreasonable for the weak man to try to escape by jumping from a cliff. Similarly, if a person is confined to a room located on the tenth floor of a building and his only means of escape is through an open window, an escape attempt would be unreasonable. In both cases, imprisonment is complete because there has been more than a mere blockage of the victim's passageway.

Would imprisonment occur in the following example? John takes Mary to his apartment for dinner. At the end of the meal, Mary gets up to leave but John steps in front of her and says: "The door is locked and I won't unlock it until you make love with me." Mary refuses, screams, and is rescued by the police. Since John has no right to demand what he demanded, the fact that Mary could have secured her release by complying does not cancel out the imprisonment. This illustrates the rule that if the price of freedom of locomotion is compliance with an unlawful demand, imprisonment is complete. If, however, a person has a legal right to demand what has been demanded, the imprisonment, as long as it is not excessive, will not render the imprisoner liable.

In addition to the completeness and reality of the confinement, the law requires that the restraint be against the will of the victim. As in the case of forcible rape (9.1), people who are intoxicated, incompetent, or unconscious may not legally consent to false imprisonment. Lack of legally recognizable consent impliedly satisfies the requirement that restraint be against the will of the victim.

It should be obvious from the foregoing discussion that every case of false imprisonment involves assault. When actual force is used to restrain the victim physically, battery may also be involved. If there is insufficient evidence of false imprisonment, assault or battery may still be chargeable. Conversely, if the imprisonment can be proved, the assault or battery will merge into that crime. Law enforcement officials would do well to look for a possible false imprisonment charge in all cases that appear on the surface to be clear-cut assaults or batteries.

C. The Intent

At common law, this misdemeanor required only a general intent. In some states today, the crime is merely a restatement of the common law definition and it only requires general intent. However, a few states now require specific intent to confine a person secretly or to imprison a person against his will.

15.2 Abduction

Before we discuss kidnapping, let us take a look at the crime of abduction which was created by statute in England about A.D. 1500. Abduction was defined by Parliament as the carrying away of a female without the consent of either of the parents, or guardians, or the victim herself for the purpose of causing her to marry someone against her will, or for the purpose of prostitution against her will.

Although our states did not adopt the English statute word for word, most states did enact abduction statutes patterned on the English law. There are two primary differences between modern abduction statutes and kidnapping statutes. Abduction can only be committed against females. In kidnapping, the victim's sex makes no difference. In addition, in line with the English law, the purpose of abduction differs from kidnapping. A kidnapper may take a person for any reason from revenge to monetary gain. An abductor takes a female either for illicit sex or to compel her to marry someone. The person she is compelled to marry may either be the abductor or someone else. Because the intent in each crime is different, it is possible for one to be guilty of both kidnapping and abduction. If Fred forcibly takes Mary from her home for the dual purpose of exacting sexual intercourse and ransom, he could be charged with both crimes. If, however, Fred merely wants sexual intercourse, he is chargeable under modern law with either crime but not with both. In the latter instance there is only one intent which would satisfy either crime but which makes the abduction a lesser offense included in the kidnap.

The element of carrying the female away by force also distinguishes abduction from the crime of seduction (9.3). In seduction, the victim is usually lured away from her house by a promise to marry or the like. Force is not an element of seduction. The legal term often used to mean lured away is *inveigled.*

Aside from these differences, the crimes of abduction and kidnapping are very similar. We will discuss the detention or taking, the unlawfulness of the taking, consent or lack of consent, whether force is essential, and other factors under the crime of kidnapping in the next section. What we have to say there will apply equally to the crime of abduction.

15.3   Kidnapping

A.   At Common Law

At common law, the misdemeanor of kidnapping was committed when a person was forcibly taken and sent from his or her country into another country. Since this was considered a more serious form of false imprisonment, the elements of the crime of false imprisonment had to be met. Although a number of states have combined the crimes of false imprisonment and kidnapping, the requirement that the victim be taken into another country has been dropped. Some form of carrying the victim away still remains, however, and this element distinguishes kidnapping from false imprisonment.

B.   Kidnapping Today—Defined

By modern statutes, kidnapping is the unlawful taking of a person against his or her will. Many states have separate statutes to prohibit the unlawful taking of a person against his or her will for ransom, providing a more severe penalty. The statutes are not in complete harmony as to whether or not kidnapping is a felony. Some say that simple kidnapping is a felony and that more serious forms of kidnapping, such as kidnapping for ransom, carry greater penalties. For the more serious kidnappings, a number of states provide the death penalty or life imprisonment. A few states consider simple kidnapping merely a misdemeanor and make the more serious forms of kidnapping felonies.

As already noted, some states combine kidnapping and false imprisonment in the same statute and make abduction a separate crime. On the other hand, there are a few states which combine abduction and kidnapping in the same statute and keep their false imprisonment laws separate. As can be seen, no two statutes may be exactly alike. For this reason, the reader is urged to consult his local statutes for the variations in effect in his state.

Even though the statutes are not exact duplicates of one another, they do have certain key elements in common which are discussed in the following paragraphs.

C. Unlawful Taking and Carrying Away or Unlawful Taking and Detention

First of all, there must be an unlawful taking of a person. This means that the kidnapper must do so without legal right or authority. Suppose an officer has a legal arrest warrant for John Doe. The officer sees John Doe and arrests him, not intending to take him to jail but intending to run him out of the state instead. The officer drives Doe to the state line. In this situation, the officer exceeded his legal authority and could be charged with kidnapping.

Mary and Richard Roe are married and have a child, Bill. Mary gets a divorce and is awarded custody of the child by the court. Richard is given visitation rights. On one visit Richard takes Bill and leaves the state in order to keep Bill away from his mother. Would this be an unlawful taking? In most states it would be. However, a few state courts have said it is not because Richard, as a parent, has a legal right to enjoy his child. In some of the states which held that this is not an illegal taking, the legislatures have responded by making it a separate crime to take a child away from the custody of a parent or guardian when that custody has been given to the parent or guardian by court order.

Most kidnapping charges are brought against people who take, carry away, and hide their victim for some monetary gain or for some other selfish motive without any real or pretended right to the victim. Not many years ago, we saw a case in which the daughter of a wealthy man was taken and buried alive. The kidnappers were not relatives and had no legal right to take the girl. (She survived.) They merely wanted money and, perhaps, publicity. Probably the most famous kidnapping involved ace-flyer Charles Lindbergh, whose son was kidnapped and later found dead.

D. Carrying Away the Victim

The main difference between false imprisonment in its pure sense and kidnapping is the fact that in kidnapping the victim is removed from one place to another. This is not a factor in false imprisonment. Most states require for kidnapping that the victim be taken from the place he was found and transported elsewhere. The distance traveled is not significant in most states. Taking a person from a sidewalk and putting him in a car would be sufficient to justify a charge of kidnapping. One or two states do require that the victim be taken with intent to transport him out of the county or state in which he is found. But even in these states, there is no requirement that the victim actually be taken out of the county or state as long as the intent can be found to have existed at the time of the taking.

E. Taking without Consent

If the victim consents to the taking there can be no charge of kidnapping. Of course, the victim must be able to consent. Children below certain ages—set either by statutes or court decisions—cannot give consent. Insane persons are deemed incapable of giving consent.

Consent obtained by fraud is no good either (6.9). In such a case, we say that the fraud vitiates the consent and that the person taking the victim is chargeable for the crime of kidnapping.

Assuming that minor children and insane persons are incapable of giving consent, can one who has legal custody of such a person consent to the incompetent's taking, thus relieving the accused of criminal liability? Yes, it is possible that no kidnapping charge could be brought. For this reason, some state legislatures have eliminated lack of consent as an essential element of kidnapping.

Where two parents are still married and living under the same roof, would the consent of only one parent relieve the kidnapper of criminal liability? We could find no cases dealing with such a situation. However, the police officer, we feel, would be on safe grounds in assuming that the consent is not binding on the other parent. Consent in such a case would be a matter of defense (6.9), and would not affect the officer's determination of probable cause to arrest.

Consent is not normally given by the victim. He is usually taken by force. When the victim is taken by force, the question of consent usually does not arise because lack of consent is implied from the circumstances of the taking. How much force is necessary to justify this implication? Can the threat of force satisfy the element of taking without consent?

As to the first question, any force used will be sufficient to justify arresting the kidnapper. This is so because most statutes do not require that force be used. The answer to the question of whether the threat of force will suffice is yes. Threats of force, or even threats to a person's reputation in a given case, may be enough to overcome the will of the victim so that it may be said that he went unwillingly. This is a question for the jury.

Can a person knowingly consent to be "kidnapped"? Yes. But his consent will eliminate any possibility of kidnapping being charged. If one consents to being kidnapped and later changes his mind, however, a kidnapping charge may be proper if, when he changes his mind and tells the "kidnappers" he has done so, they decide to continue the transportation and detention against his will. On the other hand, if the victim does not change his mind until after he has been carried off, there is no kidnapping. For example, if Sam consents to be kidnapped and taken to a house in another town and changes his mind after arriving at the house and does not communicate this change of mind to his kidnappers until they are in the house, there is no kidnapping. If the kidnappers refuse to let him leave the house, however, a charge of false imprisonment is proper. This would be so because the transportation element was not contemporaneous with the other elements of kidnapping (4.5).

If, however, Sam consents to go on a trip and, during the trip, his companions decided to detain him without his consent, the consent given by Sam applies only to the original purpose of the trip. His companions' later decision will be grounds for a charge of kidnapping. If the decision to detain Sam is made after the trip is over, a charge of false imprisonment would be proper for the reason discussed in the preceding paragraph. If the decision was actually made before the trip but not communicated to Sam until after the trip was over, kidnapping may be the proper charge. The investigating officer should look for proof of fraud used to obtain Sam's consent.

Finally, and obviously, a person cannot give consent unless he is aware of what is going on. Taking and carrying away an unconscious person or someone who is asleep would be sufficient to satisfy this element of the crime.

F. The Mental Element

Although a few states require specific intent for the crime of kidnapping, most states require only general intent for simple kidnapping. The kidnapping-for-ransom statutes, for the most part, do require a specific intent: that the victim be taken with the intent to gain ransom money.

G. The Federal Kidnapping Statute

The federal statute is found at 18 USC § 1201, and it reads as follows:

"§ 1201 Transportation

(a) Whoever knowingly transports in interstate or foreign commerce, any person who has been unlawfully seized, confined, inveigled, decoyed, kidnaped, abducted, or carried away and held for ransom or reward or otherwise, except in the case of a minor, by a parent thereof, shall be punished (1) by death if the kidnaped person has not been liberated unharmed, and if the verdict of the jury shall so recommend, or (2) by imprisonment for any term of years or for life, if the death penalty is not imposed. . . ." (Sections (b) and (c) omitted.)

The federal statute is designed to make kidnapping across state lines illegal. The statute does not require that the kidnapped person be harmed in any way. However, the issue of harm and the amount of the injury may affect the punishment which can be meted out to the offender.

It is not necessary that the government prove that the defendant meant or intended to go across state lines. All the government has to show is that the defendant did, in fact, go across state lines with the victim. In fact, part (b) of the statute raises such a presumption if the kidnapped victim is not returned within twenty-four hours after the taking.

The statute also makes conspiracy to kidnap for ransom a separate crime.

Statute 18 USC § 1202 makes it a separate crime knowingly to receive, possess, or dispose of any money or property that has been delivered as ransom for a kidnap victim.

15.4 Abuse of Process

Crimes are wrongs against society and torts are wrongs against individuals, civil wrongs. Abuse of process is generally a civil wrong. We mention this civil wrong to inform the reader that participation, knowingly, in the tort of abuse of process may lead to liability for one of the three major crimes discussed in this chapter. Prosecutions are rare but possible.

Abuse of process is defined as unwarranted misuse of process with a hidden and perverted motive which does damage to the person against whom the process was used. This involves, among others, the perverted misuse of criminal process items such as arrest warrants and search and seizure warrants. If a police officer illegally uses an arrest warrant, if he completely steps out of the line of duty and uses that warrant for a purpose not intended, he will be liable civilly, and if the elements of one of the three crimes discussed in this chapter are met, he will be criminally liable as well. For instance, if a police officer uses an arrest warrant to collect a personal debt or to secure sexual privileges, he may have also kidnapped, abducted, or falsely imprisoned his victim. He may also be liable for other crimes.

15.5   Malicious Prosecution

Another civil wrong which may cause a police officer or other person to be liable for one of the three major crimes discussed in this chapter is the tort of malicious prosecution. In some states it is a separate and additional crime created by statute.

As a tort, it is defined as the beginning of a legal action, criminal or civil, for the purpose of harassing or injuring a party. For example, suppose John wants to run his competitor, Sam, out of business and he thinks he can accomplish this by ruining Sam's reputation. John decides to swear out a criminal complaint and cause a bogus criminal action to be started against Sam. John has begun a legal action for the purpose of injuring Sam, thus satisfying the necessary elements. He would be civilly liable in all states and criminally liable for malicious prosecution in those states making such conduct a crime. If the officer gets involved and knowingly helps John by maliciously arresting Sam, it is possible that the officer is guilty of false imprisonment, and he may be prosecuted for that crime. There is even the possibility of a kidnapping charge.

As stated, some states have made it a separate crime to begin a criminal case without probable cause and in bad faith, intending to harass or injure the other party. This crime may be committed by police officers as well as private citizens.

Questions for Discussion

1. Angus entered his boss's house one night intending to kidnap the boss's three-year-old daughter for ransom. He crept up the stairs and stole into the child's room where he picked up the sleeping girl. As he turned to leave the room, he dropped the child and woke everyone in the house. The police were summoned and Angus was arrested. Of what crimes, if any, is Angus guilty?

2. Bill owns a house on Ninth Street. As Bill arrives at his home, he learns that three escaped convicts are in the house and will not let Bill in. Bill goes to the police station and tells the officer in charge that he wants to swear out a complaint charging the three with false imprisonment because he is being restrained from going into his house. Is Bill correct in his assessment of the case? Why or why not?

Chapter 16

CRIMES INVOLVING THE MANUFACTURE, SALE, AND USE OF NARCOTIC DRUGS AND ALCOHOLIC BEVERAGES

16.0   Introductory Comments: Narcotics Legislation

Perhaps one of the greatest problems our complex and growing society has faced and continues to face is drug use and abuse. Although the problem receives disproportionate attention through mass media today, it also caused great concern in the early years of the twentieth century. Our society had two choices open to it—either permit the traffic in drugs to go on uncontrolled and hope that the incidence of addiction and its corollary problems would be stable and few, or place legislative controls on drug traffic and, by direct government action, induce the stability that was felt to be needed.

The United States chose the latter course of action. Both federal and state governments enacted laws to control the traffic in drugs. Prior to 1971, federal and state laws were not in complete harmony. This created some problems when federal and state agents wished to mount an effective campaign.

The primary state law enacted in some 49 states was the Uniform Narcotic Drug Act of 1932, amended in 1942 and 1958. Additionally, states have other "home-grown" laws. The primary federal statutes were not part of an overall control scheme but were found piecemeal in taxing laws and the Pure Food and Drug Act.

Congress enacted the Comprehensive Drug Abuse Prevention and Control Act of 1970, popularly called the Controlled Substances Act. This created a need for a new approach by the states. The Commission on Uniform Laws drafted the Uniform Controlled Substances Act in 1972. In the prefatory note to this Act (Handbook of the National Conference of Commissioners on Uniform State Laws and Proceedings of the 79th Annual Conference 223–224 [1970]), the Commissioners summed up the needs as follows:

This Uniform Act was drafted to achieve uniformity between the laws of the several states and those of the federal government. It has been designed to complement the new federal narcotic and dangerous drug legislation and provide an interlocking trellis of federal and state law to enable government at all levels to control more effectively the drug abuse problem.

The exploding drug abuse problem in the past ten years has reached epidemic proportions. No longer is the problem confined to a few major cities or to a particular economic group. Today it encompasses almost every nationality, race, and economic level. It has moved from the major urban areas into the suburban and even rural communities, and has manifested itself in every state in the Union.

Much of this major increase in drug use and abuse is attributable to the increased mobility of our citizens and their affluence. As modern American society becomes increasingly mobile, drugs clandestinely manufactured or illegally diverted from legitimate channels in one part of a state are easily transported for sale to another part of that state or even to another state. Nowhere is this mobility manifested with greater impact than in the legitimate pharmaceutical industry. The lines of distribution of the products of this major national industry cross in and out of a state innumerable times during the manufacturing or distribution processes. To assure the continued free movement of controlled substances between states, while at the same time securing such states against drug diversion from legitimate sources, it becomes critical to approach not only the control of illicit and legitimate traffic in these substances at the national and international levels, but also to approach this problem at the state and local level on a uniform basis.

A main objective of the Uniform Act is to create a coordinated and codified system of drug control, similar to that utilized at the federal level, which classifies all narcotics, marihuana, and dangerous drugs subject to control into five schedules, with each schedule having its own criteria for drug placement. This classification system will enable the agency charged with implementing it to add, delete, or reschedule substances based upon new scientific findings and the abuse potential of the substance.

Another objective of this Act is to establish a closed regulatory system for the legitimate handlers of controlled drugs in order better to prevent illicit drug diversion. This system will require that these individuals register with a designated state agency, maintain records, and make biennial inventories of all controlled drug stocks.

The Act sets out the prohibited activities in detail, but does not prescribe specific fines or sentences, this being left to the discretion of the individual states. It further provides innovative law enforcement tools to improve investigative efforts and provides for interim education and training programs relating to the drug abuse problem.

The Uniform Act updates and improves existing state laws and insures legislative and administrative flexibility to enable the states to cope with both present and future drug problems. It is recognized that law enforcement may not be the ultimate solution to the drug abuse problem. It is hoped that present research efforts will be continued and vigorously expanded, particularly as they relate to the development of rehabilitation, treatment, and educational programs for addicts, drug dependent persons, and potential drug abusers.

It should be noted that as of this writing 35 states have adopted the Controlled Substance Act with only minor modifications.

The balance of the chapter will be a detailed breakdown of the Act's most important features.

16.1   An Analysis of the Uniform Act

The Act provides five lists, known as schedules, which determine the scientific names of the controlled substances. The first schedule includes all opiates which have a high potential for abuse and no acceptable medical use or are unsafe even under medical supervision. The second list contains those substances which have a high potential for abuse but are medically acceptable under severe restrictions. This schedule, however, includes those items which may lead to severe psychic or physical dependence. The third list contains those items which have a lesser abuse potential but may lead to some physical or psychological dependence. The fourth list demonstrates those substances which may lead to a limited physical or psychological dependence. The fifth list presents those items which create an even lower possibility of dependence.

Each of these schedules and each item in each schedule is established by meeting an eight-point test. These eight points are:

1. the actual or relative potential for abuse;
2. the scientific evidence of its pharmacological effect, if known;
3. the state of current scientific knowledge regarding the substance;
4. the history and current pattern of abuse;
5. the scope, duration, and significance of abuse;
6. the risk to the public health;
7. the potential of the substance to produce psychic or physiological dependence liability; and
8. whether the substance is an immediate precursor of a substance already controlled under this article.

The Act clarifies some definitional areas that caused problems under the prior narcotics laws. For example, manufacturing includes all production, preparation, propagation (growing), compounding, converting, or processing of a controlled substance. The Act also defines production as the manufacturing, planting, cultivating, growing, or harvesting of a controlled substance.

Like the previous acts, it determines who may lawfully possess or otherwise deal in controlled substances. And like previous acts, those who wish to deal in controlled substances must meet certain rigid criteria regarding training and past conduct. A person convicted of certain crimes can be prohibited from dealing in such drugs. This would include those owners of corporations as well as those who actually produce the substances.

Any person who violates the provisions of the Act can then be prosecuted. The Act makes it unlawful for any person to knowingly or intentionally possess a controlled substance unless he received it through proper channels. The Act also penalizes those registered drug manufacturers who refuse to furnish records or refuse to allow an inspection of their premises. It is also a crime knowingly to keep or maintain any type of building, vehicle, boat, or aircraft which is resorted to by persons using controlled substances or for the purpose of selling controlled substances.

This prevents the opium dens and would appear to cause those who open their houses to drug users from claiming innocent activity.

One section of the Act permits a judge to place a first offender on probation instead of sending him to prison. However, this applies only to cases of simple possession. Even though the Act gives this bit of forgiveness, it provides that a person convicted of second and subsequent offenses may be imprisoned for terms and fines twice those provided in the Act.

The Act also provides for the exchange of information between state, local, and federal law enforcement agencies. The intent is to insure that all agencies work harmoniously and to prevent duplication of effort. This law appears to declare war on illegal drug traffic.

16.2   Acquisition, Possession, and Use of Narcotic Drugs

There are several methods by which a person may obtain drugs. He may genuinely need drugs and honestly acquire them upon a written order from a physician to an apothecary or receive them honestly and in good faith directly from the doctor. Second, he may get them from a legitimate source by lying to a doctor or apothecary. Third, he may secure them through so-called underground or illegitimate sources. Finally, he can steal them. The first method involves no crime on the buyer's part. The second and third methods will in some way cause him to be subject to penalty for violation of the Act. The last method will subject him to penalties under the general criminal laws of the state.

The Act makes it a crime to obtain or attempt to obtain narcotics by fraud, deceit, misrepresentation, or subterfuge. Drug addicts are no less resourceful when it comes to getting a "fix" than alcoholics are at getting something to drink. Drug addicts have been known to see several doctors in the same building in a two- or three-hour period, getting a prescription from each. Each doctor was unaware of this fact. The addict would then take his wad of prescriptions to each of several pharmacies which were also unaware of the plot. Addicts have been known to steal prescription pads which they then use by writing out their own prescriptions and signing the doctor's name. They have even carefully removed directions from prescriptions that directed that the prescription should not be refilled. The methods that can be employed are limited only by man's imagination.

When a user of drugs purchases the drugs on the black market, he is not criminally liable for the purchase in most states, but upon receipt of the drugs, he is liable to prosecution for the crime of possessing or having narcotic drugs under his control. The most difficult problems raised by the Act involve what constitutes possession. Most states have determined that possession means that the narcotic drug is under the actual control, care, or management of the person charged and that the defendant must have more than a passing control. The perplexing problem is this: Suppose an officer discovers a group of pot or marihuana smokers sitting in a circle passing the "stick" from one person to another. Who has control? Does the person who has the "stick" at the time of the discovery have the possession or control necessary for the charge? Or should the officer charge all who are there for possession or control? Or is the one who brought the "joint" to the group the only one that can be charged? Or did his act of sharing destroy his possession?

Some states have solved the problem by finding that narcotic drugs may be jointly possessed by two or more persons. Therefore, all the participants in the "pot" party would be subject to arrest. The jury would be permitted to imply from these circumstances, if there is no proof to the contrary, that each had discretionary control over the marihuana. It is important to note that this rule is applied in only a few states.

Some states have rejected the joint possession concept and put the entire burden of proving which person or persons actually had possession or control on the state. In several recent cases dealing with the problem, the participants have been said by the courts to have "fleeting" control, which is not prohibited by the Act. It does not appear, however, that the state in these cases made any attempt to prove actual possession of any individual or individuals involved, but merely rested their case on the facts discovered at the time of arrest.

Most states agree that the narcotic drugs do not have to be in the hands of, or on the person of, the accused as long as the narcotics are found in a place or thing the defendant has control over, such as his home or automobile. Similarly, as long as the defendant has the right to control the use, distribution, and disposal of the drug, he can be charged with possession. For instance, if the accused hides drugs in the middle of a city park, the fact that the drugs are not found on him, or in or on something he owns, will not prevent his being charged with possession or control of narcotic drugs. The law recognizes constructive possession. A jury is permitted to infer that a defendant had control of the narcotic drug when the narcotics are found on his premises.

The defendant must know the drugs in his possession are illegally possessed. The state must prove he knew or should have known the nature of the substance he possessed. This may be proved by showing all the surrounding circumstances. Unless the jury is convinced that there was no way he could have known what was in his house, car, or on his person, he can be convicted on such circumstantial evidence.

Only *external* possession is chargeable. There is no penalty for internal possession. Let us illustrate the concept of internal possession. Suppose John has possession of a narcotic. He is sitting in his home one evening and hears a police officer from outside his house say, "This is the police. Open up. We have a warrant for your arrest." John takes all his narcotics and swallows them so the police won't find them. By ingesting the narcotics, he has changed his possession from external to internal. In a majority of the states, he could not be charged with possession or control of narcotics. The only possible crime chargeable may be habitual use unless the state has an internal possession statute.

Can a state constitutionally punish a user of narcotic drugs? The answer to this question is a qualified yes. As we saw early in this book (4.3), no state can make a mere state of being or status criminal without serious constitutional problems. We pointed out that in the case of *Robinson* v. *California,* 370 US 660 (1962), the Supreme Court held the California statute which made drug addiction a crime invalid. But the same Court made it clear that a state could constitutionally punish a habitual user of drugs for being under the influence of drugs. Why the difference? In the latter cases the Court was able to find a sufficient act with clearly defined terms. In the former case the Court was presented with a statute which was so vague that it could not determine whether or not the addict got to be an addict of his own free will. The Court recognized that not all addicts voluntarily reach that condition. The more specific the statute, the more likely it is to be held constitutional.

16.3 Introductory Comments: Crimes Involving the Use, Sale, and Manufacture of Alcoholic Beverages

Perhaps some of the best stories comedians tell are about alcohol and its effects. There is an old, old story often told that goes like this: "Our town is so small that we don't even have a town drunk and so poor we couldn't afford one." Most boys, whether they are from the city or not, learn to sing the old folk song "Mountain Dew." If the effects of alcohol were not so serious, all this would be very romantic and funny. Statistics which stagger the imagination show that in a large percentage of fatal traffic accidents, alcohol plays a major part. Who knows how many broken homes result from overuse of alcoholic beverages or how many crimes have been committed because of the influence of alcohol? But drinking is a social problem, and our experience shows that morals cannot be legislated. Prohibition, the "Noble Experiment," rather than having the good effect it was supposed to have, did just the opposite. More people drank than ever before. People openly and notoriously broke the law. Centuries from now, historians will probably point to Prohibition as the event which started an attitude of disrespect for the law and which caused all the problems of the 1940s through the 1970s. Of course, hindsight has always been better than foresight.

Some states still try to control the problem by allowing each county to decide whether to permit the sale of alcoholic beverages. This is called the local option. Dry areas exist in name only. People leave their dry county and go to a wet county to buy their favorite whiskey, wine, or beer.

Most states have a more realistic approach to the problem and seek to regulate it from a different point of view. The states regulate who makes the beverage in order to make sure that those who wish to drink can do so without fear of going blind or dying from drinking poisoned alcohol. States try to keep drinkers off the roads and provide severe penalties for those who cause accidents on the road. States also provide penalties for habitual drunkards. We will look at these laws in the following sections of this chapter.

16.4   Crimes Involving the Manufacture and Sale of Alcoholic Beverages

All states and the federal government make it a crime to produce alcoholic beverages in excess of a limited amount. These laws are aimed at preventing the sale of adulterated alcohol which could cause death or serious injury. Usually under some sort of revenue law, the manufacturers must be registered with the state and federal governments. The success of these laws is in direct proportion to the integrity, diligence, and size of the enforcement body. Illicit stills continue to operate. Most of these are put together with such haste and lack of safety devices that the liquor produced, sometimes called "white lightning," can cause death, permanent blindness, or other severe physical problems.

All states require that anyone who sells alcoholic beverages be licensed and make it a crime for anyone to sell liquor without a license. In addition the states make it a crime for anyone to sell or give alcoholic beverages to minors. A few states have enacted laws prohibiting the sale or gift of alcoholic beverages to persons known to be alcoholic. Some provide criminal penalties for the sale or delivery of alcoholic beverages to someone who is already intoxicated. All states delegate to municipal and county officials the right to regulate the hours during which licensed sellers may operate. Penal ordinances are provided for those who do not observe these hours. The only possible exception to this delegation of power may involve a general statewide Sunday closing statute, or "Blue Law." Some states prohibit the sale of any alcoholic beverage by the bottle or drink and some prevent only bars from selling on Sunday. Others do the opposite and prevent only the sale of "packaged goods" and allow the bars to be open. Some states require that the bars be closed while the polls are open on election days. Any violation of these provisions will cause the violator to be punished. These offenses are all *mala prohibita* offenses and require no showing of criminal intent.

16.5 Public Drunkenness

Drunkenness is a status and as such it is not criminal. A number of states provide, however, that being drunk in public areas is a criminal offense. A few states make it a criminal offense to be a habitual drunkard. Some states make it a crime to drink in public places. Such a statute is constitutional because the drinking is enough of an act for the completion of a crime. In these states, the places in which drinking is not allowed are listed in the statutes. Since the variations are so great from state to state, the reader should consult both his state statutes and municipal ordinances for the approach taken in his area.

16.6 Driving While Intoxicated

Nearly every jurisdiction has, by statute, created the offense of driving an automobile or other vehicle while intoxicated. All the state needs to prove is that the defendant was intoxicated and that, while intoxicated, he was operating a motor vehicle of some sort upon a public street or highway. A few states label the offense a felony but the majority deem it only a misdemeanor.

What constitutes intoxication is a somewhat difficult question and each state arrives at a necessarily arbitrary answer. Each has slightly different tests for determining intoxication. It all comes down to a subjective test. If a defendant in a particular case is affected by what he drank to the point where he is not "normal," he will probably be convicted of the charge. There are rafts of materials on methods for testing intoxication and the reader is urged to study some of them.

Being drunk in a parked automobile will not make the drunk guilty of this offense. Nor will the drunk be chargeable if he is sitting in a parked car with the motor running or while attempting to start the car. In states which label the offense "driving while intoxicated," there must be some perceptible movement of the car while the defendant is behind the wheel. A few states, dissatisfied with these narrow conclusions, have broadened their statutes by making it an offense to operate a vehicle while intoxicated. These states require no movement of the car but would require more than mere presence of a drunk in a parked car whose engine is not running. Most jurisdictions include in their driving-while-intoxicated statutes a provision that will allow the statute to operate equally whether the intoxication is a result of excessive use of alcoholic beverages or of narcotic drugs.

Questions for Discussion

1. John has a diagnosable illness which requires a certain narcotic drug for its control. Bill, a friend of John's, is a narcotic addict and relies on the same drug that John needs for his illness. Bill tells John that he will pay John twice the cost of the drug if John will get some of it. John agrees. John visits his doctor and after diagnosis the doctor gives John a prescription for the narcotic. John takes the prescription to the drugstore and has it filled. He then sells the drug to Bill at the agreed upon price. For what crime or crimes are John and Bill liable?

2. Officer Jones, while on routine patrol, observes a car parked in a sparsely populated area of the city with its motor running. Upon investigation, Jones observes a man intoxicated and passed out behind the wheel of the car. The key is in the ignition and the motor is warm. The officer wakes the sleeping man and after determining that he is intoxicated, places him under arrest for driving while intoxicated. Discuss the propriety of the charge.

Chapter 17

EXTORTION, BLACKMAIL, BRIBERY, OTHER OFFICIAL CRIMES, AND CRIMINAL DEFAMATION

17.0 Introductory Comments

Most of the crimes we have examined have shown the physical brutality of men which society seeks to eliminate or at least hold to a minimum. We have seen the more commonly known crimes such as larceny and false pretenses where one man secures money or property from another. In this chapter, we will examine nonviolent crimes where money or property is secured not by trick, physical force, or stealth, but is extracted by misuse of public office. In addition, we will examine a crime where one man mentally forces another to part with money, property, or influence. Finally, we will see a crime where money or property is not necessarily involved but where a man uses inflamed words to damage another's reputation.

17.1 Extortion

At common law, it was a crime for any public officer corruptly to demand money or property that neither he nor his office was entitled to. This crime was called extortion. Today the crime exists in most states as a separate and distinct crime, but extortion is sometimes found in the bribery statutes of some states.

To be guilty of the offense of extortion, the accused must be a public officer. A public officer, simply put, is one who works for a government or holds elective office. This would include, in our system of multiple governments, all municipal, county, state, and federal officials. No branch of government is exempt. Administrative, executive, judicial, and legislative officials are all subject to prosecution for the crime of extortion if all the elements of the crime are met.

The crime may be committed by one who is properly appointed or elected to office—a *de jure* officer. It can also be committed by one whose appointment or election was not technically perfect in all respects—a *de facto* officer. There are even cases where a "phony" officer has been convicted. The courts, in these cases, have prevented the self-appointed public officer from denying his office, thus making him pay for his pretense. There is one qualifying point that must be met in this situation, however. If the office he pretends to fill is nonexistent, there is no extortion. The office must be one that actually exists.

The money or property demanded by the public officer must be demanded in connection with his official capacity. It would not be extortion for an officer to demand money in an unofficial capacity not connected with the job he holds. For example, it would not be extortion for a police officer to demand money from another person for getting a building permit okayed. Such a demand is well beyond the scope of his duties as a policeman. It would be extortion for the building inspector to demand excessive fees for granting a building permit because this is within the building inspector's scope of employment.

The common law recognized three circumstances where extortion was said to exist. First, an officer was guilty of extortion if he demanded fees in excess of the fees set by law for the service to be rendered. Next, it was extortion to demand a fee for a service for which the law set no fee because it was to be rendered at the general expense of the government. Finally, it was extortion to extract a fee corruptly before the service was rendered. This was true even if the service was later performed by the official. In studying the old common law cases, it appears that at the time of the demand and payment by the victim, the victim was apparently unaware that the fee demanded was illegal. When the victims later learned of the falsehoods, they reported them.

The crime today is basically one of official corruption. The law labels it a crime and attempts to stifle a system of private favors for public services. Nowhere does it appear that the modern victim has to be unaware of the illegality of the fees demanded. To complete the crime, all that is needed is the demand for and receipt by the officer of money or property to which he is not entitled for the performance of his duty.

Although the money has to be received by the extortionist, it does not have to be placed directly in his hands. Delivery to an agent appointed by the extortionist will be enough. Likewise, delivery to a post office box or bank account belonging to the extortionist will satisfy the delivery element.

If the extortionist receives nothing but a promise of payment, the crime is not complete. Receipt of any other thing, with even the slightest value, will be enough. Thus, a written promise to pay placed on a properly executed negotiable promissory note or a personal check could be enough. Some states have enacted laws which say that a promise given to pay when the demand is made will suffice. This represents an extension of the common law.

The common law required that the fee be demanded by the official with knowledge of its illegality. Thus, the common law would excuse an official who negligently miscalculated or who by some other method made a good faith mistake. Although this is the rule applied in most states today, there are some states which, by statute, permit no excuses. This is done to eliminate the possibility of sham defenses thought up after the officer is caught.

17.2 Blackmail

As we saw, demands by public officers in their official capacities for illegal fees are extortion. Illegal fes demanded by private citizens are likewise punishable and are popularly known as blackmail. Many states call blackmail extortion by a private person. Blackmail occurs when a person, using written or oral threats of force or fright, demands money or other property to which he is not entitled.

The most common method of blackmailing a person is to threaten to expose the victim to the public by telling the public about certain past misdeeds, whether real or pretended. The crime thrives on the basic tenet that each man would like to protect his reputation or the reputation of a member of his family and will pay to do so. The threat can also be to the physical well-being of the victim or a member of his family. Some states even say that the threat can be to the property of the victim.

The statutes from state to state are not harmonious, but they all agree that there must be intent to extract or extort money from another person. Here the words used constitute the act needed for the crime. Unless a local statute requires receipt of the money or property demanded, the crime is complete upon communication to the victim of the threat to person, reputation, property, or family.

17.3   Bribery

Perhaps the best known crime of official corruption is the crime of bribery. Stories have been written and continue to be written concerning the subject. It has been said that if bribery were stopped, organized crime would cease to exist. Whether that statement is true or not is not for us to debate. Suffice it to say that if bribery were completely eliminated, it would certainly hurt the operation of crime syndicates.

There are two types of bribery. First, it is bribery to give a public official money or property of any value in exchange for an agreement by the public official to do or refrain from doing something that is against or in contradiction of his official duty. Second, it is bribery for a public official to agree to do or not do something that is in contradiction of his duty in exchange for money or property of any value.

The agreement, not the act called for in the agreement, is essential to completion of the crime. That is why the crime would be complete even if the agreement were to affect a possible, not even certain, transaction in the future. In a few states, there has to be a tender or offer of the bribe money or other property and receipt by the official. If there is a mere offer of a bribe but no agreement on the part of the official, only attempted bribery can be charged. In states which require an offer and receipt of the money, if an agreement is reached but the official refuses the money or property, or if the money is not offered, there would also be only an attempted bribery. This was not the case at common law because the crime was the offer of a bribe with an agreement *or* acceptance of bribe money with an agreement. An official who refused money after an agreement was reached could be charged with bribery and so could the offeror. Because the statutes have changed the law somewhat, many legislatures make it a punishable offense to offer a bribe, but continue to recognize bribery when an officer approves the agreement without accepting the money or other property. These states find a completed bribery when there is an agreement and either acceptance or tender of the bribe money along with the completed agreement.

Contrary to the common law, statutes have made it bribery to give or receive money or other property to influence sports officials, athletes, municipal officers, county officials, members of juries, whether grand or petit, and witnesses. The states' statutes differ on this point and should be consulted to determine the scope of the statute in the reader's state.

Unlike extortion, the thing agreed to by the officer need not be within the scope of his authority or employment. Extortion, as you will recall, involved illegal payment for doing the right thing, but bribery calls for doing or not doing the wrong thing—something contrary to the powers of the office. This is the other main distinction between the two crimes.

At common law, bribery was a misdemeanor and it continues as such in a few states. However, a large percentage of the states have made bribery a felony.

17.4 Other Crimes Chargeable Against Public Officials

In addition to extortion and bribery, there are other crimes a public official can commit in his official capacity. Some of these come to us through the common law. They are set out briefly in this section to help the reader become aware of the possibilities. The crimes cover a multitude of official "sins" and serve as a catchall in this area.

A. Nonfeasance

Whenever an official purposely fails to do his duty which he is commanded by law to perform, he is guilty of nonfeasance in public office. The only defense available is that the dangers were greater than any normal man could be expected to face.

B. Misfeasance

If he is not acting under a genuine mistake of fact, it is unlawful for any public officer to abuse his discretionary power, commit any fraud or act of oppression, or do any other act in an illegal manner.

17.5 Criminal Defamation: Libel

One of the first rights we hear of in grade school is freedom of speech. As has been pointed out throughout this book, even fundamental freedoms have limits within which the citizen must operate. The common law recognized as a misdemeanor the crime of defamation of character through libel. Regulated by statute, the crime, which some states label as a misdemeanor and some deem a felony, is defined as the act of maliciously publishing, by writing or other sign, a statement which tends to defame another. A few states add a requirement that the published matter be false, although most states do not require this. In most states, the truth of the published allegation is not in issue and does not affect the guilt or innocence of the person who publishes the material.

A defamatory publication is one which opens a person, or family if he or she is dead, to public ridicule or hatred. It is a statement which disgraces a person or causes others to lose faith in him or her. Whenever a published statement has this potential, it is defamatory.

The libel must be written or visible to the eye. It could appear in a letter or magazine, on a painting or poster, or in any other manner. Oddly enough, there is one exception to this rule. Broadcasts on the radio are considered in the same class as written matter even though the broadcast is not visible to the eye. It is libel to publish (broadcast) defamatory remarks over the radio. Likewise, it is libel to telecast defamatory remarks.

In the popular sense, we think of newspapers and books when we think of publishing. In the legal sense, publication means that one person's comments are seen or heard by a person other than the one defamed. For the crime of libel, it is not necessary for the material to be widely circulated. The only limit on this rule at common law, and in some states today, is that the published defamatory material must be of such a character as to affect seriously the public order and perhaps cause a breach of peace. However, most states merely require the possibility of injury to the person libeled.

The requirement that the material be maliciously published does not mean, in most states, that it has to be done out of hatred or with evil motives. Mere publication of defamatory material is enough. In most states libel is a general intent crime. A few states do require specific intent to injure the defamed person.

Some states include in their libel statutes the crimes of writing threatening or obscene letters, whether or not for the purpose of blackmail, and making threatening or obscene phone calls, to name just a few. The variation between the states is great.

17.6 Criminal Defamation: Slander

Slander is a companion wrong to the crime of libel. Slander is usually a civil action only, unless it is made criminally punishable by statute, as it has been in a few states such as Alabama, California, and West Virginia. The distinction between slander and libel is often thought to be that slander is a defamation in spoken or oral form while libel is written. This distinction is not entirely accurate, for libel may be committed through the use of paintings or pictures which are not traditionally classified as writings. Likewise, slander may be committed by the use of bodily signs or gestures which are not considered spoken words.

Judicial opinions concerning libel and slander have attached various labels to distinguish these offenses. The words *permanent, durable,* and *visible* have been used at times to describe libel. Slander has often been defined by such terms as *temporary, transitory,* or *visible.* As one judge noted, "Traditionally, the distinguishing characteristic of a libel has been its expression in some permanent and visible form, such as writing, printing, pictures, or effigies, whereas a slanderous statement is made in spoken words or in some other transitory form, whether visible or audible, such as gestures or inarticulate but significant sounds."

Proof of slander requires the same element of maliciousness as does libel.

17.7   Public Officials and Federal Civil Rights Violations

Sections 241 through 245 of Title 18 of the United States Code spell out those circumstances when a public official can be held criminally responsible for the violation of another's civil rights. These sections are not to be confused with Section 1983 of Title 42 of the United States Code, which can cause certain public officials to pay money damages for civil rights violations.

If two or more persons conspire to injure, oppress, threaten, or intimidate any citizen in the free exercise of any constitutionally protected right or privilege, the persons so conspiring can be fined $10,000 or be given up to ten years in prison, or both. Likewise, if two or more persons go in disguise on the highway or on the premises of another with the intent to prevent or hinder the free exercise of such a right, a crime has been committed. If any of these activities leads to the death of another, such perpetrators will be subject to life imprisonment. It is not necessary for the prosecution to show that the defendant actually knew it was a constitutional right he was conspiring to violate.

Section 242 provides that, "whoever, under color of any law, statute, ordinance, regulation, or custom, willfully subjects any inhabitant of any State, Territory or District to the deprivation of any rights . . . or to different punishments, pains or penalties, on account . . . of his color, or race . . ." is subject to a year imprisonment, a fine of $1,000 or both. Here, as in the previous section, if a death results the defendant can get a life sentence.

Physical abuse or violence is not a necessary element of this crime. People have a right to be secure in one's person and to be immune from illegal arrest. Thus, an officer has committed the crime who knows a warrant is either illegal, groundless, or fictitious, and uses his power to arrest.

This misuse of power is made possible only because the defendant is clothed with authority of state law—thus, the action taken is under color of state law. A person does not have to be an officer of the state to be convicted under this section, however. It is enough that he is a willful participant in a joint activity with the state or its agents.

The next provision, Section 243, provides criminal penalties for disqualifying or preventing members of any race, because of race, from serving on juries or grand juries. Thus, blacks cannot be arbitrarily excluded from juries.

Section 244 prevents any discrimination against a person wearing the uniform of the armed services of the United States.

The final provision is more encompassing because it applies to anyone, whether under color of state law or not, who uses force, threats, intimidation, attempts, and so forth to prevent anyone from exercising certain federally protected activities. This section lists several activities, from voting to receiving food stamps. It includes activities such as attending desegregated schools, eating in restaurants, and seeking jobs.

Question for Discussion

1. The Warrensville County School Board hires the accounting firm of Smith, Smith, and Smith to audit the books of all the schools in the county. Smith, Jr., a member of the C.P.A. firm, discovers a shortage of funds in the Warrensville High School account. Smith, Jr., corners the principal of the high school, and after ascertaining that the principal is aware of the shortage, Smith tells the principal that for a sum of $500, he, Smith, will overlook the shortage and straighten the books. The principal agrees. It is agreed that to avoid any possibility of their plan being discovered, the principal will leave the money in a booth at a particular restaurant that night where Smith will pick it up. The money is left, but before Smith can get to the restaurant, Joe, a local wino, discovers the package and takes it for his own. What is the liability of each party involved in this situation?

Chapter 18

OFFENSES BY AND AGAINST JUVENILES

18.0 Introductory Comments

The key distinction between a crime and any other form of prohibited conduct is the state of mind with which a person acts, commonly referred to as intent. In Section 6.3, we observed that the common law established a set of arbitrary rules governing when and how well a person was capable of forming this intent, based partially on chronological age. Under seven years of age, a child was conclusively presumed incapable of forming the intent to commit a crime. This presumption could not be rebutted. Children between seven and fourteen years of age were rebuttably presumed incapable of forming the intent. For persons over fourteen years of age, the presumption was in favor of capability. As a result of these arbitrary rules, children of tender years often escaped punishment for conduct which, if committed by an adult, would have constituted heinous crimes. On the other hand, for a mere fourteen-year-old child, the punishment meted out for the commission of an offense was as harsh as it would be for an adult.

Many people felt that both alternatives provided by the common law system were unjust. They argued that it was wrong to allow a child under fourteen possibly to escape all liability for his conduct. On the other hand, they felt it equally bad to subject a child, possibly as young as seven years of age, to the harshness of the legal punishment of the times, especially in light of the poor penal systems. Over the long range, failing to segregate youthful offenders from adults took its toll.

It was not until 1899, in Cook County, Illinois, that any major steps were taken to rectify this situation. In that year, the first juvenile court was created for the handling and disposition of cases involving juveniles. From that court grew the widespread juvenile court system.

18.1   Juvenile Defined

With the advent of the juvenile court system, a whole new vocabulary developed within the framework of criminal justice. Among the terms that gained popularity in this context were petition instead of complaint, summons instead of warrant, initial hearing instead of arraignment, findings of involvement instead of conviction, and disposition instead of sentence.

Of course, the most important term that required definition was juvenile. Who is a juvenile? As in the case of most legal matters, there is little uniformity among the states. Each state was and still is free to define and interpret its own juvenile court law. A juvenile is, of course, determined by chronological age, but not all states are in agreement as to what that age should be. The ages range from a child under fifteen years to one who has not yet reached his nineteenth birthday at the time the act is committed. The exact age is in all cases established by legislation. It is an arbitrary decision derived from the best judgment of the lawmakers, who must determine when a child has been sufficiently socialized by the community to know right from wrong. Once that goal is achieved, the individual is considered an adult liable for the legal consequences of his or her actions.

The term juvenile is not used synonymously with the word minor. A minor is a person under twenty-one years of age. Several states have taken the initiative in trying to treat rather than punish youths until they reach the age of majority, by creating Youth Aid Authorities which deal with the person until the age of twenty-five.

18.2   Juvenile Court Jurisdiction

Like any other court referred to in Chapter 3, the juvenile courts of each state must meet the tests of jurisdiction before they are permitted to dispose of any case.

It must be pointed out that even though all states have a juvenile court system, the makeup of the court may vary from area to area within the same state. This is dictated by practical population and economic factors. In the densely populated urban and suburban areas, there may be a separate staff, buildings, and other facilities serving the separate juvenile court. The court may be composed of one or more judges whose sole function is to serve in juvenile matters. In the less densely populated rural areas of a state, the court may work out of the same facilities and share the staff of other county offices. In fact, the judge may wear two or more hats. He may be the county judge or the like and serve as the juvenile judge also. As a result, the quality of juvenile justice may vary greatly from one area of the state to another. The quality of justice administered to juveniles is also dependent upon the qualifications of the juvenile judges, length of service, diversity of the judicial role, and size of the court's jurisdiction. Most importantly, however, it will be affected by the resources available to the judge in making appropriate dispositions of cases. For example, a part-time juvenile judge in a rural area may only have a few options available, such as release on probation or referral to a state training school. Judges in urban or suburban areas, on the other hand, may have a variety of local treatment and probation programs from which to choose. The majority of juveniles sent to state training schools from these areas are, in fact, the so-called hard core delinquents. This inequality of treatment presents a number of controversial legal and social issues.

A. Territorial Jurisdiction

Like all other courts, the juvenile court has territorial jurisdiction only within a specific geographic area, usually a county or circuit, and it has no authority to dispose of any cases outside its jurisdiction. However, there may be exceptions to this rule in light of the philosophy of the juvenile court system. Courts may, by legislative action, transfer a case to the juvenile court of another jurisdiction closer to the place where the juvenile lives so that once disposition of the case is made, that court will be better able to keep track of the youth. This procedure is perfectly permissible because of the noncriminal nature of a juvenile court proceeding. However, this is permitted only between courts of the same state.

B. Jurisdiction over the Person

Juvenile court statutes generally specify that they have jurisdiction over youths who were juveniles at the time the prohibited act was committed. Thus, in most states, even if a youth has passed the age limit for juvenile court jurisdiction by the time the hearing is held, he may still be subject to juvenile court jurisdiction if, at the time the act was committed, he was within the age limit.

Statutes in some states provide that the juvenile court judge may have discretionary authority to refuse juvenile court jurisdiction over a juvenile who has committed an act which would constitute a felony if the youthful offender were an adult. In some states, this authority may be limited to capital crimes. When the court so refuses, jurisdiction is transferred to the appropriate adult court on the grounds that the juvenile court, after evaluating the offender's psychological makeup, intelligence, and likelihood of successful rehabilitation, does not have adequate resources available to treat him. The statutes of a few states provide for concurrent jurisdiction over juvenile matters by both juvenile and adult criminal courts. In these jurisdictions, the choice of courts rests with the referring police officer or agency when the situation is initiated as a police matter.

Some states permit youths over a certain age to waive the jurisdiction of the juvenile court by demanding trial in the appropriate adult court. This is a little known privilege which is rarely utilized. Under the philosophy of the juvenile court, the decision of the juvenile court would tend to be more lenient than a guilty verdict in an adult court.

C.   Jurisdiction over the Subject Matter

Juvenile courts have jurisdiction over two basic types of situations involving juveniles—offenses committed by juveniles and offenses committed against juveniles. In the former case, offenses committed by juveniles can be subdivided into two categories—status offenses and delinquency.

Juvenile status offenses are violations of rules of conduct established by society to protect the interests and the process of socialization of youth. They are not considered criminal violations of the laws of the state, county, or city in which they are applied. Unlike criminal violations, status offenses lose their relevancy to an individual once that individual becomes an adult. Among the status offenses are such behavior as truancy from school, curfew violations, running away from home, and a category of behavior commonly known by such titles as stubborn or unruly child, ungovernable behavior, conduct injurious to a juvenile's person, or conduct unbecoming a juvenile.

Despite the noncriminal nature of status offenses, the jurisdiction over them has been awarded to the juvenile courts in most jurisdictions. There are many who feel that this jurisdiction should be transferred to other public agencies not associated with the judicial aspects of the criminal justice system. In the alternative, where juvenile courts maintain this jurisdiction, efforts are being made to dissociate this kind of conduct from more serious acts of delinquency. One method of accomplishing this has been to attach the label "persons in need of supervision" (service) (PINS) to the juvenile status offender. In fact, some jurisdictions have urged that PINS be extended to all juveniles coming within the jurisdiction of the juvenile court for whatever reason.

Delinquency is conduct engaged in by a juvenile which, if committed by an adult, would violate the penal laws of the state. Boiled down to simple language, delinquency is a crime committed by a juvenile. Some jurisdictions also attach arbitrary labels to distinguish between serious and nonserious delinquency acts. The distinction is based upon the nature and seriousness of the offense and the severity of the disposition that can or should be imposed by the juvenile court judge.

Juvenile courts also have jurisdiction over cases involving offenses committed against juveniles. Dependency and neglect cases fall within this classification. The juvenile court often extends its authority to youngsters who have not committed any overt act that demonstrates that the juvenile has offended society, but if circumstances exist that indicate the failure on the part of a parent or guardian to provide properly for the welfare of the juvenile, the court is considered to have sufficient reason to assume jurisdiction of the case. Dependency and neglect are often used interchangeably and in many jurisdictions the authority of the court to dispose of such cases is identical. However, a technical distinction does exist. In cases of neglect there is generally some parental fault. Deliberate abandonment, physical and emotional abuse, general failure to provide for the minimum needs of the child's welfare, and the outright physical abuses associated with the battered child syndrome all fall within the court's jurisdiction over neglect cases. Cases classified as dependency generally involve no deliberate parental irresponsibility. Instances of dependency include the total absence of a parent or guardian to look after the welfare of a child, lack of proper care by virtue of physical or mental incapacity on the part of the parent or guardian, cases where a parent or guardian, with good cause, wishes to give up parental responsibility, or instances where parental poverty prohibits the child from receiving minimum care.

18.3 The Juvenile Hearing

Juvenile courts used to operate under a philosophy that their function was treatment and rehabilitation, to prevent the youthful offender from involving himself in activities which could lead him into a life of crime in his adult years. Juvenile court proceedings were treated as civil in nature, not requiring all the constitutional safeguards of a criminal trial. This philosophy was called the doctrine of *parens patriae*. Under the doctrine, the court would act in place of the parents with the welfare of the child as its only goal.

A. The Delinquency Hearing

Under the doctrine of *parens patriae* and by definition of the juvenile court system, the hearing in delinquency cases was conducted in an informal atmosphere. The hearing was attended by the child, the judge, the parents, and a juvenile counselor or caseworker if one had been assigned to the case. The proceedings were conducted informally with no emphasis placed on adhering to strict rules of evidence. The juvenile was entitled to have an attorney represent him if he wanted one, but the court was under no obligation to afford the youth the services of legal counsel. The object of the hearing was to determine what happened, why it happened, and how best to dispose of the case in the best interests of the juvenile. Disposition of the case could take any number of forms, ranging from dismissal or mild reprimand to committal to a boys' or girls' school or reformatory. If the case came before the court on referral from a police officer, he too was present to disclose the circumstances surrounding his contact with the juvenile.

In 1966 the United States Supreme Court began rendering a series of decisions which have drastically affected the *parens patriae* concept as it applies to delinquency cases.

The juvenile justice system did not escape the onslaught of Supreme Court decisions in the 1960s and early 1970s emphasizing the due process requirements of the Constitution. In the 1966 case of *Kent* v. *United States*, 383 U.S. 541, the court questioned the efficacy of the *parens patriae* philosophy of juvenile courts and noted that this philosophy was not an invitation to procedural arbitrariness. The Court stated:

> There is evidence, in fact, that there may be grounds for concern that the child receives the worst of both worlds: that he gets neither the protection accorded to adults nor the solicitous care and regenerative treatment postulated for children.

One year later the Supreme Court first began to provide the contents of a general definition of juvenile due process. In the case of *In Re Gault*, 387 U.S. 1 (1967), a fifteen-year-old boy was charged with having made lewd phone calls. The boy was denied even the most basic rights accorded to adult criminals. The Supreme Court held that any juvenile "criminal" proceeding that did not provide the following was void for lack of due process:

1. Notice to the accused and his parents of forthcoming proceedings given in sufficient time to allow them adequately to prepare a defense.
2. Notice of the charges against the accused set out with particularity.
3. Notice that the accused has a right to counsel at the proceedings at which delinquency will be determined.
4. Notice that counsel will be appointed to represent the accused if he or his family is unable to afford the cost of an attorney.
5. Right against self-incrimination.
6. Right of the accused to confrontation by witnesses that testify against him.

The Supreme Court found, in the *Gault* case, that the term *delinquency* had lost its intended function of preventing the stigma of criminality from attaching to the offender. Instead, the term had taken on a new meaning, a meaning that equated delinquency with criminality, juvenile delinquent with criminal. Also, the Court recognized that some youths were sometimes being locked up in state youth reformatories for longer periods of time than they could have been jailed for had they been convicted in an adult court where all the safeguards of due process applied. This seemed incongruous and unfair, and was complicated by the varying resources available in different jurisdictions.

In 1970 the Court reversed the conviction of a twelve-year-old boy who had been declared delinquent after being accused of stealing $112. The Court said that the standard of proof used in delinquency proceedings must be the same standard necessary to achieve the conviction of an adult criminal—proof beyond a reasonable doubt. Prior to this decision the standard of preponderance of evidence, usually applied in civil cases, had traditionally been acceptable in juvenile courts.

This line of cases has unquestionably formalized proceedings in delinquency cases before juvenile courts and it would now be more difficult to say that the hearing is civil in nature. With all the safeguards now provided, the hearing takes on the aura of a criminal trial, particularly in serious delinquency cases.

This issue has not been resolved. The Supreme Court apparently has not yet determined the exact nature of juvenile proceedings. In 1971 the Court declined to rule that a juvenile facing delinquency proceedings has a constitutional right to a jury trial. The majority of the Court held that a jury trial might tend to destroy the nonadversary nature of the present system. The opinion states:

. . . there is a possibility, at least, that the jury trial, if required as a matter of constitutional precept, will remake the juvenile proceeding into a fully adversary process and will put an effective end to what has been the idealistic prospect of an intimate, informal protective proceeding.

Consequently, it is still not clear whether the Court views juvenile proceedings as criminal or civil in nature. Apparently they have settled on something in between—a quasi-criminal proceeding which is, to say the least, an unusual legal concept.

B. Dependency Hearing

The *Gault* decision and companion cases have not drastically affected the operations of juvenile courts in dependency matters. Once the court acquires jurisdiction over the parents, it may dispose of the case in a manner best suited to the welfare of the child. The *parens patriae* concept still operates in these instances.

Very often, in a dependency matter, the child is taken from the parent or parents and placed in a foster home until disposition of the case. The social worker in the case investigates the petition or complaint to determine the facts in the case. A hearing is held in which the facts are presented by the social worker. Present at the hearing are the judge and the parents. Since this is basically a noncriminal proceeding to determine what would be best for the welfare of the child, the right to counsel has not yet been guaranteed in such hearings. If the parents have the means, they can be represented by counsel. After all sides are heard, the judge will make a disposition on the basis of the facts.

The court can usually do one of three things. First, it can determine that the facts do not warrant any action against the parents of the child. In this case, the court removes the child from the foster home, returns the child to the custody of the parents, and dismisses the petition. Second, the court can find that although the facts do not warrant permanently removing the child from parental custody, the child does deserve some control by the court. In this situation, the court will return the child to the custody of his parent or parents but will retain jurisdiction by having a social worker periodically check on the child and his environment. Finally, the court may determine that extreme measures are warranted. In this case, custody of the child is taken from the parent or parents. The child is made a ward of the state, usually under the direct supervision of the state welfare department or a related social service agency. The juvenile court retains jurisdiction of the case. Attempts are made to place the child in a foster home on a temporary basis pending further developments and final disposition. The parents can, at a later time, petition the court to regain custody of the child. If the court deems that the circumstances have changed sufficiently to warrant returning custody to the parents, the court will remove the child from the foster home and place the child in his natural home. Statutes in many states provide some limited jurisdiction to juvenile courts over the parents of dependent and neglected children. Very often the parents are placed on probation. In any event, the welfare of the child and not the parents is paramount.

18.4 Adoption

Adoption is the process whereby a child is legally separated from his or her natural parents and placed as a permanent member of another family entitled to all legal rights and responsibilities as if the adopting parents were the child's natural parents. All states have established the machinery for the processing of such cases. The states approve and license certified adoption agencies to perform this function after full investigations. There are extensive regulations governing both the operations of adoption agencies and the adoption procedures themselves. Certified adoption agencies often work hand-in-hand with state welfare departments and related social agencies to insure that children are placed in suitable households where they will be loved and well cared for.

As a general rule, most state laws require that one or both natural parents, if living and locatable, must consent to putting a child up for adoption. If the parent or parents do not consent, the child is not eligible for adoption. Parental consent must be wholly voluntary. Once a child is adopted, the natural parents lose complete contact with the child. They are not informed as to the child's new home. Likewise, the new parents generally are not informed as to the identity of the natural parents. Unlike most judicial records, proceedings of adoption cases are not public records.

Because the mechanics of adopting a child involve a long, drawn-out procedure encumbered by many rules, regulations, and laws, the adoption process has opened up an area of illicit activity for the criminal mind. The legal process may encompass a time frame of several months to two years. Often, prospective parents seeking to adopt a child are so overzealous that they are not willing to wait that length of time. Likewise, there are many prospective parents who want a child of their own, yet are unable to qualify after investigation by licensed adoption agencies and they are willing to go to extremes to adopt a child. Hence, many instances arise where criminals purchase, sell, and possibly abduct children for the purpose of making a profit. A person engaged in this kind of illegal enterprise might seek out unwed mothers who give birth to unwanted, illegitimate children and are willing to sell those children for the purpose of "adoption." Likewise, there are prospective adopting parents who will pay exorbitant amounts of money to speed the process of bringing a child into their lives. In these situations it is quite often true that they choose to ignore the legal procedures established by the state. This type of black market operation does involve violations of a number of state laws. The particular violations may vary from jurisdiction to jurisdiction and thus local law needs to be consulted. Police officers should be aware that illicit activities of this kind are occurring and are prosecutable.

Questions for Discussion

1. Discuss the significance of the *parens patriae* philosophy of the juvenile courts. To what extent has this philosophy been abrogated by recent court decisions?

2. Investigate and define the jurisdiction of the juvenile court in your state.

3. Distinguish delinquency from dependency.

Chapter 19

CRIMES AFFECTING JUDICIAL PROCESS

19.0   Introductory Remarks

Most, if not all, crimes affect the judicial process in one way or another. Were it not for the commission of crimes, a criminal judicial process would not be needed. There are a certain group of offenses, known to the common law and codified by statute in most jurisdictions, which more directly affect the administration of criminal justice. These offenses directly concern the dignity of the courts and their judicial decisions and the processes by which the criminal justice system is administered. Some of the offenses in this category are covered in other, more appropriate sections of this book. For example, bribery is discussed in Chapter 17. The offenses selected for presentation in this chapter are by no means exhaustive. We have chosen to discuss only those crimes which we feel are of immediate concern to law enforcement officials. Included in this category are perjury, subornation of perjury, embracery, escape, rescue, breaking prison, and obstructing justice.

19.1   Perjury

The common law misdemeanor of perjury consisted of taking a false oath in a judicial proceeding regarding a matter material to that proceeding. A false oath meant that the accused willfully and corruptly made a sworn statement regarding something he knew to be false or that he did not believe to be true. Today, perjury remains a criminal offense in all jurisdictions and in many has been made a felony. An analysis of the elements of this offense is in order.

A.   Oath or Affirmation Duly Administered

Before perjury may be properly charged, the testimony must have been given under oath or some legally recognized equivalent. At common law, one test of the competency of a witness was his belief in a supreme being. Based on this belief, the witness would swear to tell the truth. Thus, taking an oath was one test of determining whether a witness was competent to testify. Although taking an oath by swearing to tell the truth is still the prime test today, it is no longer the exclusive test of competency. It is generally held today that to qualify as a witness, the person must understand the obligations of an oath and undertake those obligations realizing the penalties of perjury for not telling the truth. If the witness does understand and undertake those obligations without actually swearing to a supreme being, this is called an affirmation. Many jurisdictions allow an affirmation instead of an oath. In those states, the affirmation is treated as a legally recognized equivalent of an oath. Thus, a witness who refuses to take an oath may still qualify as a competent witness by affirming that he will tell the truth.

Aside from religious or other reasons why one would refuse to take an oath, the affirmation is often used in the case of children who are to be witnesses. The fact that the witness is a child will not automatically qualify him as a competent witness. In fact, in the case of children, their competency to testify will be more closely scrutinized. A child who may not be mature enough to understand the nature of an oath may still be qualified as a competent witness if, under private examination by the judge, he or she understands the importance of telling the truth and agrees to do so.

There is another ramification to taking an oath or affirmation which must be shown to exist before a perjury charge will be proper. The oath or affirmation must be lawfully administered. This refers to the legality of the oath administered. In order for an oath or affirmation to have any legal effect, the taking of the oath must be permitted or required by statute. One who has no authority to administer an oath may not legally do so, and false testimony given under such an oath may not be grounds for a perjury charge. This would be true when a person is compelled to give an oath and testify in a "hangman" court proceeding run by a group of vigilantes.

B. False Oath

As previously stated, a false oath is a willful and corrupt sworn statement which the accused knows to be false or which he does not know to be true. This does not include mistakes even if the mistake completely contradicts previous testimony on the same subject. Nor does the law make criminal a mistake caused by negligence or carelessness on the part of the witness. As will be seen in the next subsection, perjury requires proof of intent, which is an integral part of this offense.

This element may be satisfied·in any number of ways. As the rule indicates, one who swears a fact is true when he knows it is false has given a false oath. If one testifies a fact is true when he is not sure it is true, he has given a false oath. Thus, if a witness deliberately testifies that the vehicle he saw leaving the scene was a convertible when, in fact, he is not sure it was a convertible, he may be liable for perjury.

A third manner in which a false oath may be given is by testifying a fact is true when the witness does not know whether it is true or false. Consequently, if Jones testifies he observed Smith running from the scene of the crime when, in fact, Jones was nowhere near the scene to observe such an event, he has given a false oath. This would constitute perjury even if it later turned out that Jones' statement were correct. Thus, if Smith actually did run from the scene at the time Jones alleged, this would be no defense to a charge of perjury against him. In essence, the rule regarding false oath concerns not the testimony itself, but rather the fact that a lie was given under oath.

C. Willful and Corrupt

The false oath must be made willfully and corruptly. This requirement supplies the intent element in the crime of perjury. To satisfy this requirement, the false testimony must be knowingly and deliberately made. This rule eliminates the possibility of holding someone liable for perjury when he testifies to something falsely but does so mistakenly or carelessly or under an honest belief that it is true.

D. Materiality of Testimony

A perjury charge may not lead to conviction if the false testimony was given on a point not really important to the outcome of the case. This does not mean that the testimony must bear directly on the issue of guilt or innocence. As long as the false oath pertains to a point which may have some bearing on the outcome of the trial, it is material. In each case, whether false testimony, willfully and corruptly given, is material or not is a question of law for the court to decide rather than a question of fact for the jury.

E. Judicial Proceeding

At common law, perjury was an offense charged when the false oath was given in a judicial proceeding. Thus, the crime was limited to in-court false testimony. There are, however, numerous out-of-court occasions which require that testimony be given under oath or which require that an oath be taken. Since these situations did not conform to the common law requirement for perjury that the testimony be given in a judicial proceeding, a separate offense was recognized by the common law courts. The crime of false swearing was identical to perjury except that it was done in a proceeding other than judicial which also required an oath.

In the majority of jurisdictions today, the crimes of false swearing and perjury have been incorporated into a single statute under the title of perjury, so that taking a false oath in any proceeding, judicial or not, where an oath is required by law, will constitute the crime.

Historically, disputes were settled in court or privately. With the growth of government, the administrative agency developed to regulate businesses, administer welfare and insurance programs, and collect taxes. These agencies developed regulations which, when apparently broken, necessitated procedures for hearing complaints. The agency would sit as a semicourt, take testimony, and render a decision. These agencies were given the power to subpoena witnesses and records. Thus, the law recognized the need to prevent perjured testimony before these boards. In addition, depositions and interrogatories which may be used in court are taken under oath or affirmation, and false testimony in a deposition will subject a person to prosecution. Affidavits which require an oath, voter registration, and certain license applications requiring an oath can be perjured, subjecting the perjuring party to prosecution.

The word oath may convey many meanings to an individual aside from the oath to tell the truth when testifying. For example, when a public official such as the president of the United States, a senator, or representative is sworn into office, he takes an oath swearing to uphold the

Constitution of the United States and to perform his responsibilities to the best of his ability. May a violation of this oath constitute perjury? Most courts hold that this is not perjury, for that crime pertains to false swearing in a testimonial capacity. However, there are a few cases on record holding to the contrary.

F. Jurisdiction

A conviction of perjury may be proper if the court or other agency issuing the oath has jurisdiction over the matter tried or the matter sworn to. On the other hand, if the agency or officer administering the oath has no jurisdiction to so do, or if the matter in which the oath is given is beyond the jurisdiction of the agency, no perjury charge will be proper regardless of the amount of false testimony given. For example, if a juvenile court attempts to try an adult for a capital felony, any amount of false oath occurring during the trial will not constitute chargeable perjury because the lack of jurisdiction voids the legality of the entire trial (see Chapter 3).

G. Perjury by a Defendant

An obvious question that police personnel often ask concerns whether a defendant in a criminal case, who takes the stand to testify in his own behalf, can subsequently be charged and convicted separately for the crime of perjury, if it can be shown that he gave a false oath. The answer is yes in most jurisdictions. If the elements of the offense can be proven, the defendant is no less subject to the charge than any other witness. It must be remembered that the dignity and integrity of the court and of the entire judicial process of our society is downgraded by a perjurer. There is some conflict in this area, however, when a defendant is acquitted of a criminal charge for whatever reason, including his own perjured testimony. The federal courts hold that in such a case a perjury charge is not allowed. Most state courts disagree and would allow a charge of perjury to be brought for the reasons just stated. But where the defendant in a federal case has been convicted of the crime charged, the federal authorities and courts will pursue and allow a charge of perjury.

H. Requirements of Proof

Because of the many errors and mistakes that witnesses can and do make in criminal trials, whether due to error, mistake, carelessness or negligence, proof of the crime of perjury must, in fact, be fairly clear-cut.

This is not to say that the burden of proof is any greater than is required for any other criminal case. The law still requires proof only beyond and to the exclusion of every reasonable doubt. What is meant is that a mere conflict in testimony or contradictory statements made by a single witness will ordinarily not be enough to convict. Likewise, the law will not allow a conviction to be based on one man's word against another. A "your word against mine" situation does not take into account the innocent mistakes that could be made. The law requires that there be independent corroborating evidence to support one person's word against another or, in the alternative, that there be at least two witnesses to testify against the defendant in the perjury trial.

I. Consequences of a Perjury Conviction

Perjury today is a felony which in some states carries a maximum penalty of life imprisonment. In addition to these very harsh penalties, perjury, being considered an infamous crime from its earliest beginnings, often disqualifies one who has been convicted of the offense from holding a public office or from serving on a jury. Some states, such as Florida, also provide in their statutes that one who has been convicted of perjury may not be a witness in any judicial proceeding in that state after conviction. Thus, there are many sanctions imposed on one convicted of this socially degrading crime.

19.2   Subornation of Perjury

The crime of subornation of perjury is the corrupt procurement of another to commit perjury. If Green procures White to commit perjury, the separate offense of subornation may be charged against Green.

A. Perjury Committed

The crime of subornation of perjury requires that the crime of perjury actually be committed by the one procured. In the example above, if White does not commit perjury, Green cannot be convicted of subornation of perjury. In light of our previous discussion of the crime of solicitation (4.10) and the liability of parties to crimes (4.11), the reader may well ask why one who is guilty of procuring another to commit perjury is not an accessory before the fact if the one procured actually commits perjury. The answer to this question lies in the historical background of the crime of subornation of perjury. The common law regarded the procurement of one to commit perjury as a much more socially degrading crime than the actual perjury and, therefore, provided more severe penalties. If the defendant were convicted of subornation, his penalty could be much more severe than if he were convicted as an accessory before the fact to perjury. It is true that perjury was only a misdemeanor at common law. It is also true that subornation of perjury was a common law misdemeanor but it still carried a more severe penalty. Modern statutes, however, reclassify perjury as a felony with extremely harsh penalties possible. Subornation of perjury usually carries the same penalty, and it too has been elevated to a felony.

If all the other elements of the crime of subornation are satisfied except that the witness procured does not commit perjury, the proper charge would be attempted subornation of perjury. The only qualification affecting this charge is that had the witness testified as the suborner wanted him to, his testimony would have been a false oath, which would have constituted perjury.

B. By Other Than the Defendant

A brief note is needed to point out that the crimes of perjury and subornation of perjury are inconsistent in the sense that they cannot both be committed in a single incident. The procurer may not be the person who commits the perjury.

C. Corrupt Inducement by Defendant

To obtain a conviction of this crime, prosecution must show that the defendant induced the witness to commit perjury. Knowledge on the part of the defendant that the witness intends to, and subsequently does, commit perjury will not support a charge of subornation if unaccompanied by some form of inducement. The inducement must also be corrupt. Thus, the suborner must procure another to commit perjury knowingly and willfully.

D. Defendant Must Have Knowledge of the False Oath

As stated above, mere knowledge that the witness intends to commit perjury will not support a charge of subornation. If, however, this knowledge is accompanied by corrupt inducement, knowledge that the witness intends and does commit perjury becomes an indispensable element of the crime. This element may be satisfied in any of several ways. First, the defendant may know that the testimony of the witness would be given under a false oath. Generally, both the defendant and the witness must know that the testimony is false. If the witness knows the testimony is true, the defendant cannot be convicted of subornation since the witness has not committed perjury. The defendant may, however, still be liable for attempted subornation of perjury. The same rule generally applies if the defendant knows that the testimony given by the witness is true. However, there is an exception to the rule that this would not constitute subornation. If the defendant knows the testimony is true and he procures a witness to testify to that effect but the witness does not believe the testimony is true, the crime of subornation is complete. This is so because the witness took a false oath, notwithstanding the fact that the testimony given was true.

E. Matters of Proof

Like perjury, subornation of perjury requires testimony by two witnesses or one witness plus independent corroborative evidence for conviction. However, the element of procuring does not require proof by such a degree of evidence. Testimony of one witness will suffice to establish the act of procurement.

19.3 Embracery

Embracery was a well-known common law offense which today is commonly called jury tampering and may be included in other statutory forms instead of as a separate offense. It is a rarely used criminal proceeding but because of its relationship to law enforcement functions, it deserves a brief mention in this chapter.

The gist of embracery involves a corrupt attempt to influence the decision of a jury or of an individual juror. It is not necessary that this be done in the form of a bribe as described in Chapter 17. Of course, if the elements of bribery are well founded, that crime may be prosecuted.

Under our system of law, the various participants in a trial each have assigned functions. It is the responsibility of the judge to apply the law to the facts of the case. The witnesses are responsible for presenting facts and the jury is responsible for drawing conclusions. Each of these functions must be kept distinct in order to preserve the system. Allowing any of the parties, or a stranger, to influence the decision of the jury destroys the entire concept of the jury system. It is for this reason that the crime of embracery was first recognized.

Unlike the crime of subornation of perjury, it is not essential that a juror actually be influenced by the embracer in reaching a verdict. Embracery is complete when the attempt to influence a juror corruptly is made. Even another juror may be liable for the crime if he attempts to influence the verdict by corrupt means. Of course, while a jury is deliberating the fate of an accused person, each member of the jury is attempting to persuade his fellow jurors to conform to his own opinion as to the guilt or innocence of the accused. This is a perfectly permissible procedure and it is really the only means by which a jury could reach a unanimous decision. If, however, the juror attempts to influence his fellow jurors by promises, threats, money, or other unlawful means not related to the evidence presented in the trial, the crime of embracery has been committed.

It has been held that this offense applies not only to trial juries but will also be chargeable when one attempts to influence corruptly the decision of a grand jury.

19.4   Escape, Rescue, and Breaking Prison

The common law misdemeanor of escape was defined as leaving lawful custody without authorization and without the use of force. Escape differs from the common law offense of prison break in which force is an essential element. The crime of rescue involves aiding another to flee from custody. An examination of the elements of each of these offenses follows.

A.   Lawful Custody.

Our discussion of these crimes relates to custody connected with criminal proceedings, although there are some states that apply these offenses equally to custody commencing from a civil action. The term *custody,* in its legal sense, does not imply physical contact nor does it mean that the prisoner must be behind bars. If the prisoner is deprived of his fredom of mobility, he is in custody. The fact that he is in an open area with no guard standing over his shoulder does not mean he is not in custody. If he is under the general supervision of one who is responsible for and restricts his movements, the prisoner is in custody.

The rules regarding custody may have a familiar ring to the reader who has read Chapter 15 on false imprisonment and kidnapping. The distinguishing feature is that in this chapter we are discussing lawful custody. False imprisonment and kidnapping are crimes which involve unlawful custody. Escaping from unlawful custody is not a crime.

In a criminal case, lawful custody may arise in a number of ways: pursuant to an arrest warrant, by authority of a *capias* issued by a competent court that has jurisdiction and probable cause for believing a felony has been committed or for an offense committed in the presence of the arresting official or citizen. There are other ways in which a particular agency may gain custody of a person. For instance, the prisoner may be transferred from another institution or he may be serving a sentence in an institution. Regardless of the reason why the agency or officer has custody of another, the custody must be lawful before an escape will be chargeable if the prisoner departs.

B. The Act of Departing

To ascertain whether one has departed from lawful custody and thereby committed the crime of escape, it is necessary to determine the limits of his confinement. If we recognize that neither prison walls nor iron bars are required for custody, the explanation is simple. If the prisoner is in lawful custody, regardless of the location or limits, an unauthorized departure will constitute escape. Fred, an inmate at the Super State Prison, is made a trustee. He is assigned the task of chauffeuring the warden. One day Fred drives the warden to an appointment at the state capital, three hundred miles from the prison walls. While the warden is attending the meeting, Fred decides to leave permanently. Fred has committed escape.

C. The Intent

Escape and breach of prison are general intent crimes, requiring only intent to leave the bounds of lawful custody. There will be times, however, when the circumstances surrounding the departure may be reasonably explained so as to preclude the crime being charged or a conviction obtained. Consequently, the law will recognize such defenses as mistake of fact or necessity as defenses. Referring to the previous example, suppose Fred thought, and could reasonably convince a jury, that he believed the warden told him to see the sights of the capital city while the warden was in conference. In fact, the warden said no such thing. If Fred acted reasonably under the mistake of fact which he honestly believed to be true, this would be a defense to a charge of escape. Would inmate Jones of the same prison be convicted for escape if he was working in a wooded area outside the prison walls with instructions to stay there and he left without intending to leave custody permanently because a forest fire broke out in the area in which he was working? Obviously not.

D. Force

The existence of the element of force is the only element which distinguished the crime of prison breach or prison break from the crime of escape. If no force is used to effect the prisoner's departure from custody, his crime is escape. If force is used, no matter what kind or how slight, at common law, the crime was breach of prison. Today, most jurisdictions have combined escape and prison breach into a single statutory offense, but the existence or nonexistence of the element of force is still necessary for proper proof of the crime.

E. Prison

Any discussion of the crimes of escape and prison break would be incomplete without noting what definition the law attaches to the word *prison*. Those of us who have grown up with television as a part of our lives ordinarily think of the word prison to mean the state penitentiary. This is not the interpretation used when referring to the crimes of escape and prison breach. A prison is any boundary within which the mobility of a prisoner is restricted. A prisoner is defined as any person who is in lawful custody. Thus, upon being arrested, an individual is in prison. All this leads to the conclusion that if Sam uses force to effect a departure from the custody of Officer Brown who has just arrested him on Main Street at high noon, he is liable for prison breach.

F. Degrees of Liability

Escape without force at common law was a misdemeanor. If force was used, the offense was more serious. Many modern courts have graded the offense in accordance with the crime for which the prisoner has been arrested or convicted. If John escapes from custody after arrest on a misdemeanor charge, his escape is a misdemeanor. If he is arrested on a felony charge, escape will constitute a felony. The same rules apply to an escape after conviction for an offense. In at least one state, these rules have been altered so that escape after conviction for a crime is a felony regardless of the classification of the crime on which conviction was based. In that state, punishment for escape before conviction is still determined by the classification of the crime for which the arrest was made.

G. Rescue

The common law crime of rescue is often referred to today as aiding another to escape. Many statutes require that the aid be rendered knowingly. As a general rule, however, the crime of rescue does not require specific intent. Defenses such as mistake of fact will excuse one for commission of the crime of rescue. Thus, if Joe slips Barney a knife or saw blade to help him escape from lawful confinement, Joe is criminally liable for this offense.

H. Some Additional Problem Areas

The topics discussed in this section cannot be completed without mentioning three additional areas of concern to law enforcement officers. First, the reader may ask whether "jumping bail" constitutes escape. In the broadest construction of the term escape, jumping bail is considered a form of escape but most jurisdictions have a separate statute making this a chargeable offense.

Second, Title 18 U.S.C. § 1073, a federal statute, declares that crossing state lines to avoid prosecution or confinement for the commission of or attempt to commit any state felony, or to avoid giving testimony in a state felony case, is itself a felony. If we recognize the separation-of-sovereignties concept discussed under the heading of concurrent and overlapping jurisdiction in Section 2.5, there is nothing to preclude the state from charging escape or prison break even if a federal fugitive warrant has been issued, and if the prisoner is apprehended and returned to the state from which he fled. A prosecution in both the federal and state courts would be proper for the different offenses.

Third, the question often arises as to whether violation of probation or parole by leaving the jurisdiction without permission constitutes an escape. The answer is a definite no. One who is on probation or parole is under the supervision of a probation or parole officer, but the law does not treat these circumstances as custodial and, therefore, there can be no escape.

19.5 Obstructing Justice

Many of the crimes previously discussed in this and other chapters were, at early common law, grouped into a general catch-all type of offense called obstructing justice. Because of the growth of importance of some of them, they were made separate punishable offenses by the later common law and by modern statute. There still exists in many jurisdictions an obstructing justice statute to cover those cases not set apart as distinct offenses. The following is a brief discussion of a few of the acts falling within the purview of this type of statute.

In Section 19.3, we discussed the crime of embracery, which consisted of tampering with jurors by attempting to influence their decisions. The crime of obstructing justice includes the act of tampering with witnesses. At common law and today we have seen one instance of tampering with a witness through the crime of subornation of perjury. However, there are other methods by which a witness may be tampered with, causing him either to testify falsely or not at all. For example, if the defendant in a given criminal case gives the witness $1,000 and tells him not to show up at the trial, the crime is complete. Most cases of tampering with witnesses have arisen from the use of force or intimidation by one of the parties to the trial. The crime would be complete if the prosecution, for example, intentionally hid a witness material to his own or the defendant's case. The crime would be chargeable if one of the parties intentionally, by force or threat of force, compelled the witness to stay away from the trial.

Another type of conduct giving rise to a charge of obstructing justice involves hiding or destroying evidence. Both parties to a particular case may be charged with this offense. The law applies equally to secretion or destruction of evidence by either the prosecution or defense. Obviously, if the defendant, before his trial, destroys material evidence by burning or mutilation, he could be charged with the crime. Likewise, if the defendant rents a safe deposit box in a bank in another town under an assumed name and places in it material that could lead to his conviction, which is not discovered by the authorities until after his acquittal, he could be charged with the crime.

Many jurisdictions have separate statutes making resisting or obstructing an officer in the performance of his lawful duties a separate offense. However, some states still include this conduct under the general heading of obstructing justice. Any person who stands in the way of any public officer to prevent him from performing the duties of his office is chargeable with this crime. Of major concern to law enforcement officers is obstructing or resisting a peace officer in the performance of his legal duties. It is emphasized that the officer must be performing a lawful duty of his office when the obstruction takes place, but, of course, since police officers are sworn officials twenty-four hours a day, this does not mean he has to be on duty at the time. Historically, resisting arrest falls within the purview of this statute if it is not made a separate crime. Obstructing or resisting may be committed either by a person to be arrested or by a third party. For instance, if Officer Smith, armed with a valid arrest warrant for Mr. Brown, attempts to enter the Brown home to execute the warrant but his way is blocked by Mrs. Brown, she is liable for obstructing an officer.

The courts uniformly hold that fleeing an officer to avoid arrest does not constitute resisting or obstructing justice because no force is employed directly against the officer. Force is an essential element of the offense but only the slightest amount is needed. Even physically barring a passageway will suffice.

One further situation deserves mention in this area. It is the duty of citizens to come to the aid of a peace officer upon the officer's request. Since there is a duty to respond to the officer's call for help, any person refusing is guilty of a misdemeanor. This is true even though the help asked for exposes the individual to great danger. As a side note, whenever a private citizen is called to the aid of an officer, the law cloaks that individual with the same powers and authority as are possessed by the police officer.

19.6 Criminal Contempt

Another offense closely aligned to obstructing justice, and one which is directly related to the judicial process, is criminal contempt. An act which is disrespectful to the court, calculated to bring the court into disrepute, or of a nature which tends to obstruct the administration of justice is criminal contempt. Examples of contemptuous conduct are misbehavior of any person in the courtroom to the discredit of accepted decorum, or disobeyance of a lawful order by a judge for which a punishment may be imposed.

Criminal contempt differs from civil contempt in that the penalty for civil contempt is purely coercive and can be avoided by compliance with the court's order. Thus, in a case where an attorney was held in contempt for failure to wear a necktie in the courtroom while litigating a case, the penalty could have been avoided if the attorney agreed to wear a necktie. But, a witness who fails to appear to testify in court under orders of a subpoena is liable for criminal contempt. It should be noted that certain conduct can constitute both civil and criminal contempt.

Judicial opinion is split as to whether criminal contempt actually constitutes a crime under the definition given previously in this text. That question is somewhat academic in light of the fact that criminal contempt is punishable as are other criminal offenses.

Until 1968 a trial by jury was not required for criminal contempt cases in either state or federal courts. The rule remains the same in state courts, but the rule in the federal courts has changed. The Supreme Court determined that "serious" contempt cases were subject to constitutional requirements of a jury trial. Just what is a "serious" contempt case has not yet been universally defined. In one case where a twenty-four-month prison sentence was administered, it was held to be serious enough to require a jury trial, while in another case a maximum sentence of ten days in jail and a $50 fine was not considered serious. It has also been held that a six-month sentence may possibly be short enough so as not to require a jury trial.

Criminal contempt may be classified either as direct or constructive. A direct contempt is one committed in the presence of the court or the judge or so near to the court or judge when he is acting judicially as to be interpreted as hindering a judicial proceeding. An indirect or constructive contempt is an act done, not in the presence of the court or of the judge, acting judicially, but under such circumstances and at such a distance that reasonably tends to degrade the court or the judge as a judicial officer, or to obstruct the administration of justice by the court or judge. An example of constructive contempt would be violation of a court instruction to jurors not to discuss a case with outsiders during a trial.

The importance of the distinction between direct and constructive contempt is important insofar as the procedure for punishment is concerned. In a direct contempt, the judge has the power to punish summarily (without hearing evidence). In the case of constructive contempt, the judge, not having knowledge of all the facts of the case, would be required to hear evidence before making his decision.

It is fairly well accepted that all courts have criminal contempt powers, even courts that do not ordinarily exercise jurisdictions in criminal cases. However, a court may not properly punish for contempt unless the order which was violated was one the court had lawful authority to make in the first place.

Questions for Discussion

1. Sam has been charged with a crime and his trial has been set for a certain day. Sam contacts Fred and gives him $100 to testify on Sam's behalf. Sam gives Fred five facts which Fred is to testify to under oath. Three of these facts are true but two are false. The state decides to drop the charges against Sam but learns of the agreement between Sam and Fred. With what crimes, if any, can Sam and Fred be charged?

2. Bill has been charged with the crime of robbery. A jury of twelve men and two alternates has been selected. One of the alternates, Al, is a cousin of Bill. Neither the prosecutor nor the defense attorney knew this fact. Bill sees Al in the hallway of the courthouse and slips Al $50 and says, "This is for the time you will have to spend on this miserable jury," but says no more. Can Bill be charged with embracery?

3. Jack and Mack were being confined in separate cells in the lower county courthouse jail awaiting trial for their crimes. Neither man knew the other before their day of trial. On the day of trial Mack and Jack were taken from the lower county courthouse cells and put in the back seat of the same car to be transported to the main courthouse for trial. While en route to the main courthouse Mack attacks the officer driving the car, takes his gun, and forces the officer to stop the car. Mack gets out of the car and hands the gun to Jack, tells Jack to point the gun at the officer's head, and says, "Make this cop drive ten miles; if you don't I'll kill you myself." Jack does as he was asked out of fear. At the end of the ten miles he tells the officer to stop, which the officer does. Jack throws the gun away and walks ten steps and sits down. With what crimes, if any, can Mack and Jack be charged?

Chapter 20

CRIMES AGAINST
PUBLIC ORDER

20.0 Introductory Remarks

Much of police officer's working time when he is not writing reports is spent enforcing the laws against violations of a group of offenses which we categorize as offenses against public order. Every state has its laws dealing with affrays, disorderly conduct, public profanity, disturbing the peace, vagrancy, nuisance, and so forth. In this chapter we will look at the legal composition and enforcement problems that are involved in many of these offenses.

20.1 Unlawful Assembly, Rout, and Riot

Our English common law heritage recognized the right of the people to assemble peaceably for a lawful purpose. This inalienable right was brought to the United States with the colonists and embedded eventually in our basic governing document, the Constitution of the United States. In the First Amendment, this guarantee is maintained. The word peaceable is important to the definition for not every assembly is protected. In order to be protected, the assembly must be peaceable, lawful, and for a lawful purpose. If it is otherwise, the assembly is not constitutionally protected and the criminal law comes into operation.

Unlawful assembly was a misdemeanor at common law and consisted of the assembly of three or more persons for an unlawful purpose or in an unlawful manner which was violent or riotous in nature or which disturbed the peace of the community. The unlawful assembly itself constitutes commission of this crime and the unlawful act or unlawful purpose sought to be accomplished by the assembly must not occur. If the unlawful purpose of the assembly is accomplished, the crime of unlawful assembly may not be charged. Such conduct falls within the purview of another offense discussed in the following paragraphs.

The common law misdemeanor of rout consisted of any physical conduct which tended toward carrying out the unlawful purpose of the assembly. Thus, if three or more assembled to organize a lynch mob, they were guilty of unlawful assembly. When they left the place of assembly and began to move toward commission of the unlawful act, they were guilty of rout.

Riot, also a common law misdemeanor, was the actual carrying out of the unlawful purpose of an unlawful assembly. If the lynch mob successfully accomplished its goal, the participants were guilty of riot over and above their liability for any homicide they committed. To satisfy the element of riot, the unlawful purpose must have been accomplished in a violent manner or in any manner which would have instilled fear in the minds of the public or which would have constituted a breach of the peace.

Liability for common law rioting required a common purpose by at least three people. This did not mean that all three had to participate physically in commission of the unlawful act. As long as each was participating in such a manner that he was able to aid in the accomplishment of a common plan or scheme, there was concerted action. See Section 4.9 on conspiracy for a complete discussion of concerted action and its ramifications. Also, refer back to Section 4.11 on parties to crimes for ways in which one may be liable for riot.

Rioting is a felony in most states today, and it usually requires destruction of or damage to property before it is chargeable. Many statutes also provide for liability of "followers" of a riotous crowd if they fail to obey lawful orders of a police officer or other official to disband.

20.2 Affray

An affray is what we commonly call a fight except that the word *fight*, as used in its broadest sense, includes legal as well as illegal conduct. An affray is an illegal fight, in which both or all parties (if there are more than two involved) are mutually at fault. The affray, in order to be chargeable, must occur in a public place. The mutuality element prevents the offense from covering situations where a fight is occasioned by one is lawfully defending himself from an unwarranted attack by another person.

Public place is defined as any place in which members of the public could view the affray, regardless of whether the property itself was public or private. An affray was a misdemeanor at common law and it remains so in most, if not all, jurisdictions today. The characteristic of the offense which puts it in the class of crimes discussed in this chapter is that its commission in a place open to public view constitutes a breach of the peace.

20.3 Breach of the Peace, Disturbing the Peace, Disorderly Conduct

Recalling the definition of crime we gave in the beginning of this book as being a public wrong, an act or omission forbidden by law and punishable upon conviction by a prescribed punishment, it is easy to say that all crimes affect the peace and dignity of the people. This concept, however, is theoretical to a certain extent. Certainly all crimes affect all the people, but many crimes are committed in such a way that the immediate impact only involves a few people. Larceny, embezzlement, burglary, and even robbery are not generally committed under circumstances that will arouse terror in the hearts of the people of the community at the time they are committed. In fact, nobody usually has knowledge of their commission until after the fact. The offenses discussed thus far in this chapter differ in the sense that they are committed in public view and under such circumstances as to make the citizenry apprehensive of trouble. The offenses of breach of the peace, disturbing the peace, and disorderly conduct are very general and broad offenses designed to cover these types of situations not otherwise covered by statutes in a particular jurisdiction. Thus, if a state has no specific statutes covering affrays, conduct that would constitute an affray would fall within that jurisdiction's breach of the peace laws, and so forth.

We use all three offenses interchangeably here, for there is no real distinction between them. Some statutes may call this conduct a breach of the peace while others term it disturbing the peace or disorderly conduct. The same rule applies to municipal ordinance provisions covering such conduct.

To summarize, any conduct that puts fear in the hearts of the citizenry when committed in public view, and which is not dealt with by any other statute in the jurisdiction, may constitute a breach of the peace.

It is important to note one further ramification of breach of the peace laws. The common law warrantless arrest powers of private citizens and peace officers alike in misdemeanor cases hinged upon whether the misdemeanor committed in the presence of the arresting person constituted breach of the peace. Private citizens and peace officers had identical arrest powers in misdemeanor cases without a warrant at common law. They could make an arrest in misdemeanor cases only if the misdemeanor was committed in their presence and only if it constituted a breach of the peace. Not all misdemeanors constitute a breach of the peace in accordance with the definitions given above. Therefore, arrests could not be made in all cases of misdemeanors committed on view unless a warrant was first obtained. All jurisdictions have enlarged peace officers' authority to arrest without a warrant for misdemeanors committed in their presence. Generally, a peace officer may now arrest for any offense committed in his presence regardless of whether it constitutes a breach of the peace. The same is not necessarily true concerning the arrest powers of a private citizen. There are still many jurisdictions today which prohibit a private citizen from making an arrest without a warrant for a misdemeanor, unless the misdemeanor is committed in his presence and constitutes breach of the peace. For this reason also, it is important to understand the definition of breach of the peace.

20.4 Nuisance

There are many times when a police officer is required to "investigate" cases which he considers to be a nuisance. Usually he is referring here to situations which he thinks are a nuisance to have him investigate. Nevertheless, there are numerous tasks assigned to police agencies not directly considered by many to be police tasks. Every officer has answered, and every future officer will answer, calls in response to a complaint of a lost dog or a cat stuck in a tree, or complaints that the neighbor's air conditioner or radio is too loud. These are minor police problems but they are very real to the people involved and deserve the officer's time and efforts.

All municipal ordinances contain provisions prohibiting the loud playing of radios and televisions between certain nighttime hours. It is likewise prohibited for a tavern or bar to emit excessive noise so as to disturb the tranquillity of the nearby residential neighborhood, and so forth. These are nuisance ordinances and are well within the realm of the enforcement powers of a peace officer. As indicated, many nuisances are specifically covered by statute or ordinance. In addition, many jurisdictions have created separate laws to encompass those conditions not otherwise covered, and have termed them nuisance laws. A nuisance may take one of two forms under civil law which are equally applicable to the "criminal" provisions. A nuisance may be either private or public. This depends on who and how many people the nuisance affects. The distinction will also determine the extent of action that may be taken to abate the nuisance. In the case of a tavern, a warning will usually suffice as "a word to the wise." Sometimes, however, it might be necessary to secure a court order to close the establishment or take other legal action to abate the nuisance.

20.5 Malicious Mischief, Malicious Destruction of Property, Vandalism

Again we have a situation in which three offenses are used interchangeably. There is no real distinction between malicious mischief and malicious destruction of property. Vandalism is sometimes more narrowly construed to include only malicious destruction of property which is considered a treasure or object of art.

The foundation of the offense is that there be some actual damage or destruction to property belonging to someone other than the accused and that the damage or destruction be caused voluntarily, not negligently or accidentally. The offense requires no specific intent but must be committed consciously with a realization of its affect. Malicious mischief may be committed against real or personal property. If John throws paint on Bob's house, he is liable for the offense. If Sam, a high school dropout, throws bricks through the local high school windows, he has committed the offense, and when Archie smashes the windows in the school principal's car, he, too, is criminally liable for malicious mischief.

To constitute the crime, there must be some damage or destruction of the property. The damage need not be great but it must be material, usually requiring some amount of repair.

Malicious mischief was a misdemeanor at common law and remains so in some jurisdictions today. There are many states, however, that now recognize, by statute, that the malicious mischief may cause a great deal of damage or destruction and have, therefore, graded the offense as either a felony or misdemeanor, depending on the type of property damaged or destroyed, the method by which the damage or destruction is done, and the extent of the damage or destruction.

20.6   Trespass of Real Property

The word trespass is used throughout the law to represent a variety of legal conditions. In its general usage, trespass implies unauthorized violation of the person or property of another. Consequently, assault and battery is a trespass against the person of the victim. The taking of property in a larceny case without permission is a trespass, and so forth. In this section, we are concerned only with trespass as it applies to setting foot on the real property of another without permission.

Trespass is universally recognized as a civil wrong for which a tort action may be brought. The civil action in no way involves the state as a party. The only participation of the state in civil cases is to provide the forum in which the parties may litigate their problems to a successful and, hopefully, just conclusion.

Most jurisdictions also provide that trespass onto the real property of another may be a criminal offense. The seriousness of the offense will depend on the circumstances surrounding the trespass, including the manner in which the trespass occurs and what the trespasser does after he enters the land of another without authorization.

As a general rule, one who enters the land of another either intentionally or otherwise, and does nothing more, is not subject to criminal liability for trespass. Most jurisdictions require that to complete the offense, the trespasser must first be advised that he is unwelcome or advised that he is forbidden to enter the property before trespass may be charged. Statutes taking this position are generally referred to as trespass-after-warning laws. In specific instances, when a trespasser enters the land of another to engage in hunting or fishing without the permission of the owner, he may not be charged with trespass unless the owner has posted signs in a number of conspicuous places around the enclosure advising against trespassing. It is usually further required that such signs be posted for a certain time before any change in a previous custom of allowing people to enter is made. A typical statute of this type may read as follows: "Six days' notice by poster to be posted in at least four different and conspicuous places around the enclosure shall be given by parties wishing to avail themselves of the benefit of this section" (referring to the provisions making trespass to hunt or fish a violation).

The grade of the offense and the severity of punishment for trespass will vary from state to state and often from case to case. Depending on the types of activities the trespasser engages in after entering the land, his crime may be a misdemeanor of the most minor nature or may be punishable as a felony deserving a long prison sentence.

Beside the cases mentioned in the preceding paragraph, trespass may involve acts such as tearing down fences, cutting or carrying away timber, severing and taking other property which is part of the real estate, or picking vegetables, flowers, or fruit. Each state legislates its own punishment for acts such as these. A word of caution is in order at this point. If the act the trespasser commits after his entry on the land would constitute any other crime such as larceny, that crime would be chargeable instead of trespass. But as in the case of hunting or fishing after trespassing on another's property, no other separate and distinct offense would be chargeable. If another offense such as larceny is committed along with the trespass, the former is the proper charge if it can be proved. Trespass becomes a lesser included offense of the larceny.

20.7 Vagrancy

In Section 4.3, vagrancy was discussed in relation to its character as a status or an act. There are authorities in the criminal law field who would disagree with our conclusion on that point, but to go into detail at this juncture would be to dwell on the theoretical. Whichever view the reader chooses to accept, it is agreed that vagrancy is an offense punishable by the statutes of most jurisdictions.

Vagrancy, where it exists, is generally a misdemeanor and encompasses many and varying forms of conduct. Because of the breadth of these laws, vagrancy statutes have often been attacked as being unconstitutional, basically on the grounds of the "void for vagueness" doctrine of constitutional law. Nevertheless, many courts have continually upheld the validity of vagrancy laws. The supreme test of constitutionality of these provisions has not yet reached the high court of the land, but a federal district court has ruled a Florida vagrancy statute unconstitutional. This decision will probably call for a Supreme Court pronouncement.

The prime basis on which the existence of vagrancy statutes hinge is founded in theories of crime prevention rather than crime repression. Vagrancy is, and may be used as, a tool by law enforcement officers to prevent the commission of serious offenses. It is believed that removing the vagrant from the streets reduces the opportunity to commit crime. Of course, this supposition rests on the premise that it is the vagrant who will commit the more serious offenses. If this justification is true, as has been indicated time after time by the courts, it is well for the reader to recognize that the people, the legislature, and the courts are placing an enormous burden and an exceptional amount of power in the hands of police officers. In no other areas of either substantive or procedural criminal law is such unrestricted discretion given to the police. Nevertheless, in order to retain the authority to arrest for vagrancy, police officers must not use or abuse the statutes indiscriminately. Even though there are a large number of acts or conditions that are incorporated within any particular vagrancy statute, the courts have said that these provisions are specific enough to allow people to understand the provisions of the statutes and reasonably to conform their conduct to the requirements of the law. Therefore, by implication, if not by express mandate, the offense must be capable of being proved by the arresting officer and prosecutor. If the vagrancy laws are used as a catch-all or for harassment, law enforcement officers may find themselves without this authority.

To illustrate the diversity of conduct or status contained in the vagrancy laws, a typical statute may read like this: "Rogues and vagabonds, idle or dissolute persons who go about begging, common gamblers, persons who use juggling or unlawful games or plays, common pipers or fiddlers, common drunkards, common night walkers, thieves, pilferers, traders in stolen property, lewd, wanton and lascivious persons, keepers of gambling places, common brawlers, persons who neglect their calling or employment, or are without reasonable continuous employment or regular income and who have not sufficient property to sustain them, and misspend what they earn without providing for themselves or the support of their families, persons wandering or strolling around from place to place without any lawful purpose or object, habitual loafers, idle and disorderly persons, neglecting all lawful business and habitually spending their time by frequenting houses of prostitution or gaming houses, persons able to work but habitually living upon the earnings of their wives or minor children, and all able bodied male persons over the age of eighteen years who are without visible means of support and remain in idleness, shall be deemed vagrants."

20.8   Gambling and Related Offenses

The common law did not recognize gambling as an offense against society. About the only way one could get in trouble by gambling was by conducting himself in such a manner that his conduct constituted a public nuisance. This possibility exists in many states today.

Thus, unless a state has, by its constitution or statutes, declared gambling illegal, it is legal. Most states do prohibit gambling or some aspect of it. These states have declared that gambling is against public welfare and they use the police power to prohibit it.

A.   State Authorized Gambling

A number of states permit gambling under certain circumstances and under certain conditions. This is often referred to as legalized gambling. Some states, for example, permit highly regulated betting at race tracks but only at the tracks through the parimutuel system. Betting on the same races outside the system through a bookmaker is illegal in these same states.

Some states permit limited gambling at certain religious, charitable, or public events, such as at fairs. Even at these places, the types of games and the amount at stake or duration of the games is regulated.

A few states which prohibit gambling of all types exempt the "weekly" private poker or other game at a private house as long as it is unconnected with organized crime and is not conducted so as to constitute a public nuisance.

Those states which permit gambling, either in a limited form such as a parimutuel betting or in all forms as is done in Nevada, require that any person conducting such a gambling operation be licensed by the state and adhere to state regulations. Conduct of a gambling operation outside the statute will render the operator chargeable for illegal gambling.

B.   Illegal Lotteries

One form of gambling often prohibited by statutes is the lottery. There are three ingredients to a lottery. They are a chance, a prize, and a consideration paid for a chance at the prize. If any one of these is missing, there is no illegal lottery.

"No purchase required" is a term we have all seen with regard to national advertising of certain companies' big giveaways. If this were not the case, if one had to purchase oil or gas products to get a chance at the prize offered by the oil company, it would be a lottery and be prohibited in most states because it would require the payment of something of some value for the chance at the prize.

Game programs that we see on television are not lotteries because the consideration element is lacking.

The element of chance looks to a fortuitous result, a result not of skill or fixed rule following but merely "luck." If the skill of the participant is the real determining factor in the outcome of the contest or game, then it is no lottery. Perhaps the best example of the game of chance is the chain letter. Each person contacted is told not to break the chain but to send the item (money, golf balls, or whatever), write letters, and maybe "good fortune will befall you as it has so many others." The person gives up a consideration for a chance at an undetermined prize.

Another most prevalent form of lottery is the numbers racket or "bolita" operation which has for so many years been connected with organized crime. The participant purchases a number (the consideration) in the hope (the chance) that his number will be drawn to receive the big money (the prize).

States have taken measures to prevent lotteries by making it illegal to advertise lotteries, or for a person to have in his possession or under his control lottery materials, records, and tickets, or to maintain a place where a lottery operation is conducted.

The federal government prohibits the use of the mails for the purpose of conducting a lottery or for transporting records, lists, number slips, and the rest of the paraphernalia through the mails.

A few states, both now and in the past, have a state lottery for the purpose of raising state revenues.

C. Illegal Gambling Houses

A number of states, by statute, make it a crime to maintain or keep a gambling (gaming) house. In order for the crime to be chargeable there has to be more than one incidence of gambling, but none of the statutes set forth a particular length of time that the gambling house must be in operation.

It is not essential that the gambling house be open to the general public. Usually it is enough if the house is maintained for a certain restricted clientele, which includes members of an organization and their invited friends. The gambling house can be hidden. It does not have to be open to the view of the public.

The type of building is unimportant. As a matter of fact, the entire building does not have to be devoted to gambling. It could be a back room in a restaurant or drugstore, for instance. It could be a spare room in a private house, hotel, or motel. Legitimate activities could be, and usually are, conducted simultaneously with the illegitimate gambling operation.

Owners, employees, and others who benefit from the operation of a gambling house may be prosecuted as keepers. This is true whether there is active participation or tacit approval of the use of one's facilities.

One of the main questions is whether the gambling that goes on in a private home is subject to the gambling laws of the state. There are at least three positions taken by state statutes. The first is that all gambling is prohibited no matter where it is carried on. The second exempts gambling in private homes. The third type permits it in private homes as long as the home is not commonly used for gambling purposes. It is essential to be thoroughly familiar with the local statutes and ordinances. Even in a state where the statute allows gambling in private residences, if a residence becomes a public place then the gambling that goes on there may be stopped and the participants arrested. Thus, there is a distinction between commercial or organized gambling and occasional gambling. One state prohibits gambling in all places, but provides a lesser fine for gambling in the private home.

D. Related Enforcement Problems

Perhaps here as in no other area does the question of selective law enforcement come up. There is no possibility of full enforcement of all criminal laws. Human resources and funds are not available. Additionally, many people would prefer law enforcement officers to stay with major crimes, such as homicide, robbery, and burglary, and leave the vices alone. Yet, too often the vices are the breeding grounds for the so-called major crimes. This puts law enforcement on the oft-quoted horns of a dilemma. Some compromise is usually reached. Law enforcement often seeks only to prevent organized crime efforts in the area of gambling, while looking the other way when "locals" are involved in an occasional way. Likewise, law enforcement officers tend to enforce against groups whose gambling activities spawn crimes of violence and crimes against property while not touching the penny-ante bridge clubs. There are those who suggest that law enforcement should concentrate only on flagrant public gambling and leave the private gambling alone. Is this sound? What problems does it create? What is your position as a student?

These questions are moot in a few states where the statute provides a penalty for neglect of duty with regard to gambling laws. In these states no discretion is left to law enforcement officials. They must enforce the law. However, the prosecutor's discretion is left intact and he can take a *nolle prosequi* (refuse further prosecution), or fail to seek an indictment, or issue an information. This can only frustrate law enforcement officials.

The problems of discriminatory enforcement were brought to light in one California case. In *People* v. *Harris,* 182 Cal. App. 2d 837, 5 Cal. Rep. 852 (1960), the trial judge refused to allow statistical evidence showing that in two years over 350 blacks were arrested for gambling and only 25 whites were arrested on like charges, and that in one year all those arrested for gambling were black. He also refused evidence that proved there were existing white gambling clubs where no arrests were made and that the chief of police belonged to one of them. Finally, he would not allow police policy to be introduced that only black areas were to be "prowled" for gambling activities. The appellate court reversed the trial court and sent the case back for retrial. Thus, discriminatory law enforcement may be used as a defense, at least in California. It has been successful in civil cases in federal court under § 1983 of the Civil Rights Act.

Questions for Discussion

1. John Builder, president of the Builder Land Developing Corporation, has opened a subdivision in a suburban area of Big City. John and his public relations firm decide to kick off the sales of property in the subdivision with a very attractive offer. Everyone who buys a piece of property will have the recording number of his deed written on a piece of paper and placed in a fishbowl. After all the property in the subdivision is sold, a drawing will be held and the person whose deed number is drawn will have his mortgage paid off, or, if he paid cash for his property, his purchase price will be refunded. Builder puts the plan into effect, sells his first lot, and places the first number in the fishbowl. Has Builder committed any crimes?

2. Jay Hanson is shopping in his local department store. While walking down an aisle in the store, Jay observes a man shoplifting merchandise. The shoplifter was taking a two-dollar imitation ruby ring. May Jay, as a private citizen, arrest the shoplifter?

Chapter 21

ORGANIZED CRIME

21.0   Background: The Threat to a Free Society

Every law enforcement officer should read the Task Force Report: Organized Crime as written by the President's Commission on Law Enforcement and Administration of Justice in 1967. As the report states the "core of organized crime activity is the supplying of illegal goods and services . . . to countless numbers of citizen customers." However, organized crime even gets into the legitimate areas, such as business and labor unions. Achieving its ends requires pressure, force, and the corruption of public officials. The influence of organized crime can cause prices to rise. But, it is not the direct effect on prices that causes so much worry. The accumulation of wealth by organized crime means that it can be a "strong motive for murder" and may "corrupt public officials." By avoiding taxes, organized crime causes each taxpayer to pay more than he should.

Too often the public is indifferent. Most people do not know the extent to which organized crime affects their daily lives.

The principal activities of organized crime are gambling, loan sharking, narcotics, labor racketeering, and infiltration of business. Prostitution and bootlegging are no longer the mainstays of organized crime's illicit incomes.

Although an estimate, legal betting on horse races only grosses $5 billion a year, while illicit betting taps $20 billion with a profit of nearly $7 billion a year to organized crime.

The second largest source of income for organized crime is loan sharking. Loan sharking is the lending of money at interest rates greater than the law allows. The Task Force found that the average loan is 20 percent a week, although it can run as high as 150 percent a week. The profit here has been estimated in the multibillion dollar range.

The third source of income is the distribution of narcotics. Most of the activity here is restricted to the importing and first-level whole-sale distribution. The lesser wholesale transactions and street transactions are left to independents. In 1967 the heroin trade alone grossed $350 million with a $21 million profit to organized crime.

A "legitimate business" the report says, allows the acquisition of "respectability." The Illinois Crime Commission said, "There is a dis-turbing lack of interest on the part of some legitimate business concerns regarding the identity of the persons with whom they deal. This lacka-daisical attitude is conducive to the perpetration of frauds and the in-filtration and subversion of legitimate businesses by the organized crimi-nal element." A 1957 meeting in New York state by 75 racket leaders found that 9 were in the building industry, 10 owned grocery stores, 17 owned bars and restaurants, 16 were in the garment industry, and so on. One criminal syndicate owned over $300 million in real estate invest-ments.

There are four ways for organized crime to get into existing busi-nesses. It invests hidden illicit profits. It accepts business interests in pay-ment of the owner's gambling debts. Usurious loans are foreclosed. Or it uses various forms of extortion.

Organized crime in labor can prevent unionization in some in-dustries. It can steal from union funds. It can extort money from business through the use of possible labor strife. Finally, it can use union funds for syndicate business ventures.

That organized crime is everywhere is no exaggeration. However, it is most firmly entrenched in the major population areas.

Perhaps the most vile of all the activities carried on by organized crime is the corruption of public officials. Organized crime is currently directing its efforts to corrupt law enforcement at the chief or middle supervisory level. Who will investigate the investigators? Even more effective is the effort at corrupting the political leaders who "tied the hands of the police."

Efforts to eradicate organized crime have been erratic. Although there were some federal, local, and state efforts with special units, they were too few, too widespread, and too uncoordinated. The major reasons often given for lack of success are: 1) difficulties in obtaining proof; 2) lack of resources; 3) lack of coordination; 4) failure to develop strategic intelligence; 5) failure to use available sanctions; and 6) lack of public and political commitment. Thus, the President's Commission found that, "Law enforcement's way of fighting organized crime has been primitive compared to organized crime's way of operating."

This led the Commission to recommend several policies for legislation and action. The proposals covered wiretapping, grand juries, immunity, sentencing, and the protection of witnesses. Additionally they recommended that each state attorney general create a special organized unit in his office. Police departments in every major city were urged to have special intelligence units. Local prosecutor's offices were to seek manpower for organized crime units.

This same Commission also recommended that the federal government create a central computerized office into which each agency would feed all of its organized crime intelligence. This type of legislation is pending and is very controversial. The major objection to the bill is balancing the right of privacy against the need for society to protect itself from criminal activity.

From these recommendations have come some major legislation. The prime pieces of legislation already enacted specifically targeting organized crime for purposes of this chapter are the Organized Crime Control Act of 1970 and the Extortionate Credit Transactions Act. The balance of this chapter will deal with these acts.

21.1   The Organized Crime Control Act of 1970

The Organized Crime Control Act of 1970 became law on October 15 of that year as Public Law 91–452 and is found in 84 Statutes at Large page 922. It amended several sections of Title 18 of the United States Code. The major portions of this Act are reproduced here. The next section of this chapter will deal with an analysis of the Act and its purposes as seen by the Congress of the United States.

An Act relating to the control of organized crime in the United States. *Be it enacted by the Senate and House of Representatives of the United States of America in Congress assembled, That:*
This Act may be cited as the "Organized Crime Control Act of 1970."

STATEMENT OF FINDINGS AND PURPOSE

The Congress finds that (1) organized crime in the United States is a highly sophisticated, diversified, and widespread activity that annually drains billions of dollars from America's economy by unlawful conduct and the illegal use of force, fraud, and corruption; (2) organized crime derives a major portion of its power through money obtained from such illegal endeavors as syndicated gambling, loan sharking, the theft and fencing of property, the importation and distribution of narcotics and other dangerous drugs, and other forms of social exploitation; (3) this money and power are increasingly used to infiltrate and corrupt legitimate business and labor unions and to subvert and corrupt our democratic processes; (4) organized crime activities in the United States weaken the stability of the Nation's economic system, harm innocent investors and competing organizations, interfere with free competition, seriously burden interstate and foreign commerce, threaten the domestic security, and undermine the general welfare of the Nation and its citizens; and (5) organized crime continues to grow because of defects in the evidence-gathering process of the law inhibiting the development of the legally admissible evidence necessary to bring criminal and other sanctions or remedies to bear on the unlawful activities of those engaged in organized crime and because the sanctions and remedies available to the Government are unnecessarily limited in scope and impact.

It is the purpose of this Act to seek the eradication of organized crime in the United States by strengthening the legal tools in the evidence-gathering process, by establishing new penal prohibitions, and by providing enhanced sanctions and new remedies to deal with the unlawful activities of those engaged in organized crime.

TITLE I—SPECIAL GRAND JURY

Sec. 101. (a) Title 18, United States Code,[34] is amended by adding immediately after chapter 215 the following new chapter:

"Chapter 216.—SPECIAL GRAND JURY

"Sec.
"3331. Summoning and term.
"3332. Powers and duties.
"3333. Reports.
"3334. General provisions.

"§ 3331. Summoning and term

"(a) In addition to such other grand juries as shall be called from time to time, each district court which is located in a judicial district containing more than four million inhabitants or in which the Attorney General, the Deputy Attorney General, or any designated Assistant Attorney General, certifies in writing to the chief judge of the district that in his judgment a special grand jury is necessary because of criminal activity in the district shall order a special grand jury to be summoned at least once in each period of eighteen months unless another special grand jury is then serving. The grand jury shall serve for a term of eighteen months unless an order for its discharge is entered earlier by the court upon a determination of the grand jury by majority vote that its business has been completed. If, at the end of such term or any extension thereof, the district court determines the business of the grand jury has not been completed, the court may enter an order extending such term for an additional period of six months. No special grand jury term so extended shall exceed thirty-six months, except as provided in subsection (e) of section 3333 of this chapter.

"(b) If a district court within any judicial circuit fails to extend the term of a special grand jury or enters an order for the discharge of such grand jury before such grand jury determines that it has completed its business, the grand jury, upon the affirmative vote of a majority of its members, may apply to the chief judge of the circuit for an order for the continuance of the term of the grand jury. Upon the making of such an application by the grand jury, the term thereof shall continue until the entry upon such application by the chief judge of the circuit of an appropriate order. No special grand jury term so extended shall exceed thirty-six months, except as provided in subsection (e) of section 3333 of this chapter.

"§ 3332. Powers and duties

"(a) It shall be the duty of each such grand jury impaneled within any judicial district to inquire into offenses against the criminal laws of the United States alleged to have been committed within that district. Such alleged offenses may be brought to the attention of the grand jury by the court or by any attorney appearing on behalf of the United States for the presentation of evidence. Any such attorney receiving information concerning such an alleged offense from any other person shall, if requested by such other person, inform the grand jury of such alleged offense, the identity of such other person, and such attorney's action or recommendation.

"(b) Whenever the district court determines that the volume of business of the special grand jury exceeds the capacity of the grand jury to discharge its obligations, the district court may order an additional special grand jury for that district to be impaneled.

"§ 3333.   Reports

"(a) A special grand jury impaneled by any district court, with the concurrence of a majority of its members, may, upon completion of its original term, or each extension thereof, submit to the court a report—

"(1) concerning noncriminal misconduct, malfeasance, or misfeasance in office involving organized criminal activity by an appointed public officer or employee as the basis for a recommendation of removal or disciplinary action; or

"(2) regarding organized crime conditions in the district.

"(b) The court to which such report is submitted shall examine it and the minutes of the special grand jury and, except as otherwise provided in subsections (c) and (d) of this section, shall make an order accepting and filing such report as a public record only if the court is satisfied that it complies with the provisions of subsection (a) of this section and that—

"(1) the report is based upon facts revealed in the course of an investigation authorized by subsection (a) of section 3332 and is supported by the preponderance of the evidence; and

"(2) when the report is submitted pursuant to paragraph (1) of subsection (a) of this section, each person named therein and any reasonable number of witnesses in his behalf as designated by him to the foreman of the grand jury were afforded an opportunity to testify before the grand jury prior to the filing of such report, and when the report is submitted pursuant to paragraph (2) of subsection (a) of this section, it is not critical of an identified person.

"(c) (1) An order accepting a report pursuant to paragraph (1) of subsection (a) of this section and the report shall be sealed by the court and shall not be filed as a public record or be subject to subpena or otherwise made public (i) until at least thirty-one days after a copy of the order and report are served upon each public officer or employee named therein and an answer has been filed or the time for filing an answer has expired, or (ii) if an appeal is taken, until all rights of review of the public officer or employee named therein have expired or terminated in an order accepting the report. No order accepting a report pursuant to paragraph (1) of subsection (a) of this section shall be entered until thirty days after the delivery of such report to the public officer or body pursuant to paragraph (3) of subsection (c) of this section. The court may issue such orders as it shall deem appropriate to prevent unauthorized publication of a report. Unauthorized publication may be punished as contempt of the court.

"(2) Such public officer or employee may file with the clerk a verified answer to such a report not later than twenty days after service of the order and report upon him. Upon a showing of good cause, the court may grant such public officer or employee an extension of time within which to file such answer and may authorize such limited publication of the report as may be necessary to prepare such answer. Such an answer shall plainly and concisely state the facts and law constituting the defense of the public officer or employee to the charges in said report, and, except for those parts thereof which the court determines to have been inserted scandalously, prejudiciously, or unnecessarily, such answer shall become an appendix to the report.

"(3) Upon the expiration of the time set forth in paragraph (1) of subsection (c) of this section, the United States attorney shall deliver a true copy of such report, and the appendix, if any, for appropriate action to each public officer or body having jurisdiction, responsibility, or authority over each public officer or employee named in the report.

"(d) Upon the submission of a report pursuant to subsection (a) of this section, if the court finds that the filing of such report as a public record may prejudice fair consideration of a pending criminal matter, it shall order such report sealed and such report shall not be subject to subpena or public inspection during the pendency of such criminal matter, except upon order of the court.

"(e) Whenever the court to which a report is submitted pursuant to paragraph (1) of subsection (a) of this section is not satisfied that the report complies with the provisions of subsection (b) of this section, it may direct that additional testimony be taken before the same grand jury, or it shall make an order sealing such report, and it shall not be filed as a public record or be subject to subpena or otherwise made public until the provisions of subsection (b) of this section are met. A special grand jury term may be extended by the district court beyond thirty-six months in order that such additional testimony may be taken or the provisions of subsection (b) of this section may be met.

"(f) As used in this section, 'public officer or employee' means any officer or employee of the United States, any State, the District of Columbia, the Commonwealth of Puerto Rico, any territory or possession of the United States, or any political subdivision, or any department, agency, or instrumentality thereof."

§ 3334. Omitted—General amendatory provisions.

TITLE II—GENERAL IMMUNITY

Sec. 201. (a) Title 18, United States Code, is amended by adding immediately after part IV the following new part: [35]

"PART V.—IMMUNITY OF WITNESSES

"Sec.

"§ 6001. Definitions

"As used in this part—

"(1) 'agency of the United States' means any executive department as defined in section 101 of title 5, United States Code, a military department as defined in section 102 of title 5, United States Code, the Atomic Energy Commission, the China Trade Act registrar appointed under 53 Stat. 1432 (15 U.S.C. sec. 143), the Civil Aeronautics Board, the Federal Communications Commission, the Federal Deposit Insurance Corporation, the Federal Maritime Commission, the Federal Power Commission, the Federal Trade Commission, the Interstate Commerce Commission, the National Labor Relations Board, the National Transportation Safety Board, the Railroad Retirement Board, an arbitration board established under 48 Stat. 1193 (45 U.S.C. sec. 157), the Securities and Exchange Commission, the Subversive Activities Control Board, or a board established under 49 Stat. 31 (15 U.S.C. sec. 715d);

"(2) 'other information' includes any book, paper, document, record, recording, or other material;

"(3) 'proceeding before an agency of the United States' means any proceeding before such an agency with respect to which it is authorized to issue subpenas and to take testimony or receive other information from witnesses under oath; and

"(4) 'court of the United States' means any of the following courts: the Supreme Court of the United States, a United States court of appeals, a United States district court established under chapter 5, title 28, United States Code, the District of Columbia Court of Appeals, the Superior Court of the District of Columbia, the District Court of Guam, the District Court of the Virgin Islands, the United States Court of Claims, the United States Court of Customs and Patent Appeals, the Tax Court of the United States, the Customs Court, and the Court of Military Appeals.

"§ 6002. Immunity generally

"Whenever a witness refuses, on the basis of his privilege against self-incrimination, to testify or provide other information in a proceeding before or ancillary to—
"(1) a court or grand jury of the United States,
"(2) an agency of the United States, or
"(3) either House of Congress, a joint committee of the two Houses, or a committee or a subcommittee of either House,

and the person presiding over the proceeding communicates to the witness an order issued under this part, the witness may not refuse to comply with the order on the basis of his privilege against self-incrimination; but no testimony or other information compelled under the order (or any information directly or indirectly derived from such testimony or other information) may be used against the witness in any criminal case, except a prosecution for perjury, giving a false statement, or otherwise failing to comply with the order.

"§ 6003. Court and grand jury proceedings

"(a) In the case of any individual who has been or may be called to testify or provide other information at any proceeding before or ancillary to a court of the United States or a grand jury of the United States, the United States district court for the judicial district in which the proceeding is or may be held shall issue, in accordance with subsection (b) of this section, upon the request of the United States attorney for such district, an order requiring such individual to give testimony or provide other information which he refuses to give or provide on the basis of his privilege against self-incrimination, such order to become effective as provided in section 6002 of this part.

"(b) A United States attorney may, with the approval of the Attorney General, the Deputy Attorney General, or any designated Assistant Attorney General, request an order under subsection (a) of this section when in his judgment—
"(1) the testimony or other information from such individual may be necessary to the public interest; and
"(2) such individual has refused or is likely to refuse to testify or provide other information on the basis of his privilege against self-incrimination.

"§ 6004. Certain administrative proceedings

"(a) In the case of any individual who has been or who may be called to testify or provide other information at any proceeding before an agency of the United States, the agency may, with the approval of the Attorney General, issue, in accordance with subsection (b) of this section, an order requiring the individual to give testimony or provide other information which he refuses to give or provide on the basis of his privilege against self-incrimination, such order to become effective as provided in section 6002 of this part.

"(b) An agency of the United States may issue an order under subsection (a) of this section only if in its judgment—

"(1) the testimony or other information from such individual may be necessary to the public interest; and

"(2) such individual has refused or is likely to refuse to testify or provide other information on the basis of his privilege against self-incrimination.

"§ 6005. Congressional proceedings

"(a) In the case of any individual who has been or may be called to testify or provide other information at any proceeding before either House of Congress, or any committee, or any subcommittee of either House, or any joint committee of the two Houses, a United States district court shall issue, in accordance with subsection (b) of this section, upon the request of a duly authorized representative of the House of Congress or the committee concerned, an order requiring such individual to give testimony or provide other information which he refuses to give or provide on the basis of his privilege against self-incrimination, such order to become effective as provided in section 6002 of this part.

"(b) Before issuing an order under subsection (a) of this section, a United States district court shall find that—

"(1) in the case of a proceeding before either House of Congress, the request for such an order has been approved by an affirmative vote of a majority of the Members present of that House;

"(2) in the case of a proceeding before a committee or a subcommittee of either House of Congress or a joint committee of both Houses, the request for such an order has been approved by an affirmative vote of two-thirds of the members of the full committee; and

"(3) ten days or more prior to the day on which the request for such an order was made, the Attorney General was served with notice of an intention to request the order

"(c) Upon application of the Attorney General, the United States district court shall defer the issuance of any order under subsection (a) of this section for such period, not longer than twenty days from the date of the request for such order, as the Attorney General may specify."

TITLE III—RECALCITRANT WITNESSES

Sec. 301. (a) Chapter 119, title 28, United States Code,[87] is amended by adding at the end thereof the following new section:

"§ 1826. Recalcitrant witnesses

"(a) Whenever a witness in any proceeding before or ancillary to any court or grand jury of the United States refuses without just cause shown to comply with an order of the court to testify or provide other information, including any book, paper, document, record, recording or other material, the court, upon such refusal, or when such refusal is duly brought to its attention, may summarily order his confinement at a suitable place until such time at the witness is willing to give such testimony or provide such information. No period of such confinement shall exceed the life of—

"(1) the court proceeding, or
"(2) the term of the grand jury, including extensions,
before which such refusal to comply with the court order occurred, but in no event shall such confinement exceed eighteen months.

"(b) No person confined pursuant to subsection (a) of this section shall be admitted to bail pending the determination of an appeal taken by him from the order for his confinement if it appears that the appeal is frivolous or taken for delay. Any appeal from an order of confinement under this section shall be disposed of as soon as practicable, but not later than thirty days from the filing of such appeal."

§ 302. Omitted—General amendatory provisions.

TITLE IV—FALSE DECLARATIONS

Sec. 401. (a) Chapter 79, title 18, United States Code,[89] is amended by adding at the end thereof the following new section:

"§ 1623. False declarations before grand jury or court

"(a) Whoever under oath in any proceeding before or ancillary to any court or grand jury of the United States knowingly makes any false material declaration or makes or uses any other information, including any book, paper, document, record, recording, or other material, knowing the same to contain any false material declaration, shall be fined not more than $10,000 or imprisoned not more than five years, or both.

"(b) This section is applicable whether the conduct occurred within or without the United States.

"(c) An indictment or information for violation of this section alleging that, in any proceedings before or ancillary to any court or grand jury of the United States, the defendant under oath has knowingly made two or more declarations, which are inconsistent to the degree that one of them is necessarily false, need not specify which declaration is false if—

"(1) each declaration was material to the point in question, and

"(2) each declaration was made within the period of the statute of limitations for the offense charged under this section.

In any prosecution under this section, the falsity of a declaration set forth in the indictment or information shall be established sufficient for conviction by proof that the defendant while under oath made irreconcilably contradictory declarations material to the point in question in any proceeding before or ancillary to any court or grand jury. It shall be a defense to an indictment or information made pursuant to the first sentence of this subsection that the defendant at the time he made each declaration believed the declaration was true.

"(d) Where, in the same continuous court or grand jury proceeding in which a declaration is made, the person making the declaration admits such declaration to be false, such admission shall bar prosecution under this section if, at the time the admission is made, the declaration has not substantially affected the proceeding, or it has not become manifest that such falsity has been or will be exposed.

"(e) Proof beyond a reasonable doubt under this section is sufficient for conviction. It shall not be necessary that such proof be made by any particular number of witnesses or by documentary or other type of evidence."

(b) The analysis of chapter 79, title 18, United States Code, is amended by adding at the end thereof the following new item:

"1632. False declarations before grand jury or court."

TITLE V—PROTECTED FACILITIES FOR HOUSING GOVERNMENT WITNESSES

Sec. 501.   The Attorney General of the United States is authorized to provide for the security of Government witnesses, potential Government witnesses, and the families of Government witnesses and potential witnesses in legal proceedings against any person alleged to have participated in an organized criminal activity.

Sec. 502.   The Attorney General of the United States is authorized to rent, purchase, modify, or remodel protected housing facilities and to otherwise offer to provide for the health, safety, and welfare of witnesses and persons intended to be called as Government witnesses, and the families of witnesses and persons intended to be called as Government witnesses in legal proceedings instituted against any person alleged to have participated in an organized criminal activity whenever, in his judgment, testimony from, or a willingness to testify by, such a witness would place his life or person, or the life or person of a member of his family or household, in jeopardy. Any person availing himself of an offer by the Attorney General to use such facilities may continue to use such facilities for as long as the Attorney General determines the jeopardy to his life or person continues.

Sec. 503.   As used in this title, "Government" means the United States, any State, the District of Columbia, the Commonwealth of Puerto Rico, any territory or possession of the United States, any political subdivision, or any department, agency, or instrumentality thereof. The offer of facilities to witnesses may be conditioned by the Attorney General upon reimbursement in whole or in part to the United States by any State or any political subdivision, or any department, agency, or instrumentality thereof of the cost of maintaining and protecting such witnesses.

Sec. 504.   There is hereby authorized to be appropriated from time to time such funds as are necessary to carry out the provisions of this title.

TITLE VI, § 601.   Omitted—Procedural-deals with depositions.

TITLE VII §§ 701 and 702.   Omitted—Procedural-litigation concerning sources of evidence.

TITLE VIII—SYNDICATED GAMBLING

PART A—SPECIAL FINDINGS

Sec. 801. The Congress finds that illegal gambling involves widespread use of, and has an effect upon, interstate commerce and the facilities thereof.

PART B—OBSTRUCTION OF STATE OR LOCAL LAW ENFORCEMENT

Sec. 802. (a) Chapter 73, title 18, United States Code,[92] is amended by adding at the end thereof the following new section:

"§ 1511. Obstruction of State or local law enforcement

"(a) It shall be unlawful for two or more persons to conspire to obstruct the enforcement of the criminal laws of a State or political subdivision thereof, with the intent to facilitate an illegal gambling business if—

"(1) one or more of such persons does any act to effect the object of such a conspiracy;

"(2) one or more of such persons is an official or employee, elected, appointed, or otherwise, of such State or political subdivision; and

"(3) one or more of such persons conducts, finances, manages, supervises, directs, or owns all or part of an illegal gambling business.

"(b) As used in this section—

"(1) 'illegal grambling business' means a gambling business which—

"(i) is a violation of the law of a State or political subdivision in which it is conducted;

"(ii) involves five or more persons who conduct, finance, manage, supervise, direct, or own all or part of such business; and

"(iii) has been or remains in substantially continuous operations for a period in excess of thirty days or has a gross revenue of $2,000 in any single day.

"(2) 'gambling' includes but is not limited to pool-selling, bookmaking, maintaining slot machines, roulette wheels, or dice tables, and conducting lotteries, policy, bolita or numbers games, or selling chances therein.

"(3) 'State' means any State of the United States, the District of Columbia, the Commonwealth of Puerto Rico, and any territory or possession of the United States.

"(c) This section shall not apply to any bingo game, lottery, or similar game of chance conducted by an organization exempt from tax under paragraph (3) of subsection (c) of section 501 of the Internal Revenue Code of 1954, as amended, if no part of the gross receipts derived from such activity inures to the benefit of any private shareholder, member, or employee of such organization, except as compensation for actual expenses incurred by him in the conduct of such activity.

"(d) Whoever violates this section shall be punished by a fine of not more than $20,000 or imprisonment for not more than five years, or both."

(b) The analysis of chapter 73, title 18, United States Code, is amended by adding at the end thereof the following new item:
"1511.   Obstruction of State or local law enforcement."

PART C—ILLEGAL GAMBLING BUSINESS

Sec. 803.   (a) Chapter 95, title 18, United States Code,[93] is amended by adding at the end thereof the following new section:

"§ 1955.   Prohibition of illegal gambling businesses

"(a) Whoever conducts, finances, manages, supervises, directs, or owns all or part of an illegal gambling business shall be fined not more than $20,000 or imprisoned not more than five years, or both.

"(b) As used in this section—

"(1) 'illegal gambling business' means a gambling business which—

"(i) is a violation of the law of a State or political subdivision in which it is conducted;

"(ii) involves five or more persons who conduct, finance, manage, supervise, direct, or own all or part of such business; and "(iii) has been or remains in substantially continuous operation for a period in excess of thirty days or has a gross revenue of $2,000 in any single day.

"(2) 'gambling' includes but is not limited to pool-selling, bookmaking, maintaining slot machines, roulette wheels or dice tables, and conducting lotteries, policy, bolita or numbers games, or selling chances therein.

"(3) 'State' means any State of the United States, the District of Columbia, the Commonwealth of Puerto Rico, and any territory or possession of the United States.

"(c) If five or more persons conduct, finance, manage, supervise, direct, or own all or part of a gambling business and such business operates for two or more successive days, then, for the purpose of obtaining warrants for arrests, interceptions, and other searches and seizures, probable cause that the business receives gross revenue in excess of $2,000 in any single day shall be deemed to have been established.

"(d) Any property, including money, used in violation of the provisions of this section may be seized and forfeited to the United States. All provisions of law relating to the seizure, summary, and judicial forfeiture procedures, and condemnation of vessels, vehicles, merchandise, and baggage for violation of the customs laws, the disposition of such vessels, vehicles, merchandise, and baggage or the proceeds from such sale; the remission or mitigation of such forfeitures; and the compromise of claims and the award of compensation to informers in respect of such forfeitures shall apply to seizures and forfeitures incurred or alleged to have incurred under the provisions of this section, insofar as applicable and not inconsistent with such provisions. Such duties as are imposed upon the collector of customs or any other person in respect to the seizure and forfeiture of vessels, vehicles, merchandise, and baggage under the customs laws shall be performed with respect to seizures and forfeitures of property used or intended for use in violation of this section by such officers, agents, or other persons as may be designated for that purpose by the Attorney General.

"(e) This section shall not apply to any bingo game, lottery, or similar game of chance conducted by an organization exempt from tax under paragraph (3) of subsection (c) of section 501 of the Internal Revenue Code of 1954, as amended, if no part of the gross receipts derived from such activity inures to the benefit of any private shareholder, member, or employee of such organization except as compensation for actual expenses incurred by him in the conduct of such activity."

(b) The analysis of chapter 95, title 18, United States Code, is amended by adding at the end thereof the following new item:

"1955. Prohibition of illegal gambling businesses."

PART D—COMMISSION TO REVIEW NATIONAL
POLICY TOWARD GAMBLING

ESTABLISHMENT

Sec. 804. (a) There is hereby established two years after the effective date of this Act a Commission on the Review of the National Policy Toward Gambling.

(b) The Commission shall be composed of fifteen members appointed as follows:

(1) four appointed by the President of the Senate from Members of the Senate, of whom two shall be members of the majority party, and two shall be members of the minority party;

(2) four appointed by the Speaker of the House of Representatives from Members of the House of Representatives, of whom two shall be members of the majority party, and two shall be members of the minority party; and

(3) seven appointed by the President of the United States from persons specially qualified by training and experience to perform the duties of the Commission, none of whom shall be officers of the executive branch of the Government.

(c) The President of the United States shall designate a Chairman from among the members of the Commission. Any vacancy in the Commission shall not affect its powers but shall be filled in the same manner in which the original appointment was made.

(d) Eight members of the Commission shall constitute a quorum.

DUTIES

Sec. 805. (a) It shall be the duty of the Commission to conduct a comprehensive legal and factual study of gambling in the United States and existing Federal, State, and local policy and practices with respect to legal prohibition and taxation of gambling activities and to formulate and propose such changes in those policies and practices as the Commission may deem appropriate. In such study and review the Commission shall—

(1) review the effectiveness of existing practices in law enforcement, judicial administration, and corrections in the United States and in foreign legal jurisdictions for the enforcement of the prohibition and taxation of gambling activities and consider possible alternatives to such practices; and

(2) prepare a study of existing statutes of the United States that

prohibit and tax gambling activities, and such a codification, revision, or repeal thereof as the Commission shall determine to be required to carry into effect such policy and practice changes as it may deem to be necessary or desirable.

(b) The Commission shall make such interim reports as it deems advisable. It shall make a final report of its findings and recommendations to the President of the United States and to the Congress within the four-year period following the establishment of the Commission.

(c) Sixty days after the submission of its final report, the Commission shall cease to exist.

POWERS

Sec. 806. (a) The Commission or any duly authorized subcommittee or member thereof may, for the purpose of carrying out the provisions of this title, hold such hearing, sit and act at such times and places, administer such oaths, and require by subpena or otherwise the attendance and testimony of such witnesses and the production of such books, records, correspondence, memorandums, papers, and documents as the Commission or such subcommittee or member may deem advisable. Any member of the Commission may administer oaths or affirmations to witnesses appearing before the Commission or before such subcommittee or member. Subpenas may be issued under the signature of the Chairman or any duly designated member of the Commission, and may be served by any person designated by the Chairman or such member.

(b) In the case of contumacy or refusal to obey a subpena issued under subsection (a) by any person who resides, is found, or transacts business within the jurisdiction of any district court of the United States, the district court, at the request of the Chairman of the Commission, shall have jurisdiction to issue to such person an order requiring such person to appear before the Commission or a subcommittee or member thereof, there to produce evidence if so ordered, or there to give testimony touching the matter under inquiry. Any failure of any such person to obey any such order of the court may be punished by the court as a contempt thereof.

(c) The Commission shall be "an agency of the United States" under subsection (1), section 6001, title 18, United States Code, for the purpose of granting immunity to witnesses.

(d) Each department, agency, and instrumentality of the executive branch of the Government including independent agencies, is authorized and directed to furnish to the Commission, upon request made by the Chairman, on a reimbursable basis or otherwise, such statistical data, reports, and other information as the Commission deems necessary to carry out its functions under this title. The Chairman is further authorized to call upon the departments, agencies, and other offices of the several States to furnish, on a reimbursable basis or otherwise, such statistical data, reports, and other information as the Commission deems necessary to carry out its functions under this title.

§§807–810. Omitted—General amendatory provisions.

TITLE IX—RACKETEER INFLUENCED AND CORRUPT ORGANIZATIONS

Sec. 901. (a) Title 18, United States Code,[95] is amended by adding immediately after chapter 95 thereof the following new chapter:

"Chapter 96.—RACKETEER INFLUENCED AND CORRUPT ORGANIZATIONS

"Sec.
"1961. Definitions.
"1962. Prohibited racketeering activities.
"1963. Criminal penalties.
"1964. Civil remedies.
"1965. Venue and process.
"1966. Expedition of actions.
"Sec.
"1967. Evidence.
"1968. Civil investigative demand.

"§ 1961. Definitions

"As used in this chapter—
    "(1) 'racketeering activity' means (A) any act or threat involving murder, kidnaping, gambling, arson, robbery, bribery, extortion, or dealing in narcotic or other dangerous drugs, which is chargeable under State law and punishable by imprisonment for more than one year; (B) any act which is indictable under any of the following provisions of title 18, United States Code: Section 201 (relating to bribery), section 224 (relating to sports bribery), sections 471, 472,

and 473 (relating to counterfeiting), section 659 (relating to theft from interstate shipment) if the act indictable under section 659 is felonious, section 664 (relating to embezzlement from pension and welfare funds), sections 891–894 (relating to extortionate credit transactions), section 1084 (relating to the transmission of gambling information), section 1341 (relating to mail fraud), section 1343 (relating to wire fraud), section 1503 (relating to obstruction of justice), section 1510 (relating to obstruction of criminal investigations), section 1511 (relating to the obstruction of State or local law enforcement), section 1951 (relating to interference with commerce, robbery, or extortion), section 1952 (relating to racketeering), section 1953 (relating to interstate transportation of wagering paraphernalia), section 1954 (relating to unlawful welfare fund payments), section 1955 (relating to the prohibition of illegal gambling businesses), sections 2314 and 2315 (relating to interstate transportation of stolen property), sections 2421–24 (relating to white slave traffic), (C) any act which is indictable under title 29, United States Code, section 186 (dealing with restrictions on payments and loans to labor organizations) or section 501(c) (relating to embezzlement from union funds), or (D) any offense involving bankruptcy fraud, fraud in the sale of securities, or the felonious manufacture, importation, receiving, concealment, buying, selling, or otherwise dealing in narcotic or other dangerous drugs, punishable under any law of the United States;

"(2) 'State' means any State of the United States, the District of Columbia, the Commonwealth of Puerto Rico, any territory or possession of the United States, any political subdivision, or any department, agency, or instrumentality thereof;

"(3) 'person' includes any individual or entity capable of holding a legal or beneficial interest in property;

"(4) 'enterprise' includes any individual, partnership, corporation, association, or other legal entity, and any union or group of individuals associated in fact although not a legal entity;

"(5) 'pattern of racketeering activity' requires at least two acts of racketeering activity, one of which occurred after the effective date of this chapter and the last of which occurred within ten years (excluding any period of imprisonment) after the commission of a prior act of racketeering activity;

"(6) 'unlawful debt' means a debt (A) incurred or contracted in gambling activity which was in violation of the law of the United States, a State or political subdivision thereof, or which is unenforceable under State or Federal law in whole or in part as to principal or interest because of the laws relating to usury, and (B) which was incurred in connection with the business of gambling in violation of the law of the United States, a State or political subdivision thereof, or the business of lending money or a thing of value at a rate usurious under State or Federal law, where the usurious rate is at least twice the enforceable rate;

"(7) 'racketeering investigator' means any attorney or investigator so designated by the Attorney General and charged with the duty of enforcing or carrying into effect this chapter;

"(8) 'racketeering investigation' means any inquiry conducted by any racketeering investigator for the purpose of ascertaining whether any person has been involved in any violation of this chapter or of any final order, judgment, or decree of any court of the United States, duly entered in any case or proceeding arising under this chapter;

"(9) 'documentary material' includes any book, paper, document, record, recording, or other material; and

"(10) 'Attorney General' includes the Attorney General of the United States, the Deputy Attorney General of the United States, any Assistant Attorney General of the United States, or any employee of the Department of Justice or any employee of any department or agency of the United States so designated by the Attorney General to carry out the powers conferred on the Attorney General by this chapter. Any department or agency so designated may use in investigations authorized by this chapter either the investigative provisions of this chapter or the investigative power of such department or agency otherwise conferred by law.

"§ 1962. Prohibited activities

"(a) It shall be unlawful for any person who has received any income derived, directly or indirectly, from a pattern of racketeering activity or through collection of an unlawful debt in which such person has participated as a principal within the meaning of section 2, title 18, United States Code, to use or invest, directly or indirectly, any part of such income, or the proceeds of such income, in acquisition of any interest in, or the establishment or operation of, any enterprise which is engaged in, or the activities of which affect, interstate or foreign commerce. A purchase of securities on the open market for purposes of investment, and without the intention of controlling or participating in the control of the issuer, or of assisting another to do so, shall not be unlawful under this subsection if the securities of the issuer held by the purchaser, the members of his immediate family, and his or their accomplices in any pattern or racketeering activity of the collection of an unlawful debt after such purchase do not amount in the aggregate to one percent of the outstanding securities of any one class, and do not confer, either in law or in fact, the power to elect one or more directors of the issuer.

"(b) It shall be unlawful for any person through a pattern of racketeering activity or through collection of an unlawful debt to acquire or maintain, directly or indirectly, any interest in or control of any enterprise which is engaged in, or the activities of which affect, interstate or foreign commerce.

"(c) It shall be unlawful for any person employed by or associated with any enterprise engaged in, or the activities of which affect, interstate or foreign commerce, to conduct or participate, directly or indirectly, in the conduct of such enterprise's affairs through a pattern of racketeering activity or collection of unlawful debt.

"(d) It shall be unlawful for any person to conspire to violate any of the provisions of subsections (a), (b), or (c) of this section.

"§ 1963.   Criminal penalties

"(a) Whoever violates any provision of section 1962 of this chapter shall be fined not more than $25,000 or imprisoned not more than twenty years, or both, and shall forfeit to the United States (1) any interest he has acquired or maintained in violation of section 1962, and (2) any interest in, security of, claim against, or property or contractual right of any kind affording a source of influence over, any enterprise which he has established, operated, controlled, conducted, or participated in the conduct of, in violation of section 1962.

"(b) In any action brought by the United States under this section, the district courts of the United States shall have jurisdiction to enter such restraining orders or prohibitions, or to take such other actions, including, but not limited to, the acceptance of satisfactory performance bonds, in connection with any property or other interest subject to forfeiture under this section, as it shall deem proper.

"(c) Upon conviction of a person under this section, the court shall authorize the Attorney General to seize all property or other interest declared forfeited under this section upon such terms and conditions as the court shall deem proper. If a property right or other interest is not exercisable or transferable for value by the United States, it shall expire, and shall not revert to the convicted person. All provisions of law relating to the disposition of property, or the proceeds from the sale thereof, or the remission or mitigation of forfeitures for violation of the customs laws, and the compromise of claims and the award of compensation to informers in respect of such forfeitures shall apply to forfeitures incurred, or alleged to have been incurred, under the provisions of this section, insofar as applicable and not inconsistent with the provisions hereof. Such duties as are imposed upon the collector of customs or any other person with respect to the disposition of property under the customs laws shall be performed under this chapter by the Attorney General. The United States shall dispose of all such property as soon as commercially feasible making due provision for the rights of innocent persons.

TITLE X—DANGEROUS SPECIAL OFFENDER SENTENCING

Sec. 1001. (a) Chapter 227, title 18, United States Code,[99] is amended by adding at the end thereof the following new sections:

"§ 3575. Increased sentence for dangerous special offenders

"(a) Whenever an attorney charged with the prosecution of a defendant in a court of the United States for an alleged felony committed when the defendant was over the age of twenty-one years has reason to believe that the defendant is a dangerous special offender such attorney, a reasonable time before trial or acceptance by the court of a plea of guilty or nolo contendere, may sign and file with the court, and may amend, a notice (1) specifying that the defendant is a dangerous special offender who upon conviction for such felony is subject to the imposition of a sentence under subsection (b) of this section, and (2) setting out with particularity the reasons why such attorney believes the defendant to be a dangerous special offender. In no case shall the fact that the defendant is alleged to be a dangerous special offender be an issue upon the trial of such felony, be disclosed to the jury, or be disclosed before any plea of guilty or nolo contendere or verdict or finding of guilty to the presiding judge without the consent of the parties. If the court finds that the filing of the notice as a public record may prejudice fair consideration of a pending criminal matter, it may order the notice sealed and the notice shall not be subject to subpena or public inspection during the pendency of such criminal matter, except on order of the court, but shall be subject to inspection by the defendant alleged to be a dangerous special offender and his counsel.

"(b) Upon any plea of guilty or nolo contendere or verdict or finding of guilty of the defendant of such felony, a hearing shall be held, before sentence is imposed, by the court sitting without a jury. The court shall fix a time for the hearing, and notice thereof shall be given to the defendant and the United States at least ten days prior thereto. The court shall permit the United States and counsel for the defendant, or the defendant if he is not represented by counsel, to inspect the presentence report sufficiently prior to the hearing as to afford a reasonable opportunity for verification. In extraordinary cases, the court may withhold material not relevant to a proper sentence, diagnostic opinion which might seriously disrupt a program of rehabilitation, any source of information obtained on a promise of confidentiality, and material previously disclosed in open court. A court withholding all or part of a presentence report shall inform the parties of its action and place in the record the reasons therefor. The court may require parties inspecting all or part of a presentence report to give notice of any part thereof intended to be controverted. In connection with the hearing, the defendant and the United States shall be entitled to assistance of counsel, compulsory process, and cross-examination of such witnesses as appear at the hearing. A duly authenticated copy of a former judgment or commitment shall be prima facie evidence of such former judgment or commitment. If it appears by a preponderance of the information, including information submitted during the trial of such felony and the sentencing hearing and so much of the presentence report as the court relies upon, that the defendant is a dangerous special offender, the court shall sentence the defendant to imprisonment for an appropriate term not to exceed twenty-five years and not disproportionate in severity to the maximum term otherwise authorized by law for such felony. Otherwise it shall sentence the defendant in accordance with the law prescribing penalties for such felony. The court shall place in the record its findings, including an identification of the information relied upon in making such findings, and its reasons for the sentence imposed.

"(c) This section shall not prevent the imposition and execution of a sentence of death or of imprisonment for life or for a term exceeding twenty-five years upon any person convicted of an offense so punishable.

"(d) Notwithstanding any other provision of this section, the court shall not sentence a dangerous special offender to less than any mandatory minimum penalty prescribed by law for such felony. This section shall not be construed as creating any mandatory minimum penalty.

"(e) A defendant is a special offender for purposes of this section if—

"(1) the defendant has previously been convicted in courts of the United States, a State, the District of Columbia, the Commonwealth of Puerto Rico, a territory or possession of the United States, any political subdivision, or any department, agency, or instrumentality thereof for two or more offenses committed on occasions different from one another and from such felony and punishable in such courts by death or imprisonment in excess of one year, for one or more of such convictions the defendant has been imprisoned prior to the commission of such felony, and less than five years have elapsed between the commission of such felony and either the defendant's release, on parole or otherwise, from imprisonment for one such conviction or his commission of the last such previous offense or another offense punishable by death or imprisonment in excess of one year under applicable laws of the United States, a State, the District of Columbia, the Commonwealth of Puerto Rico, a territory or possession of the United States, any political subdivision, or any department, agency or instrumentality thereof; or

"(2) the defendant committed such felony as part of a pattern of conduct which was criminal under applicable laws of any jurisdiction, which constituted a substantial source of his income, and in which he manifested special skill or expertise; or

"(3) such felony was, or the defendant committed such felony in furtherance of, a conspiracy with three or more other persons to engage in a pattern of conduct criminal under applicable laws of any jurisdiction, and the defendant did, or agreed that he would, initiate, organize, plan, finance, direct, manage, or supervise all or part of such conspiracy or conduct, or give or receive a bribe or use force as all or part of such conduct.

A conviction shown on direct or collateral review or at the hearing to be invalid or for which the defendant has been pardoned on the ground of innocence shall be disregarded for purposes of paragraph (1) of this subsection. In support of findings under paragraph (2) of this subsection, it may be shown that the defendant has had in his own name or under his control income or property not explained as derived from a source other than such conduct. For purposes of paragraph (2) of this subsection, a substantial source of income means a source of income which for any period of one year or more exceeds the minimum wage, determined on the basis of a forty-hour week and a fifty-week year, without reference to exceptions, under section 6(a)(1) of the Fair Labor Standards Act of 1938 (52 Stat. 1602, as amended 80 Stat. 838), and as hereafter amended, for an employee engaged in commerce or in the production of goods for commerce, and which for the same period exceeds fifty percent of the defendant's declared adjusted gross income under section 62 of the Internal Revenue Act of 1954 (68A Stat. 17, as amended 83 Stat. 655), and as hereafter amended. For purposes of paragraph (2) of this subsection, special skill or expertise in criminal conduct includes unusual knowledge, judgment or ability, including manual dexterity, facilitating the initiation, organizing, planning, financing, direction, management, supervision, execution or concealment of criminal conduct, the enlistment of accomplices in such conduct, the escape from detection or

apprehension for such conduct, or the disposition of the fruits or proceeds of such conduct. For purposes of paragraphs (2) and (3) of this
subsection, criminal conduct forms a pattern if it embraces criminal acts
that have the same or similar purposes, results, participants, victims, or
methods of commission, or otherwise are interrelated by distinguishing
characteristics and are not isolated events.

"(f) A defendant is dangerous for purposes of this section if a period
of confinement longer than that provided for such felony is required for
the protection of the public from further criminal conduct by the defendant.

"(g) The time for taking an appeal from a conviction for which sentence is imposed after proceedings under this section shall be measured
from imposition of the original sentence.

"§ 3576. Review of sentence

"With respect to the imposition, correction, or reduction of a sentence
after proceedings under section 3575 of this chapter, a review of the
sentence on the record of the sentencing court may be taken by the defendant or the United States to a court of appeals. Any review of the
sentence taken by the United States shall be taken at least five days before expiration of the time for taking a review of the sentence or appeal
of the conviction by the defendant and shall be diligently prosecuted.
The sentencing court may, with or without motion and notice, extend the
time for taking a review of the sentence for a period not to exceed thirty
days from the expiration of the time otherwise prescribed by law. The
court shall not extend the time for taking a review of the sentence
by the United States after the time has expired. A court extending the
time for taking a review of the sentence by the United States shall extend
the time for taking a review of the sentence or appeal of the conviction
by the defendant for the same period. The taking of a review of the sentence by the United States shall be deemed the taking of a review of the
sentence and an appeal of the conviction by the defendant. Review of
the sentence shall include review of whether the procedure employed
was lawful, the findings made were clearly erroneous, or the sentencing
court's discretion was abused. The court of appeals on review of the sentence may, after considering the record, including the entire presentence
report, information submitted during the trial of such felony and the
sentencing hearing, and the findings and reasons of the sentencing court,
affirm the sentence, impose or direct the imposition of any sentence
which the sentencing court could originally have imposed, or remand for
further sentencing proceedings and imposition of sentence, except that a

sentence may be made more severe only on review of the sentence taken by the United States and after hearing. Failure of the United States to take a review of the imposition of the sentence shall, upon review taken by the United States of the correction or reduction of the sentence, foreclose imposition of a sentence more severe than that previously imposed. Any withdrawal or dismissal of review of the sentence taken by the United States shall foreclose imposition of a sentence more severe than that reviewed but shall not otherwise foreclose the review of the sentence or the appeal of the conviction. The court of appeals shall state in writing the reasons for its disposition of the review of the sentence. Any review of the sentence taken by the United States may be dismissed on a showing of abuse of the right of the United States to take such review.

"§ 3577. Use of information for sentencing

"No limitation shall be placed on the information concerning the background, character, and conduct of a person convicted of an offense which a court of the United States may receive and consider for the purpose of imposing an appropriate sentence.

"§ 3578. Conviction records

"(a) The Attorney General of the United States is authorized to establish in the Department of Justice a repository for records of convictions and determinations of the validity of such convictions.

"(b) Upon the conviction thereafter of a defendant in a court of the United States, the District of Columbia, the Commonwealth of Puerto Rico, a territory or possession of the United States, any political subdivision, or any department, agency, or instrumentality thereof for an offense punishable in such court by death or imprisonment in excess of one year, or a judicial determination of the validity of such conviction on collateral review, the court shall cause a certified record of the conviction or determination to be made to the repository in such form and containing such information as the Attorney General of the United States shall by regulation prescribe.

"(c) Records maintained in the repository shall not be public records. Certified copies thereof—

"(1) may be furnished for law enforcement purposes on request of a court or law enforcement or corrections officer of the United States, the District of Columbia, the Commonwealth of Puerto Rico, a territory or possession of the United States, any political subdivision, or any department, agency, or instrumentality thereof.

"(2) may be furnished for law enforcement purposes on request of a court or law enforcement or corrections officer of a State, any political subdivision, or any department, agency, or instrumentality thereof, if a statute of such State requires that, upon the conviction of a defendant in a court of the State or any political subdivision thereof for an offense punishable in such court by death or imprisonment in excess of one year, or a judicial determination of the validity of such conviction on collateral review, the court cause a certified record of the conviction or determination to be made to the repository in such form and containing such information as the Attorney General of the United States shall by regulation prescribe; and

"(3) shall be prima facie evidence in any court of the United States, the District of Columbia, the Commonwealth of Puerto Rico, a territory or possession of the United States, any political subdivision, or any department, agency, or instrumentality thereof, that the convictions occurred and whether they have been judicially determined to be invalid on collateral review.

"(d) The Attorney General of the United States shall give reasonable public notice, and afford to interested parties opportunity for hearing, prior to prescribing regulations under this section."

(b) The analysis of chapter 227, title 18, United States Code. is amended by adding at the end thereof the following new items:

"3575. Increased sentence for dangerous special offenders.

"3576. Review of sentence.

"3577. Use of information for sentencing.

"3578. Conviction records."

Sec. 1002. Section 3148, chapter 207, title 18, United States Code, is amended by adding "or sentence review under section 3576 of this title" immediately after "sentence."

TITLE XI—REGULATION OF EXPLOSIVES

PURPOSES

Sec. 1101. The Congress hereby declares that the purpose of this title is to protect interstate and foreign commerce against interference and interruption by reducing the hazard to persons and property arising from misuse and unsafe or insecure storage of explosive materials. It is not the purpose of this title to place any undue or unnecessary Federal restrictions or burdens on law-abiding citizens with respect to the acquisition, possession, storage, or use of explosive materials for industrial, mining, agricultural, or other lawful purposes, or to provide for the imposition by

Federal regulations of any procedures or requirements other than those reasonably necessary to implement and effectuate the provisions of this title.

Sec. 1102. Title 18, United States Code,[1] is amended by adding after chapter 39 the following chapter:

"Chapter 40.—IMPORTATION, MANUFACTURE, DISTRIBUTION AND STORAGE OF EXPLOSIVE MATERIALS

"§ 841. Definitions

"As used in this chapter—

"(a) 'Person' means any individual, corporation, company, association, firm, partnership, society, or joint stock company.

"(b) 'Interstate or foreign commerce' means commerce between any place in a State and any place outside of that State, or within any possession of the United States (not including the Canal Zone) or the District of Columbia, and commerce between places within the same State but through any place outside of that State. 'State' includes the District of Columbia, the Commonwealth of Puerto Rico, and the possessions of the United States (not including the Canal Zone).

"(c) 'Explosive materials' means explosives, blasting agents, and detonators.

"(d) Except for the purposes of subsections (d), (e), (f), (g), (h), (i), and (j) of section 844 of this title, 'explosives' means any chemical compound mixture, or device, the primary or common purpose of which is to function by explosion; the term includes, but is not limited to, dynamite and other high explosives, black powder, pellet powder, initiating explosives, detonators, safety fuses, squibs, detonating cord, igniter cord, and igniters. The Secretary shall publish and revise at least annually in the Federal Register a list of these and any additional explosives which he determines to be within the coverage of this chapter. For the purposes of subsections (d), (e), (f), (g), (h), and (i) of section 844 of this title, the term 'explosive' is defined in subsection (j) of such section 844.

"(e) 'Blasting agent' means any material or mixture, consisting of fuel and oxidizer, intended for blasting, not otherwise defined as an explosive: *Provided,* That the finished product, as mixed for use or shipment, cannot be detonated by means of a numbered 8 test blasting cap when unconfined.

"(f) 'Detonator' means any device containing a detonating charge that is used for initiating detonation in an explosive; the term includes, but is not limited to, electric blasting caps of instantaneous and delay types, blasting caps for use with safety fuses and detonating-cord delay connectors.

"(g) 'Importer' means any person engaged in the business of importing or bringing explosive materials into the United States for purposes of sale or distribution.

"(h) 'Manufacturer' means any person engaged in the business of manufacturing explosive materials for purposes of sale or distribution or for his own use.

"(i) 'Dealer' means any person engaged in the business of distributing explosive materials at wholesale or retail.

"(j) 'Permittee' means any user of explosives for a lawful purpose, who has obtained a user permit under the provisions of this chapter.

"(k) 'Secretary' means the Secretary of the Treasury or his delegate.

"(l) 'Crime punishable by imprisonment for a term exceeding one year' shall not mean (1) any Federal or State offenses pertaining to antitrust violations, unfair trade practices, restraints of trade, or other similar offenses relating to the regulation of business practices as the Secretary may by regulation designate, or (2) any State offense (other than one involving a firearm or explosive) classified by the laws of the State as a misdemeanor and punishable by a term of imprisonment of two years or less.

"(m) 'Licensee' means any importer, manufacturer, or dealer licensed under the provisions of this chapter.

"(n) 'Distribute' means sell, issue, give, transfer, or otherwise dispose of.

"§ 842.   Unlawful acts

"(a) It shall be unlawful for any person—

"(1) to engage in the business of importing, manufacturing, or dealing in explosive materials without a license issued under this chapter;

"(2) knowingly to withhold information or to make any false or fictitious oral or written statement or to furnish or exhibit any false, fictitious, or misrepresented identification, intended or likely to deceive for the purpose of obtaining explosive materials, or a license, permit, exemption, or relief from disability under the provisions of this chapter; and

"(3) other than a licensee or permittee knowingly—

"(A) to transport, ship, cause to be transported, or receive in interstate or foreign commerce any explosive materials, except that a person who lawfully purchases explosive materials from a licensee in a State contiguous to the State in which the purchaser resides may ship, transport, or cause to be transported such explosive materials to the State in which he resides and may receive such explosive materials in the State in which he resides, if such transportation, shipment, or receipt is permitted by the law of the State in which he resides; or

"(B) to distribute explosive materials to any person (other than a licensee or permittee) who the distributor knows or has reasonable cause to believe does not reside in the State in which the distributor resides.

"(b) It shall be unlawful for any licensee knowingly to distribute any explosive materials to any person except—

"(1) a licensee;

"(2) a permittee; or

"(3) a resident of the State where distribution is made and in which the licensee is licensed to do business or a State contiguous thereto if permitted by the law of the State of the purchaser's residence.

"(c) It shall be unlawful for any licensee to distribute explosive materials to any person who the licensee has reason to believe intends to transport such explosive materials into a State where the purchase, possession, or use of explosive materials is prohibited or which does not permit its residents to transport or ship explosive materials into it or to receive explosive materials in it.

"(d) It shall be unlawful for any licensee knowingly to distribute explosive materials to any individual who:

"(1) is under twenty-one years of age;

"(2) has been convicted in any court of a crime punishable by imprisonment for a term exceeding one year;

"(3) is under indictment for a crime punishable by imprisonment for a term exceeding one year;

"(4) is a fugitive from justice;

"(5) is an unlawful user of marihuana (as defined in section 4761 of the Internal Revenue Code of 1954) or any depressant or stimulant drug (as defined in section 201 (v) of the Federal Food, Drug, and Cosmetic Act) or narcotic drug (as defined in section 4721(a) of the Internal Revenue Code of 1954); or

"(6) has been adjudicated a mental defective.

"(e) It shall be unlawful for any licensee knowingly to distribute any explosive materials to any person in any State where the purchase, possession, or use by such person of such explosive materials would be in violation of any State law or any published ordinance applicable at the place of distribution.

"(f) It shall be unlawful for any licensee or permittee willfully to manufacture, import, purchase, distribute, or receive explosive materials without making such records as the Secretary may by regulation require, including, but not limited to, a statement of intended use, the name, date, place of birth, social security number or taxpayer identification number, and place of residence of any natural person to whom explosive materials are distributed. If explosive materials are distributed to a corporation or other business entity, such records shall include the identity and principal and local places of business and the name, date, place of birth, and place of residence of the natural person acting as agent of the corporation or other business entity in arranging the distribution.

"(g) It shall be unlawful for any licensee or permittee knowingly to make any false entry in any record which he is required to keep pursuant to this section or regulations promulgated under section 847 of this title.

"(h) It shall be unlawful for any person to receive, conceal, transport, ship, store, barter, sell, or dispose of any explosive materials knowing or having reasonable cause to believe that such explosive materials were stolen.

"(i) It shall be unlawful for any person—

"(1) who is under indictment for, or who has been convicted in any court of, a crime punishable by imprisonment for a term exceeding one year;

"(2) who is a fugitive from justice;

"(3) who is an unlawful user of or addicted to marihuana (as defined in section 4761 of the Internal Revenue Code of 1954) or any depressant or stimulant drug (as defined in section 201 (v) of the Federal Food, Drug, and Cosmetic Act) or narcotic drug (as defined in section 4731(a) of the Internal Revenue Code of 1954); or

"(4) who has been adjudicated as a mental defective or who has been committed to a mental institution;

to ship or transport any explosive in interstate or foreign commerce or to receive any explosive which has been shipped or transported in interstate or foreign commerce.

"(j) It shall be unlawful for any person to store any explosive material in a manner not in conformity with regulations promulgated by the Secretary. In promulgating such regulations, the Secretary shall take into consideration the class, type, and quantity of explosive materials to be stored, as well as the standards of safety and security recognized in the explosives industry.

"(k) It shall be unlawful for any person who has knowledge of the theft or loss of any explosive materials from his stock, to fail to report such theft or loss within twenty-four hours of discovery thereof, to the Secretary and to appropriate local authorities.

"§ 843. Licenses and user permits

"(a) An application for a user permit or a license to import, manufacture, or deal in explosive materials shall be in such form and contain such information as the Secretary shall by regulation prescribe. Each applicant for a license or permit shall pay a fee to be charged as set by the Secretary, said fee not to exceed $200 for each license or permit. Each license or permit shall be valid for no longer than three years from date of issuance and shall be renewable upon the same conditions and subject to the same restrictions as the original license or permit and upon payment of a renewal fee not to exceed one-half of the original fee.

"(b) Upon the filing of a proper application and payment of the prescribed fee, and subject to the provisions of this chapter and other applicable laws, the Secretary shall issue to such applicant the appropriate license or permit if—

"(1) the applicant (including in the case of a corporation, partnership, or association, any individual possessing, directly or indirectly, the power to direct or cause the direction of the management and policies of the corporation, partnership, or association) is not a person to whom the distribution of explosive materials would be unlawful under section 842(d) of this chapter;

"(2) the applicant has not willfully violated any of the provisions of this chapter or regulations issued hereunder;

"(3) the applicant has in a State premises from which he conducts or intends to conduct business;

"(4) the applicant has a place of storage for explosive materials which meets such standards of public safety and security against theft as the Secretary by regulations shall prescribe; and

"(5) the applicant has demonstrated and certified in writing that he is familiar with all published State laws and local ordinances relating to explosive materials for the location in which he intends to do business.

"(c) The Secretary shall approve or deny an application within a period of forty-five days beginning on the date such application is received by the Secretary.

"(d) The Secretary may revoke any license or permit issued under this section if in the opinion of the Secretary the holder thereof has violated any provision of this chapter or any rule or regulation prescribed by the Secretary under this chapter, or has become ineligible to acquire explosive materials under section 842(d). The Secretary's action under this subsection may be reviewed only as provided in subsection (e) (2) of this section.

"(e) (1) Any person whose application is denied or whose license or permit is revoked shall receive a written notice from the Secretary stating the specific grounds upon which such denial or revocation is based. Any notice of a revocation of a license or permit shall be given to the holder of such license or permit prior to or concurrently with the effective date of the revocation.

"(2) If the Secretary denies an application for, or revokes a license, or permit, he shall, upon request by the aggrieved party, promptly hold a hearing to review his denial or revocation. In the case of a revocation, the Secretary may upon a request of the holder stay the effective date of the revocation. A hearing under this section shall be at a location convenient to the aggrieved party. The Secretary shall give written notice of his decision to the aggrieved party within a reasonable time after the hearing. The aggrieved party may, within sixty days after receipt of the Secretary's written decision, file a petition with the United States court of appeals for the district in which he resides or has his principal place of business for a judicial review of such denial or revocation, pursuant to sections 701–706 of title 5, United States Code.

"(f) Licensees and permittees shall make available for inspection at all reasonable times their records kept pursuant to this chapter or the regulations issued hereunder, and shall submit to the Secretary such re- ports and information with respect to such records and the contents thereof as he shall by regulations prescribe. The Secretary may enter during business hours the premises (including places of storage) of any licensee or permittee, for the purpose of inspecting or examining (1) any records or documents required to be kept by such licensee or permittee, under the provisions of this chapter or regulations issued hereunder, and (2) any explosive materials kept or stored by such licensee or permittee at such premises. Upon the request of any State or any political subdivision thereof, the Secretary may make available to such State or any political subdivision thereof, any information which he may obtain by reason of the provisions of this chapter with respect to the identification of persons within such State or political subdivision thereof, who have purchased or received explosive materials, together with a description of such explosive materials.

"(g) Licenses and permits issued under the provisions of subsection (b) of this section shall be kept posted and kept available for inspection on the premises covered by the license and permit.

"§ 844. Penalties

"(a) Any person who violates subsections (a) through (i) of section 842 of this chapter shall be fined not more than $10,000 or imprisoned not more than ten years, or both.

"(b) Any person who violates any other provision of section 842 of this chapter shall be fined not more than $1,000 or imprisoned not more than one year, or both.

"(c) Any explosive materials involved or used or intended to be used in any violation of the provisions of this chapter or any other rule or regulation promulgated thereunder or any violation of any criminal law of the United States shall be subject to seizure and forfeiture, and all provisions of the Internal Revenue Code of 1954 relating to the seizure, forfeiture, and disposition of firearms, as defined in section 5845(a) of that Code, shall, so far as applicable, extend to seizures and forfeitures under the provisions of this chapter.

"(d) Whoever transports or receives, or attempts to transport or receive, in interstate or foreign commerce any explosive with the knowledge or intent that it will be used to kill, injure, or intimidate any individual or unlawfully to damage or destroy any building, vehicle, or other real or personal property, shall be imprisoned for not more than ten years, or fined not more than $10,000, or both; and if personal injury results shall be imprisoned for not more than twenty years or fined not more than $20,000, or both; and if death results, shall be subject to imprisonment for any term of years, or to the death penalty or to life imprisonment as provided in section 34 of this title.

"(e) Whoever, through the use of the mail, telephone, telegraph, or other instrument of commerce, willfully makes any threat, or maliciously conveys false information knowing the same to be false, concerning an attempt or alleged attempt being made, or to be made, to kill, injure, or intimidate any individual or unlawfully to damage or destroy any building, vehicle, or other real or personal property by means of an explosive shall be imprisoned for not more than five years or fined not more than $5,000, or both.

"(f) Whoever maliciously damages or destroys, or attempts to damage or destroy, by means of an explosive, any building, vehicle, or other personal or real property in whole or in part owned, possessed, or used by, or leased to, the United States, any department or agency thereof, or any institution or organization receiving Federal financial assistance shall be imprisoned for not more than ten years, or fined not more than $10,000, or both; and if personal injury results shall be imprisoned for not more than twenty years, or fined not more than $20,000, or both; and if death results shall be subject to imprisonment for any term of years, or to the death penalty or to life imprisonment as provided in section 34 of this title.

"(g) Whoever possesses an explosive in any building in whole or in part owned, possessed, or used by, or leased to, the United States or any department or agency thereof, except with the written consent of the agency, department, or other person responsible for the management of such building, shall be imprisoned for not more than one year, or fined not more than $1,000, or both.

"(h) Whoever—

"(1) uses an explosive to commit any felony which may be prosecuted in a court of the United States, or

"(2) carries an explosive unlawfully during the commission of any felony which may be prosecuted in a court of the United States,

shall be sentenced to a term of imprisonment for not less than one year nor more than ten years. In the case of his second or subsequent conviction under this subsection, such person shall be sentenced to a term of imprisonment for not less than five years nor more than twenty-five years, and, notwithstanding any other provision of law, the court shall not suspend the sentence of such person or give him a probationary sentence.

"(i) Whoever maliciously damages or destroys, or attempts to damage or destroy, by means of an explosive, any building, vehicle, or other real or personal property used in interstate or foreign commerce or in any activity affecting interstate or foreign commerce shall be imprisoned for not more than ten years or fined not more than $10,000, or both; and if personal injury results shall be imprisoned for not more than twenty years or fined not more than $20,000, or both; and if death results shall also be subject to imprisonment for any term of years, or to the death penalty or to life imprisonment as provided in section 34 of this title.

"(j) For the purposes of subsections (d), (e), (f), (g), (h), and (i) of this section, the term 'explosive' means gunpowders, powders used for blasting, all forms of high explosives, blasting materials, fuzes (other than electric circuit breakers), detonators, and other detonating agents, smokeless powders, other explosive or incendiary devices within the meaning of paragraph (5) of section 232 of this title, and any chemical compounds, mechanical mixture, or device that contains any oxidizing and combustible units, or other ingredients, in such proportions, quantities, or packing that ignition by fire, by friction, by concussion, by percussion, or by detonation of the compound, mixture, or device or any part thereof may cause an explosion.

"§ 845. Exceptions; relief from disabilities

"(a) Except in the case of subsections (d), (e), (f), (g), (h), and (i) of section 844 of this title, this chapter shall not apply to:

"(1) any aspect of the transportation of explosive materials via railroad, water, highway, or air which are regulated by the United States Department of Transportation and agencies thereof;

"(2) the use of explosive materials in medicines and medicinal agents in the forms prescribed by the official United States Pharmacopeia, or the National Formulary;

"(3) the transportation, shipment, receipt, or importation of explosive materials for delivery to any agency of the United States or to any State or political subdivision thereof;

"(4) small arms ammunition and components thereof;

"(5) black powder in quantities not to exceed five pounds; and

"(6) the manufacture under the regulation of the military department of the United States of explosive materials for, or their distribution to or storage or possession by the military or naval services or other agencies of the United States; or to arsenals, navy yards, depots, or other establishments owned by, or operated by or on behalf of, the United States.

"(b) A person who had been indicted for or convicted of a crime punishable by imprisonment for a term exceeding one year may make application to the Secretary for relief from the disabilities imposed by this chapter with respect to engaging in the business of importing, manufacturing, or dealing in explosive materials, or the purchase of explosive materials, and incurred by reason of such indictment or conviction, and the Secretary may grant such relief if it is established to his satisfaction that the circumstances regarding the indictment or conviction, and the applicant's record and reputation, are such that the applicant will not be likely to act in a manner dangerous to public safety and that the granting of the relief will not be contrary to the public interest. A licensee or permittee who makes application for relief from the disabilities incurred under this chapter by reason of indictment or conviction, shall not be barred by such indictment or conviction from further operations under his license or permit pending final action on an application for relief filed pursuant to this section.

§§ 846–848. Omitted—General administrative provisions.

TITLE XII—NATIONAL COMMISSION ON INDIVIDUAL RIGHTS

Sec. 1201. There is hereby established the National Commission on Individual Rights (hereinafter in this title referred to as the "Commission").

Sec. 1202. The Commission shall be composed of fifteen members appointed as follows:

(1) four appointed by the President of the Senate from Members of the Senate;

(2) four appointed by the Speaker of the House of Representatives from Members of the House of Representatives; and

(3) seven appointed by the President of the United States from all segments of life in the United States, including but not limited to lawyers, jurists, and policemen, none of whom shall be officers of the executive branch of the Government.

Sec. 1203. The President of the United States shall designate a Chairman from among the members of the Commission. Any vacancy in the Commission shall not affect its powers but shall be filled in the same manner in which the original appointment was made.

Sec. 1204. It shall be the duty of the Commission to conduct a comprehensive study and review of Federal laws and practices relating to special grand juries authorized under chapter 216 of title 18, United States Code, dangerous special offender sentencing under section 3575 of title 18, United States Code, wiretapping and electronic surveillance, bail reform and preventive detention, no-knock search warrants, and the accumulation of data on individuals by Federal agencies as authorized by law or acquired by executive action. The Commission may also consider other Federal laws and practices which in its opinion may infringe upon the individual rights of the people of the United States. The Commission shall determine which laws and practices are needed, which are effective, and whether they infringe upon the individual rights of the people of the United States.

Sec. 1205. (a) Subject to such rules and regulations as may be adopted by the Commission, the Chairman shall have the power to—

(1) appoint and fix the compensation of an Executive Director, and such additional staff personnel as he deems necessary, without regard to the provisions of title 5, United States Code, governing appointments in the competitive service, and without regard to the provisions of chapter 51 and subchapter III of chapter 53 of such title relating to classification and General Schedule pay rates, but at rates not in excess of the maximum rate for GS–18 of the General Schedule under section 5332 of such title; and

(2) procure temporary and intermittent services to the same extent as is authorized by section 3109 of title 5, United States Code, but at rates not to exceed $100 a day for individuals.

(b) In making appointments pursuant to subsection (a) of this section, the Chairman shall include among his appointment individuals determined by the Chairman to be competent social scientists, lawyers, and law enforcement officers.

Sec. 1206. (a) A member of the Commission who is a Member of Congress shall serve without additional compensation, but shall be reimbursed for travel, subsistence, and other necessary expenses incurred in the performance of duties vested in the Commission.

(b) A member of the Commission from private life shall receive $100 per diem when engaged in the actual performance of duties vested in the Commission, plus reimbursement for travel, subsistence, and other necessary expenses incurred in the performance of such duties.

Sec. 1207. Each department, agency, and instrumentality of the executive branch of the Government, including independent agencies, is authorized and directed to furnish to the Commission, upon request made by the Chairman, such statistical data, reports, and other information as the Commission deems necessary to carry out its functions under this title. The Chairman is further authorized to call upon the departments, agencies, and other offices of the several States to furnish such statistical data, reports, and other information as the Commission deems necessary to carry out its functions under this title.

Sec. 1208. The Commission shall make interim reports and recommendations as it deems advisable, but at least every two years, and it shall make a final report of its findings and recommendations to the President of the United States and to the Congress at the end of six years following the effective date of this section. Sixty days after the submission of the final report, the Commission shall cease to exist.

21.2   The Organized Crime Control Act: An Analysis

Any time that a new law is passed, the search begins for its legislative intent. Legislative intent guides the courts in their interpretation of an act's provisions. Congressionally, this intent is found in two places.

The first place to look is to the Act to see if Congress has made a policy finding in the Act itself. In the case of the Organized Crime Control Act (OCCA), there is such a policy statement. Entitled "Statement of Findings and Purposes," the OCCA recites the problems as found by the President's Commission. The second paragraph states its purpose. The Congress feels it adds strength, new penal provision, enhanced sanction, and new remedies to "eradicate" organized crime. The question remains: has Congress found and created an effective weapon against organized crime?

The second place to find legislative intent is in the House and Senate reports. The following material is taken from a house report on the OCCA. House Report No. 91–1549 (Sept. 30, 1970) is a section by section analysis of the OCCA. The majority report is about 43 pages long. Filed with the report are some additional 40 pages of individual and dissenting views of congressmen. From this volume of material, the major features will be highlighted.

Title I of the OCCA provides for the convening of special grand juries that will deal with one subject—organized crime. Regular grand juries will go about their business, leaving to the special grand juries the ferreting out of organized crime activity. The special grand jury must submit a report on organized crime and is permitted to make the report public. This is an effort to break the cloak of secrecy surrounding organized crime.

The immunity provisions of Title II broaden the immunity from transaction immunity to use immunity so that direct and derivative evidence cannot be used against the witness. It is hoped that this will unlock some closed mouths so that information on top echelon leaders can be obtained and they may be prosecuted. The immunity will be no good if the person to whom it is granted perjures himself. Immunity orders may be granted prospectively, which was not the case in some circuit and district courts. The immunity is granted only by special court order when the court is satisfied that the testimony is needed and the witness has refused, or probably will refuse, to testify.

Title III adds a new concept, the "recalcitrant witness." The court is authorized summarily to confine the witness at a suitable place until the witness is willing to testify. This is civil confinement. Title III also deals with the fleeing witness from state proceedings investigating crime, as well as those who flee as witnesses from criminal proceedings.

The penalty for such actions as false testimony before a court or grand jury has been increased to a $10,000 fine or five years imprisonment or both, according to Title IV of the OCCA. In addition to the types of statements, burden of proof, and defense in this title, the most significant portion deals with the doing away of the "two witnesses to perjury rule" heretofore in force.

Title V recognizes the need to give protection to "star" witnesses. The right to create such facilities and maintain them is given the attorney general of the United States. State witnesses may be protected on a reimbursable basis.

Under Title VI the government is now allowed, as was the defendant before, to preserve testimony by the use of depositions. This clearly recognizes a fact of life—"star" witnesses do not always live long enough to testify at trials of organized crime leaders.

A new section entitled "Litigation concerning sources of evidence" is added by Title VII. The intention is to limit disclosure of information illegally obtained by the government to defendants who seek to challenge the admissibility of evidence because it is either the primary or indirect production of such an illegal act. There can be no challenge if the illegal act occurred five years or more before the event sought to be proved. This limits the "fruit of the poisonous tree" doctrine.

Finding that illegal gambling involves widespread use of, and has an effect on, interstate commerce and its facilities, Title VIII creates a new crime, "Obstruction of state or local law enforcement." The section applies to persons who participate in ownership, management, or conduct of an illegal gambling business. Thus, it is a federal offense to conspire to interfere with state and local law enforcement to facilitate an illegal gambling business. The conspiracy must be with some official or employee of a state or local subdivision, and one of the persons must finance, manage, supervise, direct, or own (all or part) of an illegal gambling business. Thus, the law is after high level and street level managers.

Title IX deals with racketeering. There must be a pattern of racketeering activity which is satisfied by two acts as defined in the first subsection of the title. Also note that in addition to the fine and prison term, the act allows for the forfeiture of all property connected or related to the pattern of racketeering activity.

The authority, standards, and procedures for imposing extended prison terms on dangerous special offenders is established in Title X of the OCCA.

Title XI establishes federal controls over the interstate and foreign commerce of explosives. It is designed to assist the states more effectively to regulate the sale, transfer, and other disposition of explosives within their borders. Licensing is required and certain persons cannot be sold or given explosives. Existing penalties are increased and the death penalty is now added for certain offenses in the title.

Finally, Title XII establishes a National Commission on Individual Rights, which is to conduct a comprehensive study and review of federal laws and practices relating to special grand juries and to special offender sentencing authorized under this Act, wiretapping and electronic surveillance, bail reform and preventive detention, no-knock search warrants, and the accumulation of data on individuals.

21.3 Extortionate Credit Transactions Act

As mentioned in section 21.0 of this chapter, one of the very real problems caused by organized crime is that of "loan sharking." In response the Congress passed Public Law 90–321 in 1968. It is found at Title 18, sections 891–896 of the United States Code (1970).

The Congress found that a substantial part of the income of organized crime is generated by extortionate credit transactions. Extortionate credit transactions are characterized by the use, or the express or implicit threat of the use, of violence or other criminal means to cause harm to person, reputation, or property as a means of enforcing payment. Congress even said that where extortionate transactions are purely intrastate in character, they nevertheless directly affect interstate and foreign commerce.

Thus, the person who uses force or the threat of force to person, property, or reputation can be charged under this Act and fined $10,000 or imprisoned for 20 years or both. The government has also to show the rate of interest to be in excess of 45 percent. The Act also punishes the "banker," or money source.

GLOSSARY

1. Abandonment. To give up, desert, or to relinquish voluntarily and absolutely any property.

2. Accident. Injury suffered without fault or liability. An unexpected, unforeseen, undesigned, sudden, and unexpected event.

3. Animus Furandi. Criminal intent to steal property.

4. Arrest. Restraint of a person.

5. Bailee. Person who receives property for safekeeping.

6. Bailment. Delivery of property in trust. Property is delivered to another for the purpose of keeping it safe. A person may get it to keep for money (a bailment for hire), or may get it by delivery for his temporary use for no money, or may pick up another's property and have no intention to use or keep it (a gratuitous bailment).

7. Bailor. Person who delivers personal property to another for safekeeping or person whose property has been found.

8. Certorari. Method of appeal which is granted only at the discretion of the reviewing court. *Certiorari* is not a matter of right.

9. Civil Rights. Embraces the rights due from one citizen to another, deprivation of which is a civil injury for which redress may be sought in a civil action.

10. Concurrent Jurisdiction. That of several different tribunals, each authorized to deal with the same subject matter.

11. Consent. Voluntary agreement by a person in possession and exercise of sufficient mentality to make an intelligent choice, to do something proposed by another.

12. Consideration. That thing of value given or gotten in a contractual relationship. Promises to do what one is not legally obliged to do can be consideration, as well as the giving of money or property.

13. Conversion. Any unauthorized act depriving a person of his property permanently or for indefinite time. Any sale or appropriation of property without consent of owner.

14. Covert. Hidden or not open to view; opposite is overt, action taken which is open to view.

15. De Facto. Term to denote the way things really are. It may be that the law requires one thing but that the facts as they exist tell a different story.

16. De Jure. Term used to denote that things are by law the way they are supposed to be.

17. Discretion. Right to act according to one's judgment. Courts are given discretion in many areas where there are no strict rules of law.

18. Dominion and Control. Complete ownership and right to property. Thus, one who is exercising dominion and control is acting as the owner of the property.

19. Extradition. Surrender by one (State B) to another (State A) of an individual accused or convicted of an offense outside its own territory (State B) and within the territorial jurisdiction of the other, (State A) which being competent to try and punish him, demands the surrender.

20. Fair Market Value. Theoretically what a willing seller would take and a willing buyer would offer.

21. Habeas Corpus. This writ asks the question, "Why do you hold this person?" If not answered satisfactorily, the person must be released.

22. Home Rule. As to the affairs of a municipality, which affects the relations of the citizens with their local government, they shall be freed from state interference, regulation, and control, the system of public improvements, the building of streets or alleys, . . . and all other matters of purely local interest, advantage, and convenience shall be left to the people thereof for their own determination.

23. Imminent Bodily Harm. Threatening to occur immediately, now.

24. Intangible Personal Property. Items such as a bank book or stock certificate. These things represent or stand for the ownership of the money in the bank account or ownership interest in the corporation represented by the stock certificate, unlike a ring which is tangible personal property simply because it is the thing of value.

25. Judicial Review. Testing of statutes or administrative regulations against the standards of the Constitution.

26. Jurisprudence. Philosophy or body of law that a given state or nation follows.

27. Mala In Se. Bad in itself or bad because the act is morally reprehensible.

28. Mala Prohibita. Forbidden by statute, but not otherwise wrong.

29. Malice. In law, a cool depravity and hardness of heart, involving wickedness and excluding a just cause or excuse.

30. Mandamus. Extraordinary remedy which requires a public officer to do his duty.

31. Mens Rea. Signifies evil purpose or mental culpability, guilty knowledge and willfulness.

32. Merger of Offenses. Under modern concept of the doctrine, the test is whether one crime necessarily involves the other.

33. Moral Turpitude. Anything done contrary to justice, honesty, modesty, or good morals.

34. Negotiable. Note, bond, or certificate is said to be negotiable when it can be transferred from one person to another.

35. Nolle Prosequi. Voluntary withdrawal by the prosecuting officer of present proceedings on a particular bill; is nothing but a declaration of prosecuting officer that he will not prosecute further at that time.

36. Nuisance. Anything that works harm or prejudice to an individual or the public, or which causes a well-founded apprehension of danger.

37. Overt. Manifest, open, public; issuing in action as distinguished from that which rests merely in intention or design.

38. Presumption. Rule which the law makes upon a given state of facts. Means to accept as being entitled to belief without examination of proof or that which may be logically assumed to be true until disproved.

39. Process. Method of proceeding from the beginning to the end of a trial. Narrowly, it means the series of notices and summons that inform people of court proceedings.

40. Prohibition. Extraordinary remedy whereby a person, usually a public officer, is prohibited from taking some action or further action which has been found to be illegal.

41. Provocation. Action or mode of conduct that excites resentment or vindictive feelings; a cause of anger.

42. Quo Warranto. Civil, not criminal, action; remedy or proceeding by which the sovereign or state determines the legality of a claim which a party asserts to the use or exercise of an office or franchise.

43. Rebuttal Presumption. Presumption that can be overcome by evidence showing a contrary conclusion.

44. Tangible Property. That which may be felt or touched, and is necessarily corporeal, although it may be either real or personal.

45. Testimony. Statement made under oath in legal proceeding, or evidence of a witness given under oath.

46. Willful. Governed by will without regard to reason; obstinate, done deliberately, intentional.

Index

References are to page numbers